Vegetarian's
A to Z Guide

to Fruits & Vegetables

Vegetarian's A to Z Guide

to Fruits & Vegetables

Kathleen Robinson

with Pete Luckett

FISHER
er
BOOKS™

Publishers: Bill Fisher
Howard Fisher
Helen V. Fisher

North American Editors: Helen V. Fisher
Sarah Smith

Cover Design: FifthStreet*design*

Book Design: Josh Young

Illustrations: David Langille

Photos: Brian Atkinson and Sue Tufts

Book Production: Deanie Wood

North American Edition
Published by Fisher Books
4239 W. Ina Road, Suite #101
Tucson, AZ 85741
(520) 744-6110

© 1996 Fisher Books
Printed in USA
Printing 10 9 8 7 6 5 4 3 2

**Library of Congress
Cataloging-in-Publication Data**

Robinson, Kathleen, 1959—

[Pete Luckett's complete guide to fresh fruits & vegetables]

Vegetarian's A to Z guide to fruits & vegetables / Kathleen Robinson, with Pete Luckett. -- U.S. ed.

p. cm.

Includes index.

Originally published: Pete Luckett's complete guide to fresh fruits & vegetables. Fredericton, N.B. : Goose Lane Editions, 1990.

ISBN 1-55561-091-9 (pbk.)

1. Cookery (Fruit) 2. Cookery (Vegetables) 3. Vegetarian cookery. I. Luckett, Pete. II. Title.

TX811.R58 1996

641.6'4--dc20   96-5413
                                 CIP

Notice: The information in this book is true and complete to the best of our knowledge. The information in this book is general and is offered with no guarantees on the part of the author or Fisher Books. The author and publisher disclaim all liability in connection with use of this book.

CONTENTS

For Aunt Peg

When this book was finally complete, I was amazed to discover just how many people had actually contributed to it. First of all, I am profoundly grateful to Pete Luckett, who is so generous in sharing his knowledge of fresh produce and who invited me to help him share this knowledge with others. I am indebted to my brother Peter, to whom this book owes its existence. I would also like to thank my parents, who kept me going through it all, and my sister, for her timely moments of inspiration. Finally, I owe a word of thanks to my coworkers at Pete's Frootique, especially one wee Scotsman who shepherded me through the hardest part and who introduced me to okra.

I love it. I really do. I love workin' wif fresh stuff. There is nuffin' like the feel of a ripe persimmon or a Passe Crassane pear. The color of mandarins next to Ribier grapes sen's shivers up and down me spine. I never lose me enthusiasm for the look of a box of fresh lychees or a new crate of asparagus or rapini. I love the smell tha' 'its you when you open a box of basil or a crate of coriander. All the colors an' tex'ure, the movemen', the activi'y which sur-roun's fruit an' veg . . . "Move it while it's at its peak, darlin'." It's a very busy job selling fruit and veg. But you know mos' of all, I enjoy the fruit and veg 'emselves, doin' what they do best, gettin' eaten.

The Greengrocer's Guide

I'd hazard a guess that most cookbooks are written by chefs—chefs, standing, pen and paper in hand in the midst of enormous well-equipped kitchens. This one was written by a greengrocer and his scribe, standing with pen in hand in the midst of a glorious array of fruit and vegetables. And as a chef can tell you about whisks and wooden spoons, so Pete and I can tell you about cardoon and boniato. A cookbook with a twist!

Pete is an excellent, inventive cook and he knows more about fruit and vegetables than anyone I know. If you follow the guide-lines in this book, not only will you create some wonderful meals, but you'll be doing it with the best ingredients available.

The purpose of this book is to pass on some of the enthusiasm and appreciation that Pete and I feel for fruit and vegetables and perhaps a few interesting tidbits that fuel our devotion. Over the three or four years I have worked with Pete, I have been amazed at how my knowledge of produce has grown. Pete has been in the business for 20 years and will tell you, without hesitation, that there is no other business he would rather be in.

Even before I worked for Pete I had begun to be a little adven-turous; I would buy the occasional Seckel pear or perhaps a mango if I was feeling really daring, but I did not know how to choose a good ripe granadilla, or how to cook okra. As I learned these things a whole new world opened up. I have "overheard" Pete explain 101 ways to cook 101 vegetables, and I have sampled 101 types of fruit at just about every stage of under-, over-, and perfect ripeness. This book can save you years of trial and error and years of working for Pete, lengthy endeavors for which few of us have time.

Given the access the average consumer has to fresh fruit and vegetables from all over the world, this guide to buying and prepar-ing fresh produce will broaden your culinary repertoire. On any given day, you can find at your local market apples and kiwi from New Zealand, lychees from Taiwan and Madagascar, Asian pears from Japan and China, papaya from Hawaii, pineapple from the Dominican Republic, Honduras and Costa Rica, figs, cactus pears and persimmons from Brazil, mangoes from Peru, squash from Mexico, pears from France, bananas from Ecuador, grapes from Chile and, of course, everything from broccoli to zucchini from California and Florida.

The leaps and bounds made in the technology of transport and shipping over the last 15 years mean that produce is shipped half-way around the world; it either arrives in the same perfect shape as when it left the tree or, having been picked at the right moment, arrives ripe and ready for eating. As a result, produce is no longer seasonal. The ground may be frozen and covered with three feet of snow, but we still have everything from grapes to snow peas wait-ing in the market.

Can you imagine that your great-grandfather ever had the chance to eat fresh grapes in January, or savor the crunch of a just-picked apple six months before he would get any from his trees, let alone sink his teeth into the creamy custard of a cherimoya, or the luscious sweetness of a persimmon?

The temperature of shipping containers is controlled to within a couple of degrees. We can unpack grapes for the stall at Pete's and know that the fruit looks and tastes every bit as good at that moment as it did when it was packed 4,000 miles ago. The bananas you bought yesterday were probably picked green in Ecuador, and during their two-week sea voyage ripened to the lovely yellow that caught your eye when you went shopping. The strawberries, which look so marvelous in January, were probably sitting in a field in California 24 hours earlier.

Thanks to modern transport, to air freight, container technology, refrigeration and storage facilities, an overwhelming variety of fresh produce arrives daily at supermarkets and fruit stalls. And we take all this freshness and variety for granted, even though the lettuce probably traveled farther than we did in the preceding week.

But the miracle of modern transport is not the only thing that gives us ultra-fresh fruit and vegetables. Pre-cooling has become a major factor in the last 30 years. Have you ever wondered why the broccoli from California you bought at the supermarket on the weekend looks better on Thursday than the broccoli you picked up at the farmers' market on Monday? It's because of pre-cooling—an amazing process by which the field heat is drawn out of fruit and vegetables and ice-cold air is circulated around them so that within 30 minutes of being picked, produce is at 33F inside and out. This means that not only can fresh fruit and vegetables stand up to long-distance travel, but once they reach their destination, their shelf life has increased by 10 to 20 times. This is why zucchini from Florida in January tastes every bit as delicious as field-fresh zucchini in July. It may even taste better.

The wonders of modern technology have also brought fresh herbs into the market year-round. At Pete's, basil, dill, mint and cilantro are the most common. I worked at a café in a little seaside town one summer not long ago. One week a coworker's aunt brought in a shopping bag full of bunches of herbs in their own little plastic bags, the stalks wrapped in damp paper towels. For the next two weeks, everything we served was garnished with fresh herbs: the grilled salmon was accompanied by dill; the scallops with Pernod and cream were garnished with tarragon; the tomato salad was dusted with freshly chopped basil. Every single dish got rave reviews.

I always recommend using fresh herbs; dried herbs are a poor substitute. If you are worried that you might not use a whole bunch of a fresh herb at once, Pete recommends that you chop up any excess herb and place it by the teaspoonful into the compartments of an ice-cube tray; then add water and freeze. Every time you need a teaspoonful of the herb, simply thaw out a cube and the herb will be almost as flavorful as it was fresh.

One day when a customer asked how to preserve herbs I told her Pete's little ice-cube trick. Now every few weeks she comes in and orders a couple of bunches of something rare, takes them home and freezes them. She says that she will never go back to dried herbs again.

Cooking is an art and a good cook an artist (not necessarily vice versa), and as a good artist knows how to blend colors and how to use light and shade, so a good cook knows how to blend flavors and how to use herbs. Herbs will make or break a meal. A handful of fresh herbs in a lettuce-and-tomato salad will turn it into a gourmet delight. Knowing how to use fresh herbs is a key to the art of fine cuisine.

There is, in all of this, one thing that Pete and I would like you to bear in mind. When we talk about how long you can expect to store produce once you get it home, we are talking about A-1 fruit and vegetables. If your celery is wilted when you buy it, make allowances for this. Don't go home and store it for a week. If the only alfalfa sprouts you could get were turning a little brown, eat them on the way home or use them up on your first salad. Don't plan your meal for the day after tomorrow around them, because when you go to use them, they will only be fit for the garbage.

This is a guidebook with some unusual recipes, a number of surprising combinations, some of which will win you over right away. Some may take a little more of this or a little less of that to suit your palate.

So explore, be adventurous, be daring . . . try Midnight Parsnip Snack, taste fried ñame, savor Carrots and Cumin. Go on, have a little fun!

Nutrient Analysis

Nutrient analysis was calculated using *The Food Processor® for Windows* software program, version 6.0, copyright 1987-1995 by ESHA Research. It has a database of more than 10,000 foods and provides analysis for 113 nutrients and 21 nutrient factors including food exchanges. It uses data from the USDA and other scientific sources.

Analysis given in this book does not include optional ingredients or variations. Where an ingredient amount is a range, the higher number is used. Where there is a range of servings, the lower number is used.

The following abbreviations are used:

Cal = Calories
Prot = Protein
Carb = Carbohydrates
Fib = Fiber
Tot. Fat = Total Fat
Sat. Fat = Saturated Fat
Chol = Cholesterol
Sdm = Sodium

Pete
King of Greengrocers

Once upon a time, not so very long ago or so very far away, somewhere around the middle of England, a boy was born who was destined to become a king: King of the Greengrocers. His name was Pete Luckett. He was the third of four children born to an "unwealthy" family who lived in a row house in the city of Nottingham. There was nothing special about this family, except that they were his family. When Pete was a little boy, his mum and dad did not have a crib for him, so he slept in a drawer. There was no indoor plumbing; the toilet was in the yard. A family pastime was to take an old baby buggy and gather coke or coal off the railway tracks, where it had fallen from trains. This is a standard beginning for every king. It is believed to build character. It certainly worked for Pete!

Right from his wee nipperhood, the prince loved his future kingdom—the outdoor markets. He was intrigued by the hustle and bustle, the vibrancy of selling fruits and vegetables. He used to go to the markets just to watch the barrowmen ply their trade. Pete would stand for hours and listen to them getting excited, screaming, yelling, hollering, fascinated by the patter, the lingo that is unique to English markets. He admired the beautiful stalls and the pride that the vendors took in their displays. The whole area was a wealth of color and excitement. "It was a really alive place to be."

While still a lad, about 10 or 11, his mum used to give him about one pound fifty—thirty bob—to go and buy the week's fruit and veg for the family. This was his royal duty every Saturday morning. With a shopping bag carefully clutched in his hand, the little prince would climb onto the bus and ride it into the middle of the town, to Nottingham Central Market. Pete would check out all the best buys and wheel and deal and bargain with the barrowmen. He would return home laden with produce and a huge grin on his face, usually munching some fruit he'd nicked off a barrow. His mum would give him a big smile and a pat on the head and say, "Well done, our Pete!"

At 16, Pete started working in the produce department of a high-class grocery store and for the next five years, despite occasional forays into the hotel trade, concentrated on learning all that there was to know about the fruit-and-vegetable business. After two years, he shifted from grocery stores to his first love, the open-air markets. He learned all the chat, the lines, the flattery, the gestures. It wasn't long before he could hold his own with any of the lads.

When he was 21, a stall came up for sale in Nottingham's Victoria Market and Pete opened Pete's Frootique. Competition was fierce. Pete's Frootique was one of 20 fruit stalls all in a line. "All doin' the same as me, all chattin' up the customers, all shoutin' and yellin' their wares, all with fabulous displays." Nevertheless, Pete ran his stall successfully, with a little help from friends and family. After four years, Pete decided that it was time to move, so move he did. He sold everything, lock, stock and barrel, went to Heathrow and boarded the first plane going to North America, with nothing but a handful of money and a suitcase.

The next few years were adventurous ones for Pete. He traveled across the United States, through Guatemala, Belize and Mexico, and even spent some time in French Guyana, working in Texas, Florida and Belize when he needed more money. Eventually, his wanderlust wearing thin, Pete decided to settle down and applied for immigration to Canada. Three months later he moved to Alberta but after a brief year in western Canada, Pete, going against the general trend, moved east and bought a farm in southeastern New Brunswick.

Although Pete loved farm life, it quickly became obvious that he was not going to make a living at it. A year or two earlier, a germ of an idea had been sown in Pete's head when he had read about the Saint John City Market in *Harrowsmith* magazine. It sounded like a typical English market, one that could use a greengrocer. When money was dangerously low, Pete decided to go to Saint John to take a look at this market and the possibilities of getting back to what he does best.

The general report about Saint John was not particularly favorable. Pete was warned about "the scruffiest, dirtiest, horriblest city in Canada, smelly, disgusting and not friendly." Undaunted, he got on the bus and headed toward this dragon of a city. The emerging monarch will never forget his first reaction to the home of his future kingdom. He was wonderfully impressed. "The old 'ouses, the colou', the streets, the way it was all buil', the characters tha' I saw aroun' town . . . I though' it was a real neat place. I though' it was real sharp."

The first thing Pete did was to head for the city market, where he managed to wrangle a deal with the clerk who gave him a 12-foot bench stall in the middle of the market. Within two months he had shifted to a more appropriate spot with lots of available counter space and the requisite refrigerator.

There are few uptowners who do not remember the arrival of this barrowman to the Saint John City Market and few who frequent the market today who do not know him. Every day, six days a week, one hour before the market opens, Pete's employees arrive to begin the daily task of setting up the stall, getting fruits and vegetables out of the cooler or the warm room, and loading up the Brussels sprouts, green beans, broccoli, cauliflower, bananas, strawberries, anything that would not survive the night without the benefits of either heat or refrigeration. (For Pete's first 10 years in the market, there was no heat in winter and no air conditioning in summer.)

It is impossible not to notice the influence of a decade of experience as a barrowman. Pete's Frootique is a blaze of carefully coordinated colors and shapes. The quality of his produce is second to none and his prices are excellent. Every employee keeps a keen eye on color: they never put the broccoli beside the green beans or the beets beside the potatoes, let alone the mandarins beside the

With $230 worth of produce and ten years of experience, Pete revived Pete's Frootique and a king was crowned!

navel oranges, or the Macs beside the Red Delicious. Dull colors are used to set off the bright green of broccoli or the vibrant orange of carrots. Quality is also carefully controlled. Pete's advice to his team is, "If you wouldn't buy it you'self, don' put it out."

When I shop at Pete's, I simply put produce in my basket. I don't bother with the 360-degree check. I know that if something is on the stall at Pete's, it is good. If by some unlucky occurrence customers get something that is not the best, they have no doubt that it will be unquestioningly replaced or their money refunded on the spot, with a smile. Customers are Pete's livelihood and each one of them knows it.

As the day progresses, Pete's part of the market is a hub of activity, humming with conversations, usually in full voice, the phone ringing off the hook, orders being filled, customers being waited on or loading their baskets, Pete's employees keeping the displays "sparklin'" and full to overflowing.

As Pete's Frootique has grown in the City Market, so Pete's Frootique has grown outside the market, with two more Pete's Frootiques and two warehouses. Pete's trucks and vans, which zip along the streets of Saint John and the highways of New Brunswick, cannot be missed with their brightly colored Pete's Frootique logo on the side. In the summer, the busiest season for Pete and his Frootique, there are between 30 and 40 employees. Not bad for a man who started with $230 worth of produce and a 12-foot stall!

Pete's employees are few when compared to his viewers! When Pete first arrived at the City Market he was certainly the loudest vendor there, ready with a comment about anything and everything and a joke or an antic for every occasion. Because he had a friend who worked for Canadian Broadcasting Corporation (CBC) Radio, his comments were often aired. And because he was lively, informative and funny, he was interviewed frequently. A fan at CBC Radio was talking with some friends at CBC Television and Pete's name came up. Not long after, Pete's phone rang. It was a CBC producer. The station was starting a new show and would Pete like to have a brief spot as greengrocer?

Two or three times a week, Pete says as much as he possibly can in two minutes about any fruit or vegetable he chooses. These are aired on CBC's "Midday" and once a week on the CBC "News for New Brunswick." Thanks to CBC, Pete and his Frootique have become a main tourist attraction. During the summer at Pete's, there seems to be a long string of people, loyal fans, who "watch Pete every time he's on, without fail," some apparently traveling halfway across the country just to come to the market for an autograph or a photograph, or to buy a T-shirt with Pete's distinctive logo on the front and his trademark "Toodaledoo" across the back. And Pete greets every one of them with the charm and enthusiasm that has got him where he is today. He has no lack of fans to cheer him on, no matter what he tries to do!

About the Authors

In a corner of the Saint John City Market stands Pete's Frootique, one of the noisiest and most colorful fruit and vegetable stalls in eastern Canada. Here you'll often find Pete Luckett, Canada's best-known greengrocer, regaling his customers with stories about the fragile feijoa and the curious kiwano. If you're lucky, you'll also find a vivacious fruit monger by the name of Kathleen Robinson.

Both Pete and Kathleen have had long-standing love affairs with fruit and vegetables, and together they have prepared this comprehensive guide in which you'll find some of the most current information on common and exotic produce. You'll also find Pete's tips on selecting the freshest and the best from your grocer's shelves and Kathleen's tidbits on how to care for fruit and vegetables once you've taken them home. Best of all, Pete and Kathleen have included more than 200 of their favorite recipes, so that like them, you'll be able to savor everything from atemoya and fiddleheads to yucca root and zucchini.

Kathleen Robinson is a writer, performer and enthusiastic purveyor of fruit and vegetables. She has worked as a waitress, interior decorator, cook, sales clerk and teacher in England and Canada.

VEGETABLES

ARTICHOKES

Artichokes are not something you eat in a hurry. Eating one of these vegetables is a lengthy but delicious task. And, amazingly, after you've finished, there seems to be more on your plate than when you started—all those nibbled leaves and leftover fuzz.

Artichokes could correctly be called *flowers*; they are the flower heads of a thistle. Although various types of artichokes are available to Europeans, almost all North American, or globe, artichokes are grown in Castroville, California, where they grow more artichokes than anywhere else in the world. If you shop at a specialty market, you may also find artichokes imported from outside North America.

Artichokes are available off and on all year. Their peak season is from March through May, but they may be a little scarce in July and August. Look for tight, compact heads with thick, blemish-free leaves. A good head will be heavy for its size and feel fresh and crisp. Someone once told me that a good artichoke will squeak if you squeeze it. This may be an old wives' tale, but give your intended a squeeze; if it does squeak, you'll only enjoy it more!

Avoid artichokes with loose, spreading leaves and discoloration. The exception to this rule are the "winter-kissed" artichokes that appear on the market at the beginning of November. The bronze markings on the leaves are a result of being touched by the first frost, thus slowing the maturing process and enhancing the flavor. Size has nothing to do with taste. Big artichokes are simply easier to stuff and have larger hearts.

Artichokes may be refrigerated in a closed plastic bag or a plastic container with a tightly fitting lid for up to a week.

They are a good source of folate and vitamin C, and provide considerable potassium and iron. Four ounces of cooked artichoke contain 53 calories.

To prepare the artichokes, simply wash them and, if you can't break off the stems, cut them off flush with the base. Pull off and throw away the little leaves at the base and any tough, discolored leaves. Immediately dip the artichokes into acidulated water, then lay them on their sides and cut off the top one-third. Or cut the spiky top off each leaf with a pair of stainless-steel scissors. They are now ready to steam. (Until I was lucky enough to buy some inexpensive artichoke steamers, I used to leave the stems on. Then I could stand them up on their stems in a pot and, because they would be out of the water, they would steam rather nicely.)

The usual way of eating a cooked artichoke is to tear off the outer leaves, one at a time, dip them in a sauce and then scrape the flesh off with your teeth. This continues until you reach the central part of the artichoke, the "choke" of inedible, light fuzz. Then scrape or cut off the fuzz, exposing the heart, the most delectable part of the artichoke, which may be eaten with a knife and fork.

Artichokes discolor after they have been cut. To prevent this, have ready a bowl of acidulated water in which to plunge the artichokes. Acidulated water is simply 1 quart of water mixed with 3 tablespoons of vinegar or lemon juice. Contact with carbon, iron, steel or aluminum will also darken artichokes and give them a harsh flavor. So, use a stainless-steel knife for cutting and a stainless-steel or enamel saucepan for cooking.

Boiled or Steamed Artichokes

This is the simplest way to cook artichokes and it is particularly delicious. Because there is nothing but you and the artichokes and your chosen sauce, you can experience not only the richness of the vegetable, but also the fun of eating it.

1 tsp salt
4 Tbsp olive oil
4 large artichokes, washed and trimmed

Using a saucepan big enough to hold your artichokes, add the salt and olive oil to about 3 inches of boiling water. Steam the artichokes until the stem end is soft when pierced with a fork. This could take anywhere from 20 minutes to 1 hour depending on the size of the artichokes. Keep an eye on the liquid, adding more boiling water, if necessary, to prevent scorching. Turn the vegetables upside down and let them drain for a couple of minutes.

Serve them with a bowl of melted butter, mayonnaise or Hollandaise sauce. *Serves 4*

Each serving contains: Cal-179, Prot-4g, Carb-13g, Fib-6g, Tot. Fat-14g, Sat. Fat-2g, Chol-0mg, Sdm-647mg

Stuffed Artichokes

This stuffing is my favorite. If you are planning to stuff artichokes, it is worth remembering that breadcrumbs are especially compatible with this vegetable.

4 large artichokes, washed and trimmed
4 Tbsp melted butter
1 clove garlic, minced
1/4 cup mushrooms, chopped
2 cups fresh breadcrumbs
1 Tbsp capers, minced
Salt and pepper
1 Tbsp fresh thyme, finely chopped
1/4 cup parsley, chopped
1/4 cup Parmesan cheese, grated
Melted butter
1 cup vegetable stock

Steam the artichokes until they are tender enough that the leaves can be spread apart easily.

While the artichokes are cooking, melt the butter in a skillet and sauté the garlic and mushrooms until the mushrooms are tender; then mix in the breadcrumbs, capers, salt, pepper, thyme and parsley. Remove from the heat.

Drain the artichokes and let them cool until they can be easily handled; then hold the vegetable upside down on the counter and push down with the palm of your hand to spread the leaves apart. Remove the tiny central leaves and carefully spoon out the "choke." Fill the cavity with stuffing and push a little between the outer leaves. Sprinkle each artichoke with some grated Parmesan cheese.

Tie each artichoke around the middle so that it will keep its shape. Stand the artichokes upright in a casserole and brush with melted butter. Pour the stock around the bottoms of the artichokes and put the whole thing in the oven at 375F for 30 minutes. Baste frequently with the liquid in the pan. *Serves 4*

<u>Each serving contains:</u> Cal-350, Prot-11g, Carb-28g, Fib-8g, Tot. Fat-23g, Sat. Fat-14g, Chol-63mg, Sdm-847mg

ASPARAGUS

The only way to really enjoy asparagus is to eat it when it is as fresh as possible. Despite all the innovations of modern technology, we still cannot preserve asparagus in any truly acceptable form. Some years when we have a good crop, we can get almost enough at a reasonable price; but in those years when the harvest is not particularly plentiful, we all suffer.

Asparagus is available all year but is usually sold at very high prices, because it is imported, except during the North American harvest from April to June. When buying asparagus look for stalks with tight, compact heads; some heads may have a purple hue, which is natural to the variety. The thickness of the stalks is a matter of taste; some people prefer thick stalks, some like them thinner. It makes little difference in the flavor of the vegetable itself. Avoid asparagus with ruffled tips or wrinkles in the stalks, which indicate that the vegetable is old and probably tough.

Asparagus, like mushrooms, should not be bought until the last possible moment. They are better off with your supplier than in your refrigerator. But once you get them home, either wrap the stem ends in wet paper towels and put the asparagus in a plastic bag, or stand them up with the stem ends in a little water. If necessary, asparagus will keep like this for 4 days in the refrigerator.

Asparagus is an excellent source of vitamin C and folate and a good source of potassium. Four ounces of the raw vegetable have only 30 calories.

There are some tips to bear in mind when dealing with this vegetable. The very first thing to remember is never, absolutely never, soak asparagus. To wash this vegetable, simply hold the stalks upside down under cold running water and shake them a bit to release any sand that might be trapped in the tips. The second important thing to remember is that because most asparagus is now a hybrid variety, 90% of the stalk is edible. It is not necessary to peel it, even less to cut the stalks right off. When trimming asparagus, you need only cut the smallest inch or so off the stalk, except of course if you buy a particularly old bunch of the vegetable. Then you might need to cut off a little more. The third and final tip is *do not overcook asparagus*. There is almost nothing worse than overcooked asparagus. Bear these rules in mind and you will get the most from your asparagus.

The easiest thing to do with asparagus is simply to use it raw, tossed into a salad or with a mayonnaise-based sauce. Asparagus is one of those vegetables that need little embellishment. As far as Pete and I are concerned, there are only two ways to eat asparagus: lightly steamed with butter and lemon juice or in a cold asparagus sandwich. A good cold asparagus sandwich is a moment of bliss and a good excuse to eat French bread. The cooked, cooled vegetable with a little lemony mayonnaise and some delicious white bread is well worth a try!

Steamed Asparagus and Variations

1-1/2 to 2 pounds asparagus, washed and trimmed
1/4 cup melted butter
2 Tbsp lemon juice
1 lemon, thinly sliced
Salt and pepper

Because the stalks of asparagus tend to be thicker than the tips, they need a little more cooking, so the very best way to cook asparagus is to tie the stalks together in a bunch and stand them up, either in an asparagus pan, if you are lucky enough to have one, or an old coffee pot, such as Pete uses. What I do, because I have neither, is to put the vegetable in the deepest available pot and make a little hood out of aluminum foil to make sure the vegetable is well covered.

Pour a couple of inches of water into the bottom of the pot, put on a lid and bring the water to a rapid boil. Add the asparagus. It should only take about 10 minutes for the vegetable to be cooked perfectly. The asparagus is ready when the stems feel tender when pierced. But don't sacrifice the spears for the stems; if the spears are tender, remove the asparagus from the pot immediately.

Put the cooked asparagus on *warm* plates. Pour the melted butter and the lemon juice over the vegetable. Garnish with a slice of lemon, and sprinkle with salt and freshly ground black pepper. *Serves* 4

With toasted almonds: instead of lemon juice, throw on a handful of toasted sliced almonds.

With pine nuts: instead of lemon juice, add some toasted pine nuts.

Asparagus belongs to the lily family, along with onions, leeks and garlic, not to mention tulips and gladioli . . . rather odd cousins!

Each serving contains: Cal-160, Prot-6g, Carb-12g, Fib-5g, Tot. Fat-12g, Sat. Fat-7g, Chol-31mg, Sdm-190mg

With cream: warm a little cream, either half-and-half or whipping cream. Cook over low heat until it thickens somewhat and pour it over the cooked asparagus, in place of lemon juice. Grate on a little nutmeg and serve with white pepper and salt.

With an egg: for a delicious brunch treat, lay the asparagus on a warm plate and slide a poached egg on top. Pour some warm Hollandaise sauce over the egg and, if you want to be truly decadent, sprinkle with a little freshly grated Parmesan. Serve with thin slices of toasted French bread.

Danish Asparagus

This is how we used to eat asparagus at my grandmother's. She had an asparagus patch, which explains the rather generous amount of this delicacy for each person. This is a main course, but it can be served in smaller quantities if you don't have an asparagus patch or are unwilling to take out a mortgage to prepare this dish.

> **4 hard-cooked eggs**
> **1 cup melted butter**
> **Rind of 1 lemon, finely grated**
> **3 Tbsp fresh lemon juice**
> **1/4 cup parsley, minced**
> **4 pounds asparagus, washed and trimmed**
> **1 Tbsp sesame seeds**
> **Nutmeg (optional)**

Mash the eggs and combine them with the butter in a small saucepan. Cook over low heat long enough to blend completely. Remove from the heat; stir in the lemon rind, lemon juice and parsley. Keep warm.

Cook the asparagus until just tender. Lay the cooked vegetable on a warmed platter; pour the sauce over the vegetable and sprinkle with sesame seeds.

You might like to have some whole nutmeg and a grater handy. My uncles claim that nutmeg makes this dish just that much better. *Serves 4*

Each serving contains: Cal-606, Prot-18g, Carb-23g, Fib-10g, Tot. Fat-53g, Sat. Fat-31g, Chol-336mg, Sdm-543mg

AVOCADOS

These extraordinary pear-shaped packages are one of the pure undiluted luxuries of the produce world. Technically they are a fruit, and over the last decade or so, they have become as readily available as tomatoes in most markets, although not in the same quantity. Despite their availability, avocados have not become ordinary.

One either loves or loathes the avocado. Its wonderful velvety, buttery texture and rich, nutty taste either win you over at once or turn you off. Get two avocado lovers together and watch them.

One day while I was working at Pete's, a man who had bought about 10 avocados the week before appeared at my cash register. I commented on the fact that he was not buying avocados this week, even though they were less expensive than they had been the week before. He looked at me in astonishment, turned up his nose and said, "Those are a completely different type of avocado and their taste does not compare with the ones I bought last week." It was then that I became aware of the amazing and obvious differences in the varieties.

Avocados are available all year round but their peak season is from December to May. They are ready to eat when they yield to gentle pressure. Often the best bet is to buy avocados before they are ripe and let them ripen at home by putting them in a loosely closed paper bag at room temperature. Keep checking them because there is a fine line between perfect ripeness and over-ripeness. Once the fruit is ripe, you may store it in the warmest part of your refrigerator for up to 3 days. Pete claims that avocados taste better if you take them out of the refrigerator for a while before you serve them. When buying avocados, keep an eye out for dark patches on the skin and soft or sunken spots; an avocado should be uniformly soft or hard.

Avocados are an excellent source of folate and a good source of potassium and magnesium. The real killer is their caloric content due to the oil in the fruit (30% in some varieties). Four ounces, about half a medium-sized avocado, have almost 160 calories. (But they are worth every single one!)

Avocados can be cooked, but few would argue that cooking improves them. Pete says that he has never cooked an avocado and never would, so neither will we. Cut in half, the pit cavity provides a natural spot to pop in a little egg salad, which is especially good with avocado. You can also put a few slices on a green salad or serve them arranged decoratively on a plate and drizzled with a little of your favorite vinaigrette. I make a salad with sliced avocados, minced shallots and cherry-tomato halves with snow peas broken over the top. I let the whole thing sit in a vinaigrette for about half an hour and then pour off the excess dressing: it's excellent.

In North America, all avocados come from California and Florida. The Florida avocados have smooth, shiny, green skins and tend to be larger and more watery than those grown in California. Pete's own particular favorite is the Hass avocado, grown in California. It is oval and has a dark-green knobby skin that turns purple or black when ripe; its flesh could not possibly be richer. "A perfectly ripe Hass avocado is almos' a miracle, darlin'," exclaims Pete. It is like eating butter out of a shell. Amazing!

Egg-Stuffed Avocados

3 large avocados, halved lengthwise
1 lemon, cut up so that you can rub it on the avocados
1/2 green pepper, chopped
1/2 English cucumber, chopped
1 Serrano or Jalapeño pepper, seeded and minced
3 hard-cooked eggs, chopped
12 pitted black olives, chopped
Mayonnaise
Sour cream
Salt
Alfalfa sprouts
Sprigs of fresh cilantro (coriander) or parsley

Scoop out the flesh of the avocados without damaging the shells. Discard the pit. Put the flesh into a bowl. Rub the inside of each shell lightly with the lemon to prevent discoloring. Mash the avocado flesh with a fork. Add the green pepper, cucumber, hot pepper, eggs and olives. Mix well. Add enough mayonnaise and sour cream (in a ratio that appeals to you) to hold everything together. Season with salt. Line the avocado shells with a layer of alfalfa sprouts and stuff them with the salad mixture. Top each shell with a sprig of cilantro (coriander) or parsley. *Serves 6*

Each serving contains: Cal-339, Prot-7g, Carb-16g, Fib-5g, Tot. Fat-30g, Sat. Fat-7g, Chol-120mg, Sdm-315mg

Guacamole

Guacamole may be served with corn or tortilla chips (it's especially nice if you heat the chips), with fresh vegetables, or scooped into a tomato shell. Guacamole is a very personalized creation: feel free to add a little homemade mayonnaise or sour cream. If you like a little crunch, add some chopped sweet peppers, olives or a small diced cucumber.

2 large, very ripe avocados
1 medium tomato, peeled, seeded and chopped
1/2 small onion minced
3 cloves garlic, minced
2 Serrano or Jalapeño peppers, finely chopped
Juice of 1 lime
Chili powder to taste
Sprigs of fresh cilantro (coriander) or parsley
Salt and pepper

Guacamole is best made just before you are going to serve it, because it darkens when exposed to air. To slow the darkening, you can add lemon juice to the guacamole or put a piece of plastic wrap over the surface.

1/2-cup serving contains: Cal-183, Prot-3g, Carb-12g, Fib-5g, Tot. Fat-16g, Sat. Fat-2g, Chol-0mg, Sdm-87mg

Scoop the flesh out of the avocado shells and mash well. Blend the remaining ingredients with the avocado flesh. *Makes about 2-1/4 cups*

Avocado-Cilantro Soup

This recipe comes from a woman who shops at Pete's and regularly buys avocados and bunches of cilantro (coriander). She says this soup is one of her staples.

2 ripe avocados, peeled and cut up
1/2 English cucumber, seeded and chopped
3 to 4 large green onions, chopped
2 cloves garlic, minced
1-1/2 cups yogurt
Juice of 1/2 lime
1 cup vegetable stock
1/2 tsp cayenne pepper
1/4 cup fresh cilantro (coriander), chopped
Salt and pepper
Cilantro (coriander) leaves
Paprika

Put everything except the salt, pepper, cilantro leaves and paprika into a food processor or blender. Process until smooth. Chill. If mixture is too thick, thin with milk. Season with salt and pepper. Garnish with fresh cilantro leaves and a sprinkle of paprika. *Serves 4*

This marvelous herb is known by three names: cilantro, Chinese parsley *and* coriander.

Each serving contains: Cal-238, Prot-6g, Carb-16g, Fib-5g, Tot. Fat-19g, Sat. Fat-4g, Chol-12mg, Sdm-125mg

BEANS

Snap and *wax beans*, as green and yellow beans are commonly called, are available all year, their peak season being from May to August. Look for smooth, crisp beans that are free from blemishes or spots. They should snap easily if they are fresh. Pete buys his yellow beans when they are a little green at either end, like an unripe banana. He says that is the best way to make sure they are fresh and tender. Avoid beans that are flabby or wilted, or those with thick, fibrous pods, an indication that they are too mature.

Yellow and green beans are stored the same way. Put them, unwashed, into plastic bags and refrigerate. They will keep for 3 or 4 days.

Beans are a good source of vitamin C, folate and potassium; they also provide some iron. Four ounces of cooked beans have 40 calories.

When beans are ready to use, wash them well in cold water. Snip off the stems and tops. Beans can be left whole, or cut or broken straight across in 2-inch pieces. The Chinese prefer long oblique slices; the French, long, thin slivers. If the beans are small enough, they are particularly delicious left whole.

These little green morsels are one of summer's delights. If you are lucky enough to have a garden, or an above-average greengrocer (like Pete), you will know the delicious taste of truly fresh green beans. Green and yellow beans are interchangeable. For a little extra color, mix them together.

A key factor when dealing with beans is cooking time. Beans should be cooked as little as possible—just long enough to take away the raw taste but not so long that they lose their snap. It is important to keep testing them so that they do not overcook.

Boiled Beans and Variations

2 pounds beans, washed, trimmed and left whole or cut up
4 Tbsp butter, chopped
Salt and pepper

In a large saucepan, boil just enough water to cover the beans. Drop in the beans, a few at a time, so the water never stops boiling. If it does, stop, put a lid on the saucepan and bring it back to a boil. Remove the lid while cooking the beans or they will lose their bright color. Boil for 3 to 10 minutes, depending on the age and size of the beans. Taste them as they cook. The instant they are done to your liking, drain them. Put the pot back on the stove and toss the beans with the butter until the butter has melted. Season with salt and pepper. *Serves 4*

With toasted almonds: toss the beans with the butter and 1/2 cup toasted sliced almonds.

With garlic and pine nuts: substitute 1/4 cup olive oil for the butter. In a skillet, heat the oil and sauté 3 finely chopped cloves of garlic until tender. Add 1/2 cup toasted pine nuts. Toss with the beans.

With fresh herbs: toss the beans with olive oil or butter and 1-1/2 teaspoons fresh tarragon, dill, marjoram or garlic and basil.

With cream: toss the beans with butter and add 1/2 cup cream—a mix of whipping cream and half-and-half is nice, or you can use one or the other.

With tomato: toss the beans with the butter and add some heated tomato sauce. Sprinkle with fresh, chopped parsley before serving.

Chilled Beans and Variations

Cook the beans as above but toss them with 4 tablespoons of olive oil instead of the butter, after you have chilled them. *Serves 4*

With mustard-flavored mayonnaise: add 2 or 3 tablespoons Dijon-style mustard and 2 or 3 tablespoons bacon bits to 1/2 cup home-made mayonnaise. Toss with the beans.

Dilled vinaigrette: toss the beans in a vinaigrette made with dill vinegar or add 3 or 4 tablespoons of freshly chopped dill to your favorite dressing.

Each serving contains: Cal-172, Prot-4g, Carb-16g, Fib-8g, Tot. Fat-12g, Sat. Fat-7g, Chol-31mg, Sdm-198mg

Pete claims that beans are simply wonderful boiled a bit and served with lots of butter, black pepper and a little squeeze of lemon juice. Easy and tasty.

Each serving contains: Cal-190, Prot-4g, Carb-16g, Fib-8g, Tot. Fat-14g, Sat. Fat-2g, Chol-0mg, Sdm-80mg

Beans, Etc.

1-1/2 pounds beans, washed, trimmed and cut up
1 Tbsp olive oil
1 Tbsp butter
1/2 cup mushrooms, sliced
1 medium onion, very thinly sliced
2 cloves garlic, mashed
3 large tomatoes, peeled, seeded and chopped
1/4 cup minced fresh basil
1/3 cup parsley, minced
Salt and pepper

Boil the beans in 1 cup salted water for 5 minutes. Drain and chill.

In a skillet, heat the oil and butter. Sauté the mushrooms, onion and garlic until the onion is soft and transparent. Add the tomatoes, basil, parsley, salt and pepper. Cook for 5 minutes, stirring frequently.

Add the beans and mix well. Cook for 3 to 5 minutes or until the beans are just tender. *Serves* 4

Each serving contains: Cal-159, Prot-6g, Carb-23g, Fib-8g, Tot. Fat-7g, Sat. Fat-2g, Chol-8mg, Sdm-124mg

Beans à la South of France

1-1/2 pounds beans, trimmed, washed and cut up
1 large onion, minced
1 clove garlic, minced
1 small red pepper, cut in strips
3 Tbsp butter
1/4 cup thyme, chopped
Salt and pepper
1/4 cup parsley, minced

Cook the beans in boiling, salted water until tender-crisp. While the beans are cooking, sauté the onion, garlic and red pepper in the butter, stirring constantly for 5 minutes or until the onion is transparent. Add thyme. Drain the beans and add them to the onion mixture. Season. Cook over medium heat for 4 minutes, stirring to coat the beans with the onion. Sprinkle with parsley and serve hot. *Serves* 4

Each serving contains: Cal-151, Prot-4g, Carb-17g, Fib-7g, Tot. Fat-9g, Sat. Fat-5g, Chol-23mg, Sdm-169mg

YARD-LONG BEANS

I would be doing an injustice to you and to the long bean if I did not mention this Asian wonder—the yard-long bean, also called the *Chinese pole bean*. Usually only about half a yard long, the yard-long bean is similar to our common green bean, not botanically but in taste. Cut into 2-inch sections, yard-long beans are superb in a stir-fry or added to a stew during the last 15 minutes of cooking. They are also delicious braised. But do not bother cooking them any other way, because the yard-long bean does not do well when compared with our own green bean.

There are essentially two types of *dau gok*, an alias for this bean: the pale-green type tends to be slightly sweet and fleshy; the dark-green variety is a little drier and not quite as delicate in taste. This creature does not keep. Buy it and use it. If you must, you can store it in a plastic bag in the refrigerator for 2 days, but no longer. One cup of the Chinese pole bean has about 45 calories, lots of vitamin A, some vitamin C and a little potassium.

BEETS

Four different varieties of beets are commonly cultivated: the garden beet, which we all know and love; the leaf beet, more commonly known as Swiss chard; the sugar beet, from which we get most of our sugar; and the mangold, which is a major source of livestock feed in Europe. Perhaps we should have more respect for the apparently dull beet!

Beets are available almost all year round, their peak season being from June to October. They are especially good in the early summer, when we get the delicious beet greens, the leaves still attached to the root. Look for beets having a good round shape, smooth, firm flesh and a rich, deep-red color. The smaller vegetables are tender, the larger ones tougher. If the green tops are attached, they should be fresh in appearance, although it will not affect the quality of the root if the leaves are slightly wilted. Avoid spotted, pitted beets, or those with scales. If you are buying the greens without the beet attached, look for thin-ribbed leaves that are fresh and clean.

If the beet greens are fresh, you can store them in your refrigerator and use them as soon as possible. Beets themselves will keep for up to 3 weeks in a plastic bag in the vegetable drawer of your refrigerator.

Beets are a good source of potassium and an excellent source of folate. The greens provide some calcium; they are also a good source of iron and an excellent source of potassium and vitamins A and C. Four ounces of cooked beets have about 40 calories. Four ounces of cooked beet greens have 30 calories.

Pete's favorite way to cook beet greens is as quickly as possible, to preserve much of their texture and nutritional value. It is preferable to boil or steam the greens in, or over, a small amount of water for about 10 minutes. Serve them with black pepper and butter. You might like to add some bacon bits or Parmesan cheese for a little extra flavor.

Aunt Gill's Beets

My Aunt Gill is a beet lover and her beets are always a cause for celebration, because they are so delicious. Cooking them is easy enough, but the preparation is a little more work.

Put the beets in a large pot and boil in water for about 1 hour, or until the skins slip off. Then peel and grate them. You have to work quickly so the beets don't get cold. Aunt Gill recommends using a paper towel so you don't burn your fingers.

If you have a microwave, you can grate the beets after they have cooled and then heat them again. When they are all grated, add butter, salt and lots of freshly ground black pepper.

This is pure beet in all its delicious glory. For something a little more exciting, you can blend the beets with anything recommended below, but do try them plain first!

Each serving contains: Cal-67, Prot-3g, Carb-15g, Fib-3g, Tot. Fat-0g, Sat. Fat-0g, Chol-0mg, Sdm-116mg

Baked Beets and Variations

In an ovenproof dish combine 1 pound cooked sliced beets with any of the following. Bake at 350F for 15 minutes or until heated through. *Serves 2 to 3*

With onion and herbs: combine sliced beets with melted butter, chopped onion, vinegar and 2 tablespoons of tarragon, marjoram, thyme or dill.

With yogurt: add yogurt and black pepper to cooked beets.

With onion and orange: combine beets with chopped onion and orange sections and reheat in oven.

Scandinavian Pickled Beets

1/2 cup cider or white vinegar
1/2 cup water
1/2 cup sugar
Salt and pepper
6 large beets, cooked, peeled and thinly sliced
2 Tbsp caraway seeds
A sprig of fresh dill, chopped

Each serving contains: Cal-162, Prot-3g, Carb-40g, Fib-3g, Tot. Fat-1g, Sat. Fat-0g, Chol-0mg, Sdm-156mg

Combine the vinegar, water, sugar, salt and pepper. Boil for 5 minutes. Cool. Pour the liquid over the beets and sprinkle with caraway seeds. Cover and refrigerate overnight. Before serving, drain and sprinkle with chopped dill. *Serves 4*

Beets Parmesan

16 tiny beets, cooked and peeled
2/3 cup cream or half-and-half
Salt and pepper
1/3 cup Parmesan cheese, grated
A sprig of dill, chopped

Mix the beets and the cream. Season with salt and pepper. Simmer over low heat, stirring constantly, until the beets and cream are heated through. Add the Parmesan cheese and cook until the cheese is melted. Sprinkle with chopped dill. Serve hot. *Serves* 4 *to* 6

Each serving contains: Cal-140, Prot-7g, Carb-13g, Fib-2g, Tot. Fat-7g, Sat. Fat-5g, Chol-21mg, Sdm-325mg

Chilled Buttermilk-Beet Soup

4 large beets, peeled and grated
2 Tbsp butter
4 cups vegetable stock
1/2 cup green onions, finely chopped
1 tsp sugar
2 cups buttermilk
1 Tbsp fresh dill, chopped
Salt and pepper

Sauté the beets in butter for 5 minutes. Add the vegetable stock and simmer until tender. Add the green onions and cook for 5 minutes. Blend in a food processor or blender until smooth. Chill. Stir in the sugar, buttermilk and fresh dill. Season with salt and pepper to taste. *Serves* 6

Each serving contains: Cal-125, Prot-5g, Carb-17g, Fib-3g, Tot. Fat-5g, Sat. Fat-3g, Chol-13mg, Sdm-238mg

BELGIAN ENDIVE

This delicacy has intrigued me ever since I first stuck the price into the basket of Belgian endive at Pete's. *French endive,* or *Witloof chicory* as it is also called, is expensive. It comes packed as though it were crystal—in little wooden boxes, beautifully wrapped in waxy purple paper. I quickly understood that this was not just an ordinary vegetable. It is a lovely looking creature. Imagine the end of a baseball bat, shrink it down and make it a little more pointed—that is the shape of Belgian endive. The heads are slender and smooth and almost completely white, except for a little yellow or green around the edge of the leaves. It has a mildly bitter flavor.

Belgian endive is available all year, with its peak season during the summer months. Look for firm, crisp heads with pure-white leaves, light yellow around their edges and tips. Heads should be between 4 and 6 inches long. The vegetable is very clean and only needs to be wiped off with a damp cloth to be ready for eating. It stores well if you are careful. Wrap it in damp paper towels and refrigerate it for up to 5 days, making sure the heads are well covered. Endive needs to be protected from the light.

Belgian endive is a good source of vitamin A and potassium and an excellent source of folate. Four ounces of the vegetable have 20 calories.

Belgian Semi-Waldorf

My sister named this salad and it does vaguely resemble a Waldorf salad. It is delicious and easy. I find that the taste improves if you let it sit in the refrigerator for a day before you serve it; the flavors mellow.

> **1/2 pound Belgian endive, cleaned and thinly sliced**
> **2 apples, diced**
> **1 carrot, sliced**
> **1/4 cup raisins soaked for 1 hour in hot water**
> **1/4 cup freshly shelled walnuts**
> **1/2 cup mild cheese such as Mozzarella, cubed**
> **1 tsp lemon juice**
> **1 tsp sugar**
> **1/2 cup vinaigrette, page 17**
> **1/4 cup fresh parsley, coarsely chopped**

Mix the Belgian endive, fruit, carrot, nuts and cheese. Add the lemon juice and sugar to the vinaigrette and blend well. Pour the vinaigrette over the endive mixture and toss well. Sprinkle with parsley and serve. *Serves 4 to 6*

It is important to remember that if you are using Belgian endive simply as a salad green, a little goes a long way. You can slice the heads and add a handful to a salad, or you can serve the individual leaves stuffed with almost anything. The taste of Belgian endive mixes beautifully with mild cheese, apples or beets, almost anything that is a little sweet.

<u>Each serving contains:</u> Cal-302, Prot-5g, Carb-26g, Fib-4g, Tot. Fat-22g, Sat. Fat-4g, Chol-11mg, Sdm-207mg

VINAIGRETTE

1/4 cup lemon juice

1/4 cup vegetable oil

1 Tbsp wine vinegar

1 tsp dill

1/4 tsp salt

1/4 tsp oregano

1/4 tsp pepper

2 tablespoons contain: Cal-124, Prot-0g, Carb-2g, Fib-0g, Tot. Fat-14g, Sat. Fat-2g, Chol-0mg, Sdm-133mg

In a small bowl, whisk together the lemon juice, oil, vinegar, dill, salt, oregano and pepper. *Makes 1/2 cup*

Belgian Endive with Pimento and Cheese

This makes a delicious, different and simple lunch dish. Pete's friend, who gave me this recipe, also says that to spruce it up, you need only pour Hollandaise sauce over the top. Definitely high-class!

4 heads Belgian endive

2 Tbsp chopped pimento

8 slices Swiss cheese

Each serving contains: Cal-146, Prot-10g, Carb-4g, Fib-1g, Tot. Fat-10g, Sat. Fat-7g, Chol-34mg, Sdm-664mg

Boil the endive in 1/2 cup of salted water, just long enough to soften the heads a bit. Slice each head in half. Lay them on a greased cookie sheet or in a buttered casserole, side by side. Sprinkle with pimento, lay the cheese across the top and broil until the cheese is melted and a bubbly golden. *Serves 4*

Braised Belgian Endive

Most Belgian endive fans prefer the vegetable cooked this way.

3 small carrots, sliced

2 small onions, sliced

2 Tbsp butter

1 pound Belgian endive, cut in 1/2-inch slices

2 cups vegetable stock

1 Tbsp lemon juice

1 bay leaf

Salt, pepper and thyme

1 Tbsp cornstarch, dissolved in

1 Tbsp water

Each serving contains: Cal-122, Prot-3g, Carb-16g, Fib-5g, Tot. Fat 6g, Sat. Fat-4g, Chol-16mg, Sdm-171mg

Sauté the carrots and onions in the butter for 5 minutes. Lay the sliced endive on top. Pour the vegetable stock over the endive and add the lemon juice and the bay leaf. Season with salt, pepper and thyme. Over medium heat, bring the mixture to a boil and cook gently for 10 to 15 minutes. Add the cornstarch and mix it into the sauce. Remove bay leaf. Adjust the seasoning. Serve hot. *Serves 4 to 6*

BOK CHOY

If you ask for Chinese cabbage in some grocery stores, you might be mistakenly led to *bok choy*. Although its taste is cabbage-like, bok choy bears no resemblance to Chinese cabbage. It is an uncommonly pretty vegetable in its mature stage, with pure, silvery-white central stalks and dark, bluish-green leaves. Baby bok choy is comparatively rare and not as attractive, being all one shade of green, the leaves only slightly darker than the stalks. Like Chinese cabbage, bok choy is two vegetables in one—the leaves and the stalks—which should be cooked separately. The leaves take much less cooking time and have a slightly hot taste; the stalks are succulent and crunchy.

Bok choy is available all year. Look for vegetables with big leaves if you want them for soup, and longer narrower stems if you are planning on a stir-fry (bok choy's forte). Buy clean-looking bok choy with clear, white stalks and crisp, bright-green leaves. Slippery brown spots on the leaves indicate overchilling, which reduces the vegetable's flavor.

It is better to use bok choy as soon as possible rather than store it. You can, however, refrigerate it, unwashed in a plastic bag, for 2 days. Don't forget that it does not hold up to storage well. To wash it, simply hold it under cold running water just before using and drain it well.

Like many other Chinese vegetables, bok choy is low in calories, with only 15 per 1/2 cup. Bok choy is also rich in vitamins A and C and a good source of potassium.

Pete likes to add a handful of chopped bok choy stalks and leaves to a salad for a little extra crunch. The next time you are having a simple soup, throw in a few thin strips of bok choy leaves; they only need to simmer for 5 minutes. You can also toss in the stalks, chopped up. Because they need to cook a little longer, put the stalks in before the leaves.

Your next stir-fry is simply waiting for bok choy. Slice up the stalk and add it first; then shred and add the leaves. The stalks take about the same time to stir-fry as celery; the leaves, literally seconds. An interesting variation with the bok choy leaves is to cut them into long very thin strips and fry them for an instant in a generous amount of oil. They need only a little salt and pepper for seasoning and can serve as a bed for something special, or as a dish on their own.

Simple Bok Choy Stir-Fry

This is essentially a "how-to" recipe. It is fast and easy.

>   **2 Tbsp peanut oil**
>   **1-1/2 pounds bok choy, cleaned, the stems cut into 1-inch slices, the leaves thinly sliced**
>   **1 tsp brown sugar**
>   **1/4 tsp garlic, minced**
>   **Salt to taste**
>   **1 tsp fresh ginger, minced**
>   **2 Tbsp bacon bits**

In a frying pan or wok, heat the oil until it smokes. Drop in the chopped stems of the bok choy and fry over high heat for about 4 minutes, or less, until the stems are soft on the outside but still crunchy.

Add the bok choy leaves, sugar, garlic, salt and minced ginger. Cook, stirring constantly, for another 2 minutes or until the mixture is tender but still crispy. Sprinkle with bacon bits. *Serves 4*

Each serving contains: Cal-100, Prot-4g, Carb-5g, Fib-3g, Tot. Fat-8g, Sat. Fat-1g, Chol-0mg, Sdm-188mg

BROCCOLI

Broccoli must be as close to perfection as anything in the vegetable world. It is easy to use in a wide variety of ways; it is beautiful to look at, tastes wonderful, has lots of vitamins and minerals and 32 calories in 4 ounces. Broccoli is one of North America's favorite vegetables, and rightly so! You can eat it raw, steamed, in a quiche, in a salad, in a soufflé, on its own in a vinaigrette, with a sauce, without a sauce—the possibilities are almost endless.

Broccoli is available throughout the year, the peak season being from October to April. Look for tightly closed, compact bud clusters and firm, tender stems. The head should be a deep green, sometimes with a hint of purple. Avoid broccoli that is wilted, bruised or flabby, or with woody stalks.

To store broccoli, simply put the unwashed head in a plastic bag and place it in the refrigerator for no more than 3 days. Broccoli is very perishable, so it is a good idea to use it promptly.

There is never a good excuse for boiling broccoli: it is one of the worst things you can do to this fine vegetable. Boiling all but destroys both its flavor and its texture. The best way to cook this vegetable is to steam it, and not for long. Broccoli should be crisply tender when cooked.

Broccoli is also splendid in a stir-fry. Don't forget to eat the stems; just peel and slice them thinly, or cut them into spears. As a rule, it is unwise to cook the stems with the florets as they are tougher and take longer to cook; you risk overcooking the one in order to make the other edible. Simply add the stems before the florets, and give them an extra 5 to 7 minutes cooking time. When the stem pieces are slightly soft, add the florets.

Italian Broccoli

3 Tbsp olive oil

1 clove garlic, minced

1 bunch broccoli, cut into florets

1 red bell pepper, sliced

1-1/2 cups dry wine, red or white

Salt and pepper

1 Tbsp roasted pine nuts

In a deep frying pan, heat the oil. Sauté the garlic until it turns gold; add the broccoli. (If you are using the stems, they should be peeled, cut into 2-inch slices and cooked for about 7 minutes. Test them before you add the florets.) Cook, stirring constantly, for 2 or 3 minutes.

Add the bell pepper, wine, salt and pepper to taste. Cook over low heat for about 5 minutes, or until the broccoli is tender but not mushy. Stir occasionally. Sprinkle with pine nuts. Serve hot. *Serves 3*

Broccoli-and-Cheese Quiche

This is actually a little more heavy-duty than a quiche.

1 bunch broccoli, cut into florets

1 cup onion, sliced

1 cup mushrooms, sliced

3 Tbsp butter

4 eggs, lightly beaten

1 cup cream or half-and-half

1/2 cup milk

1/4 tsp Dijon-style mustard

Salt, pepper and nutmeg

1 cup sharp Cheddar cheese, grated

1 unbaked 9-inch pie shell (Add a little lemon peel to the pastry for this quiche to make it extra special!)

Fry the broccoli, onions and mushrooms in the butter until slightly tender. In a medium saucepan, beat the eggs into the cream and milk, add the mustard and season to taste with salt, pepper and nutmeg. Heat very gently until close to boiling but do not boil.

Each serving contains: Cal-273, Prot-6g, Carb-11g, Fib-5g, Tot. Fat-16g, Sat. Fat-2g, Chol-0mg, Sdm-136mg

Each serving contains: Cal-439, Prot-21g, Carb-18g, Fib-5g, Tot. Fat-33g, Sat. Fat-18, Chol-292mg, Sdm-495mg

Broccoli is rich in vitamins A and C, folate and potassium. As a member of the cabbage family, it may be helpful in the prevention of some types of cancer. Broccoli is also low in calories, with only 33 calories in 4 ounces of the raw vegetable, or 3/4 cup of the cooked.

Each serving contains: Cal-837, Prot-41g, Carb-55g, Fib-8g, Tot. Fat-52g, Sat. Fat-30g, Chol-373mg, Sdm-922mg

Sprinkle the cheese into the pie shell, top with the vegetables and pour the egg mixture over the top. Bake at 400F for 15 minutes; then reduce the heat to 375F and bake for another 30 minutes or until set. Let stand for 5 minutes before serving. *Serves 4*

Broccoli-Mushroom Casserole

1 bunch broccoli, florets and stems peeled and sliced

1 pound fresh mushrooms, sliced

1 cup chopped onion

3 Tbsp butter

Salt and pepper

1/4 cup vegetable stock

4 eggs

1-1/2 cups cottage cheese

1 cup sour cream or yogurt

3 cups egg noodles

2 Tbsp butter

1/4 cup fine breadcrumbs

1-1/2 cups aged Cheddar cheese, grated

Sauté the broccoli, mushrooms and onion in butter. Remove from the heat and toss with the salt, pepper and stock.

Beat the eggs in a bowl; whisk in the cottage cheese and the sour cream or yogurt.

Cook the egg noodles in salted water until slightly underdone. Drain and butter.

Mix the broccoli and cheese mixtures together with the noodles and place in a 9 x 13-inch baking pan. Top with the breadcrumbs and grated cheese. Bake, covered, at 350F for 30 minutes and, uncovered, for an additional 15 minutes. *Serves 4*

Broccoli Soup

1 large onion, chopped

1 medium carrot, grated

1 clove garlic, minced

2 Tbsp oil

6 cups vegetable stock

1 bunch broccoli, cut into florets, stems peeled and cut into chunks

1 tsp rosemary

Salt, pepper and nutmeg

1 cup sour cream or yogurt

Parmesan cheese

Sauté the onion, carrot and garlic in a frying pan with the oil. When the onion is soft, add the vegetable stock and the broccoli. Bring to a boil and simmer until the broccoli is tender.

Set aside a few florets for a garnish and purée the rest.

Heat the soup and add the rosemary, salt, pepper and nutmeg. Stir in the sour cream or yogurt. Blend thoroughly. Do not allow the soup to boil. Sprinkle with Parmesan cheese and garnish with the reserved florets. *Serves 4*

Each serving contains: Cal-311, Prot-10g, Carb-25g, Fib-8g, Tot. Fat-21g, Sat. Fat-10g, Chol-30mg, Sdm-271mg

BRUSSELS SPROUTS

I can still remember the first time that I was served these tiny Belgian natives. I sat in open-mouthed astonishment gazing at the tiny boiled cabbages sitting on my plate. Another surprise was tasting them, because they certainly didn't taste like boiled cabbage. That was about 20 years ago. Since then I have almost become fond of Brussels sprouts.

Brussels sprouts are readily available almost all year, the peak season being from September until mid-February. If you have the chance, buy small, firm, bright-green heads that feel heavy for their size. The small heads have the sweetest taste. Avoid soft, wilted, puffy heads with loose or yellow leaves.

To store Brussels sprouts, simply remove any yellowish or loose leaves and put the unwashed sprouts in a plastic bag. They may then be put in the refrigerator and stored for 4 or 5 days. But use Brussels sprouts as quickly as possible, because their flavor can get quite strong as they sit around.

Brussels sprouts are rich in vitamin C and folate. They are also a good source of potassium and iron. Like the other members of the cabbage family, Brussels sprouts may be influential in the prevention of certain types of cancer. Four ounces of Brussels sprouts contain about 45 calories.

The secret to cooking Brussels sprouts is to make a shallow "X" in the stem ends after trimming: this little "X" will ensure even cooking.

Boiled or Steamed Brussels Sprouts and Variations

It takes less water to boil Brussels sprouts than to steam them. For boiling, use about 1 inch of water and allow approximately 7 minutes cooking time. For steaming, allow 15 to 20 minutes and use 2 to 3 inches of water. Cooking time depends on the size and freshness of the sprouts. They are cooked when the stem ends feel tender when pierced. *Use 1 pound of sprouts for 4 servings*

Each serving contains: Cal-49, Prot-4g, Carb-10g, Fib-6g, Tot. Fat-0g, Sat. Fat-0g, Chol-0mg, Sdm-28mg

With butter: simply toss the cooked sprouts with melted butter and sprinkle with some freshly ground black pepper.

With mushrooms: mix sautéed mushrooms with the butter and toss together with the sprouts.

With sour cream: heat sour cream and pour over sprouts. Top with bacon bits.

A real gourmet treat: toss 1 pound of cooked Brussels sprouts in 4 tablespoons of butter, 4 tablespoons of finely minced shallots, 1/2 teaspoon of caraway seeds, a pinch of marjoram and 2 tablespoons of vinegar. Serve hot.

Brussels sprouts are a favorite of many devout vegetable lovers and are considered by some to be the national vegetable of Great Britain. Their taste is certainly unique and can easily be enhanced. But there are two key points to bear in mind when dealing with Brussels sprouts: do not buy them when they're too big and do not cook them too long.

Brussels Sprouts Roma

1 pound Brussels sprouts, washed and trimmed

2 cloves garlic, finely chopped

2 Tbsp olive oil

Salt and pepper

2 Tbsp freshly squeezed lemon juice

Rind of 1 lemon, grated

1/4 cup Parmesan cheese

1 Tbsp fresh dill, coarsely chopped

Boil or steam the Brussels sprouts until almost tender. Meanwhile, fry the garlic in the oil; when golden, add the sprouts. Season with salt and pepper.

Sauté the mixture, stirring carefully, for 3 minutes. Add the lemon juice and cook for another minute. Sprinkle with lemon rind and Parmesan cheese. Garnish with dill before serving. *Serves* 4

Each serving contains: Cal-142, Prot-7g, Carb-12g, Fib-6g, Tot. Fat-9g, Sat. Fat-2g, Chol-5mg, Sdm-212mg

Brussels Sprouts, Sour Cream and Chestnuts

1-1/2 pounds Brussels sprouts, trimmed and washed

1/4 cup sliced almonds

4 Tbsp butter

1 pound cooked or canned chestnuts, water chestnuts or jícama, thinly sliced

Salt and pepper

1/4 tsp nutmeg

1/4 cup sour cream

1/4 cup minced parsley

Steam or boil the sprouts until they are almost tender. Drain.

Each serving contains: Cal-285, Prot-8g, Carb-27g, Fib-15g, Tot. Fat-18g, Sat. Fat-9g, Chol-37mg, Sdm-241mg

The cabbage family, which includes broccoli, Brussels sprouts, kale, kohlrabi, collards and cauliflower, is a diet recommendation of the American Cancer Society. It is believed to be helpful in the prevention of certain types of cancer.

Toast the almonds in the butter; then add the Brussels sprouts and chestnuts. (If you use canned chestnuts or water chestnuts, let them drain and gently pat them dry.) Season with salt, pepper and nutmeg. Cook over low heat, shaking the pan frequently, until the sprouts are tender.

Add the sour cream, stirring carefully. Heat until warm. Sprinkle with the parsley before serving. *Serves 4 to 6*

CABBAGE

Red, green and Savoy—all three cabbages are interchangeable, one difference, besides color, being the mild taste of the crinkly leafed Savoy. Some people also find red cabbage has a little spicy warmth.

Pete is particularly fond of Savoy cabbage and so, behold some further details on and information concerning Savoy cabbage. In his fondness for Savoy cabbage Pete gives away his roots, for Europeans love this vegetable, from its purplish-green outside to its solid, deep-green heart. Savoy is probably the most versatile of all the cabbages. Its big, "easy-peel-away" leaves make excellent cabbage rolls. Its crinkly outer leaves, which resemble napa, can be used instead of the Chinese cabbage in Oriental cooking. As Pete points out, the flavor of cooked Savoy cabbage is so delicious that it needs nothing but butter and freshly ground black pepper—no sauce, nothing to mask that sweet, distinctive flavor.

Cabbage is available all year and new cabbage is available from May to September. The difference between old and new cabbage is incredible. Pete says that the only time cabbage is good as a cooked vegetable is when new cabbage is available, the taste of the new cabbage being so much more delicious. The rest of the year, cabbage is good for salads, soups, slaws, pickling and sauerkraut.

When buying cabbage, look for firm heads that are heavy for their size. The outer leaves should be of a soft color, crisp and fresh in appearance and without blemishes. Savoy cabbage is deep green, occasionally with a distinct purplish color, and has a softer head but should still have firm, crisp leaves. Avoid heads that are too white and overmature. If the leaf bases are separated from the stem, the cabbage may be strong in flavor and coarser. The best way to keep cabbage is to refrigerate it, uncut and unwashed, in a plastic bag, where it will keep for up to a week.

Raw cabbage is a wonderful source of vitamin C and an excellent source of fiber. Four ounces of raw cabbage have only 30 calories.

Steamed Cabbage

1 medium head of cabbage, cut in wedges
1/2 cup melted butter
Salt and pepper

Boil 1/2 inch of salted water in a heavy pot. When steam begins to rise, add the cabbage. Cover tightly and turn the heat down. Test after 5 minutes; it could take up to 10 minutes for the cabbage to become crisply tender. Drain well. Toss with melted butter and season with salt and pepper. A handful of caraway seeds would not go amiss in this recipe. *Serves* 4

With vinaigrette: toss the cabbage with a few tablespoons of oil and some bacon bits. At the last moment, add a few drops of vinegar, or pour on a little vinaigrette (see page 17 for recipe).

Each serving contains: Cal-260, Prot-4g, Carb-12g, Fib-5g, Tot. Fat-24g, Sat. Fat-14g, Chol-62mg, Sdm-342mg

Lemon Cabbage

2 to 3 pounds cabbage, shredded
3 Tbsp butter
3 Tbsp flour
Juice and rind of 2 lemons
Salt and pepper
1 lemon, sliced paper-thin
Dill for garnish

Bring 1-1/2 to 2 cups salted water to a boil, add the cabbage and cook until just tender. Save the cooking liquid.

Melt the butter in a saucepan. Mix in the flour and cook over low heat for a minute. Gradually add the cabbage water. Cook over medium heat until the sauce is smooth. Add lemon juice and rind, salt and pepper to taste. Put the cabbage in a casserole and pour the sauce over it. Heat at 350F for 15 minutes. Garnish with lemon slices and dill. *Serves* 4

Each serving contains: Cal-195, Prot-6g, Carb-27g, Fib-8g, Tot. Fat-10g, Sat. Fat-6g, Chol-23mg, Sdm-217mg

Cabbage, Etc.

1 small onion, sliced
1 cup carrot, sliced
1/2 pound mushrooms, sliced
3 Tbsp butter
1 medium-size cabbage, trimmed and shredded
1/2 cup vegetable stock, heated
1 Tbsp butter
1 Tbsp flour
3 large tomatoes, peeled, seeded and chopped
1 cup tomato juice
1/4 cup parsley, minced
3 Tbsp cream
1 Tbsp fresh basil, chopped
Salt and pepper

Sauté the onion, carrot, and mushrooms in the butter until soft. Add the cabbage and the boiling vegetable stock. Cook over high heat for 3 minutes, stirring constantly. Remove from the heat.

Melt the remaining butter; stir in the flour and cook for 1 minute. Add the tomatoes, tomato juice and parsley, stirring constantly until the mixture begins to thicken. Stir in the cream. Combine the tomato sauce with the cabbage mixture and mix well. Season with the basil, salt and pepper. Cover and simmer for 10 minutes, stirring frequently. Serve very hot. *Serves 6*

Each serving contains: Cal-185, Prot-5g, Carb-20g, Fib-5g, Tot. Fat-11g, Sat. Fat-7g, Chol-31mg, Sdm-316mg

Braised Cabbage

1/4 cup butter
1 medium head of cabbage, shredded or coarsely cut
Salt and pepper
1 cup vegetable stock or dry white wine, or a mix of the two

Melt the butter in a large, heavy frying pan. Add the cabbage and stir over medium heat until it wilts and turns brown at the edges. Add salt, pepper and the stock or wine. Cover and simmer for about 30 minutes, or until the cabbage is just tender.

You may wish to add some chopped fresh dill or basil and a tablespoon of vinegar. *Serves 4*

Each serving contains: Cal-182, Prot-4g, Carb-13g, Fib-5g, Tot. Fat-12g, Sat. Fat-7g, Chol-31mg, Sdm-228mg

CARDOON

Cardoon looks like a rather long, large, flat celery stalk. Like celery, cardoon grows in bunches but with thicker, fleshier, silvery-gray stalks and larger, longer leaves. It can grow to lengths of more than two feet.

Cardoon, occasionally called *artichoke weed*, looks like a relative of celery but is in fact part of the thistle family. The plant grows wild in the pampas grass of Argentina and as a weed in Australia. It is almost revered in France and Italy, where it has been considered a delicacy for 300 years. Unfortunately, this rather lovely vegetable is not as popular with North Americans and may be a little difficult to track down. This may be in part due to the fact that some people find that cardoon is an acquired taste, the flavor of the vegetable being a combination of artichoke, celery and parsnip. Its texture, when cooked, is rather soft and fleshy.

Cardoon is available from November to March. It should look and feel a little soft; don't expect it to be crisp like celery. Cardoon, which is small and slender, will be more tender. The stalks, however, should be firm. Don't worry if the tops of the cut stalks are a little brown or limp; the leaves are often removed just prior to shipping and the cardoon browns quickly once cut. You can keep the vegetable wrapped in plastic in the refrigerator for up to 2 weeks.

Cardoon is a good source of potassium. Four ounces of this vegetable have only 26 calories!

Pete says the key to cardoon is that it has to be carefully trimmed and must be precooked before it can be cooked. Chop off the top leafy portion of the vegetable and save it to use as flavoring for soups and casseroles. Remove the outer ribs and use them for flavoring as well. If the sides of any of the inner ribs are tough, remove them. Cardoon ribs have tough strings, looking like those found in celery, but more pronounced, so pull these off before cooking.

If you can get cardoon from France or Italy, it is nice raw, sliced into a salad. The California cardoon, most common on the North American market, is better cooked because it has a tendency to be bitter.

To cook the vegetable, cut it into 2-inch chunks and boil it in lightly salted water until tender, about 15 to 20 minutes. Although this may sound like a bit of a bother, don't skip the precooking. Otherwise, you'll find yourself serving a nasty, bitter vegetable. You can then add the cooked vegetable to stews or soups, or you can stir-fry it and serve it with a cheese sauce or a delicious Mornay sauce. Cardoon dipped in a light egg batter and deep-fried until crisp is a great Italian treat.

If you have a favorite way of cooking celery, substitute cardoon; the two are readily interchangeable. But be careful to use only light sauces or dressings because this delicate vegetable is easily overwhelmed.

Some people recommend that cardoon be treated with acidulated water, because the vegetable discolors quickly once cut. As it has to be cooked and turns rather brown anyway, Pete says he sees little point in the acidulated-water treatment. Its color does not affect the taste.

French Cardoon

5 cloves garlic

1 large onion, cut into chunks

1/4 cup parsley

1 bay leaf

1-1/2 tsp fresh thyme

1 red pepper, seeded and cut in strips

2 pounds cardoon, cut into 1/2-inch slices

1/4 cup fresh parsley, chopped

1 Tbsp olive oil

1 Tbsp flour

Salt and pepper

Combine 2 cloves of the garlic with the onion, parsley, bay leaf, thyme and red pepper in a pot with 2-1/2 quarts of water. Simmer. Add the cardoon and cook for 30 minutes or until tender. Drain and reserve the cooking liquid.

Crush the remaining garlic in a bowl, and add the parsley. Mix well.

Combine the olive oil and flour in a saucepan big enough to hold the cardoon. Add the parsley mixture and stir gently. Add up to 1 cup of the cooking liquid, enough to make a thick sauce.

Add the cardoon to the sauce and reheat until the cardoon is good and hot. Season with salt and pepper to taste. *Serves 4 to 6*

Each serving contains: Cal-99, Prot-3g, Carb-16g, Fib-5g, Tot. Fat-4g, Sat. Fat-1g, Chol-0mg, Sdm-268mg

Cardoon au Gratin

6 Tbsp butter

4 Tbsp all-purpose flour

1-1/2 cups milk

1 cup Cheddar or Swiss cheese, grated

1 tsp Dijon-style mustard

1-1/2 to 2 pounds cardoon, cut up, cooked and drained

1/4 cup breadcrumbs

Melt 4 tablespoons of the butter in a saucepan. Stir in the flour and cook for about 1 minute. Heat the milk and stir it into the mixture. The sauce should be quite thin because it will thicken as it cooks. Feel free to add more warmed milk as you go along to keep the consistency as you like it. Cook for 2 minutes. Add 3/4 cup of the cheese and the mustard.

Each serving contains: Cal-463, Prot-15g, Carb-33g, Fib-4g, Tot. Fat-31g, Sat. Fat-19g, Chol-89mg, Sdm-787mg

Meanwhile, melt the remaining 2 tablespoons butter in a large frying pan. Add the cardoon and heat, stirring gently and constantly. When the cardoon and the cheese sauce are both hot, blend the two and pour the mixture into a well-buttered casserole. Sprinkle with breadcrumbs and the remaining 1/4 cup cheese. Bake at 350F for 15 minutes or until bubbly and golden. *Serves* 4

You can add 1/2 cup of sliced, sautéed onions to this mixture. Or you can omit the cheese and mustard, add 1 cup of sliced, sautéed onions and season with a little nutmeg instead.

Cardoon and Cream

Hopelessly simple and beautifully delicious.

1-1/2 to 2 pounds cardoon, cut up, cooked and drained
1/2 cup whipping cream
1/2 cup cream or half-and-half
Salt, pepper and nutmeg

Each serving contains: Cal-179, Prot-3g, Carb-10g, Fib-3g, Tot. Fat-15g, Sat. Fat-9g, Chol-52mg, Sdm-287mg

Mix everything together well and simmer in a large saucepan until the cream is reduced by half. Serve as hot as possible. *Serves* 4

CARROTS

The vegetable world is full of wonderful little treats and the carrot is one of Nature's finest surprises. From carrot soup to carrot muffins and carrot cake, this lowly vegetable doubtlessly has uses we have not even thought of, perhaps some even stranger than the snowman's nose. Carrots are dual-purpose: useful simply as a vegetable and, because of their sugar content, as an ingredient in desserts such as carrot cake and carrot pudding. And, wonder of wonders, carrots are one of the vegetables that children truly enjoy eating.

Carrots are available all year round. The stored ones wear rather thin and get a little old at about the same time the new crop of Florida and California carrots become available in markets across the country. As well as the traditional large carrots, tiny baby carrots, popular in Europe, are now easily available. Look for carrots with a rich golden-orange color. They should be smooth, clean, firm and well-shaped. Choose even-sized carrots. Usually the smaller the carrot, the more tender and sweet it is. If you are buying bunched carrots, look for fresh-looking, bright-green leaves. Avoid cracked, soft or shriveled carrots. Be especially careful in the spring: if prepackaged carrots have not been stored properly, there will often be soft spots or decay.

Pete has some advice: the next time you go shopping, look for a bag of really fresh carrots or, if you can, get a bunch with their tops on. Take them home, give one carrot a good wash, peel it if you must, and sit down and eat it. Really taste this little wonder. Pete will just about guarantee that you'll be surprised. He claims that we are so spoiled by always having good carrots readily available that we don't appreciate them enough.

Each serving contains: Cal-100, Prot-1g, Carb-11g, Fib-3g, Tot. Fat-6g, Sat. Fat-4g, Chol-16mg, Sdm-98mg

To store prepackaged carrots, simply place them in their bag in the refrigerator. For bunched carrots, remove the green tops and store them unwashed in a plastic bag; they store well for 2 weeks. Pete surprised me by mentioning that fresh carrot greens provide excellent flavoring for soups, stews and casseroles. So next time, don't throw them out!

Ah, yes, we all know, don't we, what a good source of vitamin A carrots are, one of the richest in fact. Vitamin A keeps your eyesight in good condition and is important in bone formation. Carrots are also a good source of vitamin C and potassium. Four ounces of raw carrot have only 45 calories.

Take some time and have some fun experimenting with carrots. Try adding puréed or mashed carrots to equal amounts of your favorite mashed vegetables, whether they be potatoes, parsnips or beets.

Steamed Carrots and Variations

2 pounds carrots, peeled and julienned
4 Tbsp butter
Pepper

Steam or boil the carrots in salted boiling water until just tender. Drain, toss with the butter and season with pepper. Steamed carrots with butter and pepper are truly delicious without any other additions. *Serves 8*

With fresh herbs: toss the buttered carrots in 2 tablespoons of chopped fresh dill, tarragon or marjoram.

Steamed, glazed carrots: add 2 tablespoons of honey or, for real excitement, maple syrup to the melted butter. Shake over low heat until the butter and honey or syrup combine and glaze the carrots. Sprinkle with chopped parsley and dill.

Nutty, glazed carrots: to make things even more exciting, throw in a handful of toasted, slivered almonds.

Cognac-glazed carrots: for a real treat, add 2 tablespoons of cognac to the glazed carrots.

Carrots and Cumin

1 pound carrots, sliced

1-1/2 cups vegetable stock

1 cup onion, chopped

1 clove garlic, minced

2 Tbsp butter

1 tsp cumin seed

Salt and pepper

Simmer the carrots in the vegetable stock for 5 minutes or until almost tender. Save 1/2 cup of the cooking liquid.

Sauté the onion and garlic in the butter until soft and transparent. Add the cumin seed and cook for 1 minute. Pour in the reserved liquid and add the carrots, salt and pepper. Cook until the carrots are tender, about 5 minutes. *Serves* 4

This is a Moroccan favorite that my brothers enjoy. They brought the recipe home and it became a family specialty.

Each serving contains: Cal-124, Prot-2g, Carb-17g, Fib-4g, Tot. Fat-6g, Sat. Fat-4g, Chol-16mg, Sdm-172mg

Carrot-Alfalfa Winter Salad

This does not have to be a winter salad. A friend of my mother's used to make this salad in the winter about 20 years ago when good vegetables were hard to find. It is so good we never stopped making it, even though good salad vegetables are now available all year round.

2 cups carrots, grated

2 cups alfalfa sprouts

1/4 cup raisins

1/4 cup peanuts

1 clove garlic, minced

1 Tbsp lemon juice

1 Tbsp oil

1/4 cup yogurt

2 Tbsp mayonnaise

1 tsp chopped parsley, chives and/or tarragon

Salt and pepper

Combine the carrots, sprouts, raisins and peanuts. Toss them together well. Blend the garlic, lemon juice, oil, yogurt, mayonnaise, herbs, salt and pepper in a bottle; give it a good shake and pour the dressing over the vegetables. Toss and serve at once. *Serves* 4

Each serving contains: Cal-200, Prot-4g, Carb-17g, Fib-3g, Tot. Fat-14g, Sat. Fat-2g, Chol-6mg, Sdm-136mg

Carrot Quiche

4 cups carrots, grated

1 unbaked 9-inch pie shell

4 eggs

1/4 cup cream or half-and-half

1 cup Swiss or Cheddar cheese, grated

Salt, pepper and nutmeg

Spread the grated carrots on the bottom of the pie shell. Beat the eggs and cream or half-and-half together. Stir in the cheese and season as desired. Pour the mixture over the carrots. Bake at 425F for 10 minutes.

Reduce the heat to 350F and continue baking for 30 minutes or until the custard is set. Let stand for 10 minutes before serving. *Serves 4*

Each serving contains: Cal-259, Prot-16g, Carb-15g, Fib-3g, Tot. Fat-15g, Sat. Fat-8g, Chol-243mg, Sdm-265 mg

Carrot Mincemeat

Now we get to see how versatile carrots really are, just for the real doubters among us.

2 cups carrots, grated

2 cups raisins, golden and dark, mixed

1 lemon, cut into pieces

5 cups chopped apples, preferably Cortlands

1 cup candied citron peel

2 cups sugar

2 tsp cinnamon

1 tsp nutmeg

1 tsp cloves

1/2 cup cider

1/2 cup molasses

Toss the carrots, raisins and lemon into the food processor. If you are not the lucky owner of one, put these ingredients in the blender one at a time and crush them. Put the carrot mixture into a medium-sized saucepan and add the apples, citron peel, sugar, cinnamon, nutmeg and cloves. Blend well. Add the cider and molasses, and simmer over low heat until the carrots and apples are soft.

Use your own preferred method for preserving. Carrot mincemeat freezes well. *Makes 2-1/2 quarts, enough for three 9" pies*

1/2-cup serving contains: Cal-232, Prot-1g, Carb-60g, Fib-2g, Tot. Fat-0g, Sat. Fat-0g, Chol-0mg, Sdm-10mg

Steamed Carrot Pudding

No one is as fond of steamed puddings as the English, and very few people seem to make them with such proficiency. Pete, being English . . . well, he claims that this is one of the things that makes him look forward to Christmas. This is a real favorite, made at least once a year chez Pete, when it provides a wonderful, light alternative to the traditional plum pudding.

2 Tbsp sour milk
1/2 tsp baking soda
1 tsp salt
1 tsp cinnamon
1/2 tsp allspice
1/4 tsp nutmeg
1/2 cup flour
1 cup grated carrots
1 cup grated potato
1 cup soft breadcrumbs
1 cup raisins
1/2 cup currants
1/2 cup candied citron peel
1 cup brown sugar
3/4 cup butter

Combine the sour milk and baking soda; set aside. Add the salt, cinnamon, allspice and nutmeg to the flour and blend well. Add the sour milk and everything else to the flour mixture.

After it's been well oiled, fill your best pudding mold with the batter. If you don't have a pudding mold, a ceramic bowl will do. Cover mold with a cloth or foil and steam for 3 hours. *Serves 12*

If you have a favorite traditional sauce, such as a brandy butter or even a custard sauce, that you serve with plum pudding, it will be as good with this delicious pudding.

Each serving contains: Cal-263, Prot-2g, Carb-39g, Fib-2g, Tot. Fat-12g, Sat. Fat-7g, Chol-32mg, Sdm-378mg

CAULIFLOWER

An attractive head of cauliflower requires a lot of work and for this reason, cauliflower tends to be expensive. In order to keep the curd (or head) white, the outer leaves are gathered around the bud and hand-tied to protect it from sunlight. There is a new purplish-green variety of cauliflower available in some markets which doesn't require as much attention as the white. It keeps its green color when cooked.

Cauliflower is available all year, with peak supplies from September to November. Look for clean, firm, snowy-white heads with nice tight curds. A yellowish hue indicates over-maturity. Often you can find smudgy or speckled heads for sale at a reduced price. If the damage is not too extensive and can be easily removed, just scrape it off or cut it out, unless you are buying the vegetable for its appearance.

The best way to store cauliflower is simply to put it in the refrigerator as soon as you get home. It will keep in a plastic bag for a week, but using it as soon as possible is recommended as old cauliflower acquires a strong taste and smell.

Cauliflower is an excellent source of vitamin C and folate and a good source of potassium. Four ounces of raw cauliflower have about 30 calories.

Cauliflower is delicious steamed and served with almost any sauce. Try it with a curry, béarnaise or Mornay sauce. The easiest way to steam a cauliflower, if you don't have a steamer, is simply to put it in a saucepan with a tightly fitting lid with a few inches of salted water in the bottom. Put the lid on and boil the water for 10 to 15 minutes. The lower part of the cauliflower will be boiled, but the rest of the vegetable will be steamed.

Cauliflower is equally delicious cooked or raw, with your favorite vinaigrette or mayonnaise. Try adding it to a green salad or include some on a tray of crudités. When searching for a snack, break off a chunk of cold, fresh cauliflower and eat it as though it were an apple. You'll probably find it to be a refreshing change.

Cauliflower Cheese

This is an English meal, usually served as a main dish with a salad or a green vegetable. It was one of Pete's favorites when he was growing up.

1 Tbsp butter
1 Tbsp flour
1-1/4 cups milk
1-1/4 cups aged Cheddar cheese, grated

1 tsp Dijon-style mustard

Salt and pepper

1 medium cauliflower, washed, trimmed and broken into florets

1/4 cup fine dry breadcrumbs

Paprika

Melt the butter in a saucepan and stir in the flour. Pour the milk into a saucepan and let it heat a bit before adding it to the butter-and-flour paste. Cook the mixture over low heat, stirring constantly until it's smooth and thickened. Add 1 cup of the cheese and the mustard. Season with salt and pepper, if desired. Stir constantly until the cheese is melted. Feel free to add more milk if the sauce gets too thick. Keep warm.

Cook the cauliflower in boiling salted water for 3 or 4 minutes or until almost tender. Drain.

Put the cauliflower into a buttered baking dish. Pour the cheese sauce over the top and sprinkle with the remaining cheese and breadcrumbs mixed together. Dust with paprika. Bake at 400F for about 5 minutes or until the top is nicely browned. *Serves 4*

Each serving contains: Cal-261, Prot-13g, Carb-13g, Fib-1g, Tot. Fat-18g, Sat. Fat-11g, Chol-55mg, Sdm-453mg

Cauliflower-and-Mushroom Bake

1 large cauliflower, washed, trimmed and broken into florets

1/4 cup butter

3 cloves garlic, minced

1 Tbsp fresh basil, chopped

Salt and pepper

1 pound mushrooms, sliced

1 large onion, chopped

1 medium green pepper, cut in strips

1 small red pepper, cut in strips

3 cups cooked rice, preferably brown

1-1/2 cups Parmesan, Swiss or Cheddar cheese, grated

Sauté the cauliflower in 2 tablespoons of the butter with the garlic, basil, salt and pepper. Set aside. Sauté the mushrooms, onions and peppers in the remaining butter. Stir everything together and place in a large well-buttered baking dish. Bake, covered, at 350F for 30 minutes. *Serves 6*

Each serving contains: Cal-340, Prot-16g, Carb-34g, Fib-5g, Tot. Fat-17g, Sat. Fat-10g, Chol-40mg, Sdm-612mg

Cauliflower Blue-Cheese Salad

1/2 cup yogurt

1 Tbsp mayonnaise

1 tsp lemon juice

3 Tbsp blue cheese, crumbled

1 medium cauliflower, washed, trimmed and broken into florets

4 Tbsp parsley

Cream the yogurt, mayonnaise, lemon juice and blue cheese together until blended. Toss the cauliflower and parsley together and add the yogurt mixture. Stir carefully. This salad looks exquisite served with sliced tomatoes, and the dressing tastes wonderful with them too. *Serves 4 to 6*

Each serving contains: Cal-80, Prot-4g, Carb-5g, Fib-1g, Tot. Fat-6g, Sat. Fat-2g, Chol-11mg, Sdm-139mg

Cauliflower Soup

1 cauliflower, washed, trimmed and broken into florets

1 medium onion, chopped

1/4 cup butter

2 Tbsp flour

2 cups vegetable stock

1 cup white wine

1 cup cream

Salt and pepper

3 Tbsp chervil, chopped

Boil the cauliflower in 1 cup water. Drain and reserve the water. Set the vegetable aside.

Cook the onion in the butter until soft. Blend in the flour, add the stock and wine and bring to a boil, stirring constantly. Add the cauliflower water along with the cream, salt and pepper. Add cauliflower and heat well.

Let the soup stand for a moment or two, and sprinkle with chervil before serving. *Serves 6*

Each serving contains: Cal-228, Prot-3, Carb-10g, Fib-2g, Tot. Fat-18g, Sat. Fat-11g, Chol-56mg, Sdm-155mg

CELERIAC

To those unfamiliar with celeriac, or *celery root*, this particular vegetable varies in size from that of a small apple to that of a large cantaloupe. Its beige exterior is covered with bumps, crevices and grooves; little rootlets protrude from the base and stubby stalks from the top. This ungainly globe, which is often scruffy and dirty, is not an appetizing sight. But it's definitely worth exploring.

Celeriac is available from late fall to early spring. If you have any doubt that what you have located is actually the elusive celeriac, simply check for its very distinct aroma of celery. Choose medium-size spheres; the larger ones tend to be woody inside. The smoother the exterior, the easier it will be to peel, and although you can leave the skin on if you're going to boil it whole, celeriac needs to be peeled at some point. To store, simply cut off the rootlets at the base and the stalks on the top; put what is left into a plastic bag and refrigerate for no more than a week.

Celeriac is not loaded with vitamins, but is a good source of potassium and vitamin C. A 4-ounce portion has 47 calories.

To prevent celeriac from turning brown when peeled, submerge the pieces of the vegetable in a bowl of acidulated water. (Acidulated water consists of 3 tablespoons of lemon juice or vinegar to 1 quart of water.)

This rather unattractive root vegetable has been unjustly ignored by most North American cooks. I have noticed that the majority of people who buy it at Pete's have European origins. When I ask them about how they cook it, their answers vary. When I asked him about it, Pete clarified things a little and made a few suggestions.

Inside the unattractive exterior of celeriac is a lovely mottled, white flesh with a delicious, unique taste and an intriguing texture. Celeriac is equally at home in soups, salads, fritters and stuffings; it can be baked, boiled, braised, puréed or eaten raw.

Pete's Introductory Celeriac Salad

When I asked Pete how to use celeriac, he gave me this recipe.

1/2 cup mayonnaise

1 Tbsp Dijon-style mustard

Salt and pepper

1/2 cup cream

3 medium-sized celeriac (2 pounds), peeled and cut into pieces a little larger than match sticks

1 Spanish onion, thinly sliced

Lettuce

1/2 tsp caraway seeds

1/4 cup minced parsley

Fold the mayonnaise, mustard, salt and pepper into the cream. Drain the pieces of celeriac, dry them on paper towels, and fold them into the dressing along with onions. Toss with two forks.

Place the mixture in a salad bowl lined with lettuce and sprinkle with caraway seeds and parsley. *Serves 4 to 6*

German-Style Celeriac

Another easy introductory salad involves marinating the celeriac.

- **3 Tbsp olive oil**
- **2 Tbsp white wine vinegar**
- **1 tsp sugar**
- **1 tsp caraway seeds**
- **1 clove garlic, minced**
- **2 medium-sized celeriac (1 pound), peeled and cut into julienne strips**
- **Salt**
- **1/4 cup mayonnaise**
- **2 green onions, chopped**

Mix the oil, vinegar, sugar, caraway seeds and garlic; add the celeriac and season with salt. Cover the mixture and leave it at room temperature for 2 hours, stirring occasionally.

Just before serving, drain off the marinade, which can be saved and used as a vinaigrette, and stir in the mayonnaise.

Sprinkle with green onions and serve. *Serves 4 to 6*

Celeriac-and-Potato Soup

- **1 large onion, sliced**
- **2 Tbsp butter**
- **3 medium-sized celeriac (2 pounds), peeled and cut into chunks**
- **1 pound potatoes, peeled and cut into chunks**
- **1 tsp fresh tarragon, chopped**
- **3 cups vegetable stock**
- **2 cups milk**
- **Salt, pepper and nutmeg**
- **Paprika**

Sauté the onion in the butter in a covered pan over low heat until soft. Add the celeriac, potatoes and tarragon. Toss for a minute or two. Then add the vegetable stock and the milk. Simmer, covered, for 30 minutes or until the vegetables are tender. Purée the soup very quickly in a food processor or blender. (I like to purée about three-quarters of the mixture and mash the rest of it with a potato masher, later adding it to the soup.)

The soup does well with a little texture. If you like your soup thinner, add some hot milk until it is the right consistency. Season with salt, nutmeg and pepper (white pepper if you have it). Sprinkle with a little paprika just before serving. *Serves 4*

Each serving contains: Cal-319, Prot-10g, Carb-51g, Fib-13g, Tot. Fat-11g, Sat. Fat-6g, Chol-32mg, Sdm-339mg

Celeriac Royale

2/3 cup homemade mayonnaise

2/3 cup yogurt

1 tsp Dijon-style mustard

1 Tbsp fresh dill, chopped

1 Tbsp chives, chopped

1 Tbsp parsley, chopped

1-1/2 pounds celeriac, peeled and coarsely grated

2 hard-cooked eggs, chopped

Mix the mayonnaise, yogurt, mustard, dill, chives and parsley together. Pour the sauce over the celeriac and garnish with the eggs. *Serves 6*

Each serving contains: Cal-248, Prot-5g, Carb-9g, Fib-4g, Tot. Fat-22g, Sat. Fat-4g, Chol-89mg, Sdm-263mg

Baked Celeriac and Potatoes

Arrange 1 cup each of thinly sliced, peeled celeriac and potatoes in layers in a well-buttered baking dish. Dot with butter and cover with vegetable stock. Bake at 350F until tender, about 45 minutes. Sprinkle with 1/4 cup shredded Mozzarella cheese. *Serves 3*

Each serving contains: Cal-156, Prot-4g, Carb-14g, Fib-2g, Tot. Fat-10g, Sat. Fat-6g, Chol-28mg, Sdm-155mg

Mashed Celeriac and Potatoes

Using 2 cups peeled celeriac and 1 cup potatoes, proceed as if you were going to make mashed potatoes, boiling the celeriac along with the potatoes. When cooked, mash the celeriac and potatoes together, using vegetable stock instead of milk. Add some finely minced garlic, salt, pepper and nutmeg. Purée everything together, adding stock until you reach the desired consistency. Serve very hot. It's a delicious change from ordinary mashed potatoes. *Serves 4*

Each serving contains: Cal-51, Prot-1g, Carb-12g, Fib-2g, Tot. Fat-0g, Sat. Fat-0g, Chol-0mg, Sdm-124mg

CELERY

Pete's favorite way of cooking celery is to sauté it and eat it with lots of butter and freshly ground black pepper.

Celery stuffed with cheese was a special treat when I was a child. One of my favorite treats is still celery with cheese, or just plain old celery.

At Pete's, the cash registers are squeezed in among the fruit and vegetables: one between the limes, garlic, ginger and grapefruit, one between the turnip and cabbage and one between the romaine and celery. My favorite is the one next to the celery. Occasionally an outer rib or two will fall off the stalk and, presto, I am suddenly standing beside a snack!

Pete trims all the celery that he sells at the stall and when this happens I find I am standing beside a whole box of snacks! Celery is particularly refreshing at Pete's because, sprinkled with ice, it is moist, cold, green and superbly crunchy. It's hard to beat.

I am always amazed by the shoppers who search through the display for a small stalk of celery (it is not a *bunch* or a *head* but a *stalk*) because, they say, they could never eat a large stalk in a week. I help them find a small one and expound on the virtues of celery, encouraging them to eat one piece in the morning and one at night or a couple of pieces at night when they are watching TV. My efforts are not always in vain. A couple of customers have started buying bigger stalks. Try it yourself; it is a great snack anytime and all but totally devoid of calories. If I begin eating a stalk at night, I will eat at least half of it before I go to bed!

Celery is available all year with no peak season. There are actually two different and distinct types of celery: Golden Heart, which is bleached white, and Pascal, which is green. Pascal is the type which can most often be found in our markets. No matter which variety you are buying, look for the same characteristics. Leaf stalks should be crisp and firm with a pronounced snap when you break them, but guess about this part—greengrocers don't take too well to customers testing their celery by breaking pieces. A nice tight stalk usually means good celery. Leaflets should look fresh. Avoid stalks that look wilted, shriveled or limp.

Store celery in a plastic bag in the refrigerator for up to 2 weeks. You have one and only one chance to revive your celery if you forget it and it wilts. Soak it in icy, salted water until it perks up again.

Celery is full of fiber and is not bad in the mineral and vitamin departments. A "detergent vegetable," raw celery is excellent for your teeth when eaten raw. Best of all, you can it eat to your heart's content, without the cheese, of course, no matter how strict your diet: an entire pound (3 to 4 large pieces) has only 50 calories and most of them are used up when your body processes the vegetable.

It takes a little thought, but you need not waste anything in a stalk of celery. The leaves are delicious in soup. The outer stalks are great cooked. The inner stalks are wonderful on a tray of crudités or stuffed with cheese. Slice the stalk thinly and add it to a stir fry, or sprinkle a handful into your next vegetable or egg salad. The key thing is not to forget you have celery in the refrigerator.

Sautéed Celery

1 stalk celery
1/4 cup butter
Salt and pepper
Tarragon or thyme

Wash the stalk well. Slice it into 1-inch pieces, cut at a 45° angle. Melt the butter in a frying pan and add the celery. Sauté for 5 minutes, stirring frequently. Add more butter if needed. Season with salt and pepper, and sprinkle with some chopped fresh tarragon or thyme. *Serves 4*

Each serving contains: Cal-103, Prot-0g, Carb-0g, Fib-0g, Tot. Fat-12g, Sat. Fat-7g, Chol-31mg, Sdm-193mg

CHAYOTES

This relative newcomer to the vegetable market is a versatile creature. This little squash comes in various colors, from white to dark green, with or without spines, with ribs or without. Weighing close to 1 pound, chayotes are roughly pear-shaped, 5 to 7 inches long and about the same in diameter. The female squash, which is smooth and meaty, is preferable to the spiny male.

Chayotes are available all year and are particularly abundant during the winter months, from November to March. Look for firm, young, unblemished vegetables, the harder the better. Avoid chayotes that are wrinkled or even vaguely soft. Pete has tested all three colors of chayotes, dark green, light green and white, and says that they all taste exactly the same. Store chayotes in a cool, dark, well-ventilated spot for up to 1 month. You can also refrigerate them, lightly wrapped, for up to a month.

Chayotes are a good source of fiber and vitamin C. Four ounces of raw chayote have 32 calories.

You can use chayote in any recipe which calls for summer squash, and then some. But it is worth bearing in mind that chayote takes longer to cook than most summer squash because of its solid consistency.

Authorities differ on treatment: some recommend vigorous seasoning; others feel that its delicate flavor is one of the chayote's most attractive features. You can choose for yourself. Pete's own choice is to add lots of different tastes to the chayote, as you will see in his stuffed-chayote recipe.

Easy Chayotes

This is the easiest way to cook chayotes, as the name suggests, and a good introduction to the vegetable.

Plan on about half a chayote per person. Cut the squash in half and cook in boiling water until tender. Scoop the flesh out of the shells and mash it with a little butter, toss in some chopped fresh oregano and a little spicy seasoning salt. That's it!

Each serving contains: Cal-126, Prot-1g, Carb-6g, Fib-3g, Tot. Fat-12g, Sat. Fat-7g, Chol-31mg, Sdm-121mg

Cheese-Stuffed Chayotes

3 large chayotes
3 Tbsp butter
1 cup Cheddar cheese, grated
1 tsp Dijon-style mustard
Tabasco® sauce
Salt and pepper
1/4 cup dry breadcrumbs

Cut the chayotes in half lengthwise and cook them in boiling, salted water until tender. Drain and cool. Spoon out the flesh, taking care not to damage the skin, which is alarmingly easy to do. Throw out the cores. Mash the flesh.

Heat 2 tablespoons of the butter and sauté the chayote flesh, stirring constantly, for 2 minutes. Stir in the cheese, mustard and a dash of Tabasco sauce, and cook until the cheese melts. Remove from the heat and season with salt and pepper.

Stuff the squash shells with the mixture and place them side by side in a shallow baking dish. Sprinkle shells with breadcrumbs, and dot with the remaining butter. Pour 1/2 inch of water around the base of the chayotes and bake at 350F for 30 minutes or until golden. Add more boiling water if necessary. *Serves 6*

A chayote is the fruit of a particularly useful plant, yielding spring shoots, which are eaten like asparagus; tuberous roots, which are eaten like potatoes; and blossoms, which are reputed to produce amazing honey. Next time you see chayotes, pick up a few because when they are in good condition, they will keep for up to a month.

Each serving contains: Cal-169, Prot-6g, Carb-9g, Fib-3g, Tot. Fat-13g, Sat. Fat-8g, Chol-35mg, Sdm-281mg

Chayotes à la Pete

2 medium-sized chayotes
1 large onion, chopped
2 cloves garlic, minced
2 Tbsp butter
2 Serrano or Jalapeño peppers, finely minced
1 cup breadcrumbs
2 eggs
3/4 cup Gruyère or aged Cheddar cheese, grated
3 Tbsp bacon bits
1 to 1-1/2 cups milk
Pepper

Boil the chayotes whole for about 30 minutes or until they begin to feel soft. Remove them from the water and let them cool until you can handle them. Scoop out the flesh very carefully; the skin becomes very tender once it has been cooked.

Put the chayote flesh in a piece of cheesecloth or a clean towel and wring it until the squash flesh is quite dry.

Fry the onion and garlic in the butter until the onion is soft and translucent. Add the hot peppers.

Mix the breadcrumbs with the chayote. Add the eggs and blend well. Mix in the grated cheese (saving a small amount for a garnish), the bacon bits and the onion mixture. Add enough milk to make the mixture moist but not soupy. Stir well. Season with pepper.

Spoon the combination back into the chayote shells, heaping up the shells with the filling. Sprinkle with the extra grated cheese. Bake at 350F for 20 minutes, or until golden. *Serves 4*

<u>Each serving contains:</u> Cal-383, Prot-18g, Carb-33g, Fib-5g, Tot. Fat-20g, Sat. Fat-10g, Chol-151mg, Sdm-583mg

CHINESE CABBAGE AND NAPA

This is a wonderful vegetable, perfect for cabbage haters. Very few people dislike this vegetable, even die-hard disdainers of cabbage.

I asked Joe, the man who used to run the Nipa Hut, a little restaurant in the corner of the Saint John City Market, to explain the difference between napa and Chinese cabbage. Joe always buys napa and insists that it is a completely different creature from Chinese cabbage, not even a substitute. He said that the main difference is that napa is a little coarser and its flavor a little hotter.

For the average person, there is no difference between napa and Chinese cabbage. For all but the most discerning tastes, the two are interchangeable, except that I like to put the former in sandwiches because it is more succulent. Pete's personal recommendation is that you try the two in the same recipe and see which one you prefer. If you can tell the difference, I will be surprised.

Appearance, however, is another matter. Chinese cabbage looks very business-like, slender like a stalk vegetable. Sometimes the upper parts of the leaves will flare outwards; sometimes they'll curl inwards. Napa is a little more frivolous, tending to be fat with pale-green, crinkled leaves, like the leaves of a Savoy cabbage, tightly bound around a central head. Both are good cooked quickly or eaten raw. They can be used instead of ordinary cabbage in any recipe, but cook more quickly.

Chinese cabbage is available year round. Buy firm, tight heads with nice clean color and crisp texture. If you plan on cooking it, the limper cabbages, which have a slightly milder flavor, are preferable. Napa is also available all year round. Buy tight, heavy heads with unblemished leaves.

Both Chinese cabbage and napa may be stored, wrapped in plastic, in the bottom of your refrigerator for up to 2 weeks. If you plan on using them raw, keep them for as brief a time as possible, only a couple of days.

These vegetables are excellent sources of vitamin C and folate and provide some vitamin A and potassium. One cup of either vegetable has only 15 calories.

When you buy Chinese cabbage or napa, you are really getting two vegetables in one. The leaves and the central ribs need to be dealt with in different ways in order to get full enjoyment from the vegetable. Both are a welcome addition to a stir-fry. Cut the leaves from the ribs. Slice the ribs like celery and the leaves in very thin strips. Simply put the ribs in to cook a few minutes before you add the leaves. The ribs are delicious raw in salads because of their juiciness, and they are equally good in strips with a vegetable dip. If lettuce is getting boring, or too expensive, try making a salad with chopped Chinese cabbage leaves. Thin laces of the leaves are also good dropped into a soup at the last minute.

Potter's Cabbage

1 Tbsp butter

3 large shallots, sliced

1-1/2 inches fresh ginger root, peeled and grated

1 large carrot, grated

3 Tbsp bacon bits

2 pounds Chinese cabbage, rinsed and cut in quarters lengthwise

1/2 cup dry white wine

1-1/2 cups vegetable stock

Salt and pepper

1 Tbsp butter

Melt the butter in a skillet, and sauté the shallots, ginger and carrot until soft. Add the bacon bits. Put half the mixture in the bottom of a 2-quart casserole. Cover with the cabbage and the other half of the vegetable combination. Bring the white wine and stock to a boil and pour the liquid over the vegetables. Season with salt and pepper. Cover and bake at 350F for 60 minutes.

Remove the casserole from the oven and drain off the liquid. Boil the liquid over high heat until only 2 tablespoons are left. Add the remaining butter and pour over the cabbage mixture. *Serves 4*

Each serving contains: Cal-155, Prot-6g, Carb-14g, Fib-5g, Tot. Fat-7g, Sat. Fat-4g, Chol-16mg, Sdm-381mg

Sweet-and-Sour Chinese Cabbage

This is also great with other types of cabbage; use red cabbage for a colorful side dish.

> **2 Tbsp butter**
> **2 to 3 pounds Chinese cabbage, coarsely chopped**
> **Salt and pepper**
> **1 cup vegetable stock, heated**
> **2 tart apples, cored and thinly sliced**
> **1/4 cup cider vinegar**
> **1 Tbsp honey**
> **1 tsp caraway seeds**
> **1 Tbsp cornstarch**
> **1/4 cup cold water**

Melt the butter in a large saucepan. Add the cabbage, a generous amount of pepper and a little less salt. Sauté, stirring constantly, for about 2 minutes. Add the boiling vegetable stock and apples. Cook for about 3 minutes or until the cabbage is slightly tender but still crisp. Add the vinegar, honey and caraway seeds.

In a small bowl, dissolve the cornstarch in the water. Gradually add the cornstarch liquid to the vegetable mixture. Simmer, stirring constantly, until the sauce thickens. Add more honey or vinegar if the sauce is not sweet or sour enough. Simmer for a minute or two. *Serves 6*

Each serving contains: Cal-114, Prot-4g, Carb-18g, Fib-4g, Tot. Fat-5g, Sat. Fat-2g, Chol-10mg, Sdm-234mg

Sautéed Chinese Cabbage

> **3 Tbsp butter or peanut oil**
> **1 pound Chinese cabbage, trimmed and shredded**
> **Salt and pepper**

Heat the butter or oil in a frying pan. Add the cabbage. Cover and cook for 2 or 3 minutes, stirring occasionally to keep the cabbage from scorching. Season with salt and pepper.

Fennel seed or ground cumin is especially tasty with this recipe. *Serves 4*

Each serving contains: Cal-91, Prot-2g, Carb-2g, Fib-1g, Tot. Fat-9g, Sat. Fat-5g, Chol-23mg, Sdm-228mg

The flavor of this leafy vegetable wanders somewhere between cabbage and kale. It has thick, meaty leaves like a cabbage but grows in a loose-leafed shape. It bears a remarkable resemblance to English Spring cabbage. African slaves introduced collards to the southern United States hundreds of years ago, and it is still the South that grows and consumes most of North America's collards.

COLLARDS

Collards are one of the oldest members of the cabbage family. The key to their popularity and longevity is hardiness, because they are able to withstand drought and very high temperatures. As for the cold, a light frost only improves their taste.

Collards are available off and on all year round, their peak season being from December to April. Look for young, firm, crisp leaves, and avoid larger, older plants with yellowed, wilted or insect-damaged leaves. Collards may be washed before being stored. But if you don't have the time or inclination to wash them when you buy them, it is not necessary. To wash collards, simply put them in a sink full of lukewarm water. Swish them around a few times and let the sand and dirt sink to the bottom. Rinse in cold water as many times as necessary, until water comes through clean. Refrigerate them wrapped in damp paper towels in a plastic bag for 3 to 5 days.

Collards are very good for you. They are an excellent source of vitamin A and provide some calcium, potassium and zinc. Four ounces of raw collard greens have 23 calories.

There are two schools of thought on cooking collards. Some experts suggest cooking them as long as possible; others think that collards should be cooked for no longer than 5 or 10 minutes. This is simply a matter of personal preference. If they are cooked for a long time, collards develop a mellow taste and become quite soft. If cooked briefly, the texture is like that of sautéed cabbage and the flavor pronounced.

You can serve collards alone or combined with a starchy vegetable like potatoes, or with rice or beans. They are also tasty with a cream or cheese sauce. You can even slide a poached egg or two in there for a little more protein. Feel free to be aggressive when seasoning collards; they blend well with garlic and onions or ginger or they can be complemented by crunchy fried croutons. Try them with raisins, some grated ginger root and pine nuts.

African Collards

A friend of mine came back from Ethiopia with this recipe and never misses an opportunity to make it. It is one of my favorites.

1-1/2 pounds collards, washed and chopped

2 large shallots, minced

2 Tbsp butter

3 Tbsp bacon bits

1/2-inch chunk of fresh ginger, grated

1 Serrano or Jalapeño pepper, minced

Salt, pepper, nutmeg, cinnamon and cardamom to taste

1 cup dry rice, cooked

3 Tbsp butter

1/4 cup raisins, soaked in boiling water for 15 minutes, then drained

1/3 cup slivered almonds, toasted

2 green onions, sliced

Drop the collards into a large pot of boiling, salted water. Boil until tender, testing often. Drain well.

Sauté the shallots in 2 tablespoons butter until tender, about 2 to 3 minutes. Add the collards, bacon bits, ginger, pepper and spices. Stir long enough to heat the collards through. Remove from the heat.

Combine the rice, 3 tablespoons butter, raisins and nuts. Fold the rice mixture into the collards. Sprinkle with green onions.

Serve at room temperature. *Serves* 4

Each serving contains: Cal-344, Prot-7g, Carb-36g, Fib-9g, Tot. Fat-21g, Sat. Fat-10g, Chol-39mg, Sdm-252mg

CORN

Although modern technology has made many kinds of produce not only more available but deliciously fresh, as if we had just picked them from the garden, fresh, affordable corn on the cob is one of those treats available about six months of the year.

Corn on the cob is the ultimate kid's food because it must be eaten with the hands and invites a mess. In order to truly enjoy corn, even adults tend to get a bit messy. Its juicy sweetness seems to be enhanced by sticky fingers and the feel of melted butter everywhere. Mmmm, dreaming of it yet?

Corn on the cob is available at Pete's all year round and at a pretty reasonable price, but this is not the norm. In most places, the peak season for fresh corn is from June to September. It is during the latter part of the summer that there is an abundance of this delightful yellow vegetable and the price drops accordingly. Select fresh-looking ears with tight green husks and a fresh, sweet smell. The kernels should be plump, juicy and packed tightly onto the cob. Avoid soft, shriveled ears with spots, signs of decay or worm damage. Large, tough kernels can indicate over-maturity. Pete recommends small-kernel corn because it is usually sweet and tender.

The best way to store fresh corn is to wrap it, unhusked, in a damp paper towel in a plastic bag in the refrigerator, but for an absolute maximum of 2 days. Cooked fresh corn is a good source of folate and has about 80 calories in one small ear.

It is almost a crime to eat fresh corn on the cob any other way than all by its glorious self, but just in case you happen to run into a windfall of fresh corn, or you are a corn farmer who finds himself with a surplus, here are a few recipes with corn as well as a few different ways to cook it.

Each serving contains: Cal-133, Prot-4g, Carb-31g, Fib-3g, Tot. Fat-2g, Sat. Fat-0g, Chol-0mg, Sdm-21mg

Corn used to be one of the vegetables that had to be eaten almost before it was picked, but thanks to recent developments in the world of hybrids and technology, most of the corn we buy now will keep its sweetness for a few days rather than just a few hours. Pre-cooling, a process that takes place moments after the corn is picked, removes the field heat much more quickly than ordinary refrigeration, thereby slowing the sugar-conversion process and prolonging the life of the cob. The corn stays sweeter and fresher longer.

Roasted Corn (2 methods)

1. Pull back the husk and remove the silk. Replace the husk and if necessary, tie with a string. To increase moisture and create some steam, soak the corn in salted water for 5 minutes. Drain and place the ears in a shallow baking dish. Bake at 350F for 30 minutes.

2. Husk the corn and rub with butter. Wrap individually in aluminum foil, shiny side in, and roast at 375F for 30 minutes.

Barbecued Corn

This is the easiest of all. Bury the unhusked corn in the coals. The husks will turn black; but don't worry, the corn inside will be fine. It should take from 10 to 15 minutes. You will have to carefully turn back one of the husks to test for doneness.

Boiled Corn

In a large pot, boil enough water to cover the corn. Husk the corn just before cooking. Do not salt the water. Put the ears in the boiling water and when it returns to a boil, cover the pot and boil 6 to 9 minutes. Do not overcook! Serve with butter, salt and pepper.

Steamed Corn

Arrange on a steamer and steam over boiling water for 6 to 10 minutes, until tender.

Grilled Corn (2 methods)

1. Pull back the husks and remove the silk. Soak corn and husks in cold water for 20 minutes. Drain well. Baste the corn with butter or barbecue sauce, or olive oil and salt or any other personal favorite. Pull the husks back up and tie them in place. Grill for 20 minutes, turning frequently.

2. Husk the corn and grill under the broiler or over an open fire for about 10 minutes, turning frequently.

Microwaved Corn

Husk corn, brush with butter and wrap in plastic or waxed paper. Microwave on HIGH (100%) about 2-1/2 minutes per ear.

Corn Frittata

1 shallot, minced

1/2 cup red or green pepper, finely chopped

4 ears of corn, kernels cut from the cob

2 Tbsp butter

1/4 cup roasted green chiles

5 eggs

3 Tbsp milk

1/4 cup Cheddar cheese, grated

1 tsp fresh thyme, chopped

Salt and pepper

Sauté the shallot, pepper and the corn in the butter for 3 to 5 minutes, until tender. Beat everything else together and pour over the corn. Fry the frittata over low heat for 5 minutes, shaking the pan occasionally to prevent sticking. When the bottom is brown and set, either flip the frittata (using a plate) or place it under the broiler until the top is set. *Serves 4*

<u>Each serving contains:</u> Cal-274, Prot-13g, Carb-23g, Fib-3g, Tot. Fat-16g, Sat. Fat-7g, Chol-290mg, Sdm-268mg

"Corn Pone"

This is not corn pone—a corn bread made in the southern United States—but rather a corn pudding. My brother insisted on calling it corn pone when we had it as children. The name stuck.

4 eggs

1 cup milk

10 ears of corn, kernels cut from the cob

1/2 cup cream or half-and-half

A sprig of basil, minced

Salt, pepper and nutmeg

3 Tbsp bacon bits

Beat the eggs well and add everything else except the bacon bits. Mix thoroughly. Pour the mixture into a 1-quart casserole, sprinkle bacon bits on top and bake at 350F for almost an hour, or until set. *Serves 4*

<u>Each serving contains:</u> Cal-417, Prot-17g, Carb-55g, Fib-6g, Tot. Fat-18g, Sat. Fat-8g, Chol-247mg, Sdm-297mg

CUCUMBERS

Cucumbers are a rather unusual vegetable. Technically they are a fruit, but we eat them as vegetables, treat them as vegetables and generally think of them as vegetables. Anyway, cucumbers are ready to be exploited. You can cut them up and put them in salads or sandwiches as I do. They can also be peeled and eaten as a fruit. They have an amazing capacity to retain water and to remain cool: the inside of a cucumber can be up to 20 degrees cooler than the outside—which explains the old expression "cool as a cucumber."

Garden cucumbers are available all year, but are at their peak in the summer. There are essentially three types of cucumbers. One of these is the long, brilliant-green English cucumber, grown in greenhouses (the only kind of cucumber available in England), which is favored over our "ordinary" cucumber by Europeans. The English cucumber is sweeter and more tender than the garden cucumber, and let's not forget that it is also burpless!

There is the garden cucumber which is often waxed (for a longer shelf life) and must, therefore, be peeled, resulting in some loss of flavor. And there is the tiny cucumber that is so good for pickling. Some parts of the world are also blessed with lemon cucumbers, which are about the size of an orange, shaped like a kiwi with pale skin and a delicious flavor. Unfortunately, these delicacies do not travel well and are locally available only where they are grown.

The easiest way to cook cucumbers is to poach or steam them. They are delicious!

When choosing a cucumber, it is important to look for ones that are firm, fresh and deep green in color. Light green or yellow ones tend to be older. Avoid soft, rubbery cucumbers or very big ones. Greenhouse, or English, cucumbers should be slender and well-shaped.

Cucumbers tend to give off a very strong odor, so refrigerate your cucumbers, cut or whole, in a plastic bag. Cover cut or cooked cucumbers very tightly with plastic wrap or aluminum foil. Unpeeled, a cucumber will last for a week. English cucumbers, however, don't like the refrigerator, so keep them wrapped in a cool place.

Cucumbers are a dieter's best friend. A 6-inch cucumber has only 25 calories. Four ounces of raw cucumber have only 17 calories. An unpeeled cucumber is a fair source of vitamin A and iron. As a further bonus, when you eat a cucumber you do your teeth a favor because it is an important "detergent vegetable," wonderful for dental health. The cucumber's final benefit is to your skin: cucumbers are still considered a beauty aid. To keep your skin soft and smooth, and (reputedly) to lighten freckles, rub a cucumber slice or two over your face.

Sautéed Cucumbers with Cream or Yogurt

3 cucumbers, peeled, split, seeded, and cut in 1/4-inch slices
2 Tbsp butter
Salt and pepper
1 Tbsp tarragon or dill, finely chopped
1 tsp cornstarch (to prevent curdling)
1/4 cup cream or plain yogurt

Blanch the cucumber for 3 minutes. Drain well. Melt the butter in a frying pan, add the cucumbers and toss briefly until heated through but still crisp. Sprinkle with salt, pepper and the herb. Gently stir the cornstarch into the cream. Add the cream mixture to the cucumbers and cook for a minute. *Serves* 4

With mushrooms: add 1 cup of thinly sliced, sautéed mushrooms to the cucumbers before adding cream or yogurt.

Each serving contains: Cal-106, Prot-2g, Carb-8g, Fib-2g, Tot. Fat-8g, Sat. Fat-5g, Chol-21mg, Sdm-137mg

Poached or Steamed Cucumbers

3 average-size cucumbers, peeled, split, seeded and cut into 1/4-inch slices
2 Tbsp butter
Pepper

Poach the cucumbers in, or steam them over, boiling salted water for 2 minutes or until they are pale and clear. Drain and stir in the butter; when the butter has melted, grind pepper over them. Or sprinkle the cooked cucumbers with freshly chopped mint, dill, chives, tarragon or parsley. *Serves* 4

Each serving contains: Cal-80, Prot-2g, Carb-6g, Fib-2g, Tot. Fat-6g, Sat. Fat-4g, Chol-16mg, Sdm-63mg

Cool Cucumber-Buttermilk Soup

4 average-size cucumbers, peeled and cut into chunks
1 cup vegetable stock
3 cups buttermilk
1 clove garlic
1 tsp fresh mint leaves
1 Tbsp fresh dill
Salt and pepper
Fresh chives, chopped

Purée everything in a blender or food processor. Chill for at least 4 hours and garnish with fresh, chopped chives. *Serves* 4

Each serving contains: Cal-122, Prot-8g, Carb-19g, Fib-3g, Tot. Fat-2g, Sat. Fat-1g, Chol-6mg, Sdm-269mg

Danish Cucumber Salad

2 English cucumbers, sliced
Salt
2 cups plain yogurt
1 Tbsp fresh dill, chopped
1 clove garlic, chopped
1 Tbsp wine vinegar

Sprinkle the cukes with a little salt. Combine the yogurt, dill, garlic and vinegar. Fold the cucumbers into the yogurt mixture and refrigerate for at least 2 hours before serving. *Serves 4 to 6*

Each serving contains: Cal-97, Prot-5g, Carb-10g, Fib-1g, Tot. Fat-4g, Sat. Fat-3g, Chol-16mg, Sdm-127mg

Cucumber Chips

3 cucumbers, peeled, split, seeded and sliced 1 inch thick
1/3 cup all-purpose flour
Salt and pepper
2 Tbsp butter
1 Tbsp grated onion
1 clove garlic
1/4 cup parsley, finely chopped
2 Tbsp fresh dill, minced

Dry the pieces of cucumber by laying them on paper towels or a clean cloth. Mix the flour, salt and pepper in a paper bag. Add the cucumbers and shake.

Melt the butter in a frying pan and sauté the onion and garlic for 1 minute. Add the cucumbers. Sauté the mixture over medium heat for 4 or 5 minutes, stirring constantly with a fork. Do not overcook or the cucumbers will get mushy.

Drain the chips on paper towels. Sprinkle with parsley and dill before serving. *Serves 4*

Each serving contains: Cal-121, Prot-3g, Carb-15g, Fib-2g, Tot. Fat-6g, Sat. Fat-4g, Chol-16mg, Sdm-132mg

CURLY ENDIVE AND ESCAROLE

Curly endive is a rather confusing vegetable, in name only. It is called not only *curly endive* but also *chicory* and on occasion, incorrectly, *escarole*. It is indeed chicory, but not escarole: escarole is Batavian endive. Curly endive is a very attractive leafy green vegetable that resembles an excited leaf lettuce, having narrow, ragged-edged leaves that curl at the ends. North Americans tend to use curly endive in salads, where its pungent flavor adds a little sparkle. In European and Middle Eastern cooking, curly endive is

Curly endive and escarole are not the same thing but they can substitute for each other. Not only do they look quite similar, they are both strong-flavored, leafy vegetables and can be used in salads, sparingly, in soups or alone.

used as a cooked vegetable or in soups. I remember being distinctly *unfond* of it as a child, but Pete has a few ideas that provide a chance for those of us who have been reticent to try it again, or those of us who have never been daring enough to give it a taste.

Curly endive is available all year, its peak season being from July to October. Look for fresh, clean heads with crisp ribs and leaves. Avoid flabby, wilted-looking heads of yellowish-green color. Curly endive is one of the few vegetables that should be washed before storing. Wash it under cold running water and shake as much water off as possible; pat it dry with a paper towel; put it in a plastic bag and store it in the refrigerator, where it will be happy in the cold for 3 days.

Curly endive is a good source of vitamin A and it contains some iron too. Four ounces of raw curly endive have 23 calories.

The easiest way to use curly endive is to use the inner whitish leaves in salads, along with lettuce. You can use the darker outer leaves too, but they tend to be too bitter for most people's taste. The outer leaves can be torn up and added to soups, stews or casseroles, where they will add a little bite.

Escarole is, in fact, endive but not curly endive. It is a broad-leaved variety. The heads look rather flat with coarse, broad, white-ribbed, somewhat curly leaves that join in a yellowish heart. Escarole has a slightly bitter flavor and a crisp texture. It can be used in salads, where the tender, yellowish inner leaves add a little zip. The outer leaves are good in a soup. You can safely use escarole in any recipe for curly endive and vice versa.

Curly Endive, Sesame and Mushroom Stir-Fry

2 Tbsp sesame seeds

2 Tbsp pine nuts

2 Tbsp oil

1 medium head endive, trimmed, washed and coarsely shredded

1/2 cup scallions or green onions, thinly sliced

3/4 cup mushrooms, thinly sliced

1 Tbsp grated fresh ginger

Salt and pepper

1/4 cup raisins, plumped in very hot water for 20 minutes

Sauté the sesame seeds and pine nuts in oil until they are golden. Add the endive, scallions, mushrooms and ginger. Season with salt and pepper. Continue cooking and stirring for several minutes, until the endive is tender.

Sprinkle the raisins over the endive. Serve immediately. *Serves 4*

Each serving contains: Cal-175, Prot-5g, Carb-14g, Fib-3g, Tot. Fat-13g, Sat. Fat-2g, Chol-0mg, Sdm-81mg

Braised Escarole and Red Onion

2 cloves garlic, minced
2 Tbsp olive oil
1 red onion, sliced
1 large head escarole, trimmed, washed and coarsely shredded
8 capers, whole
Salt and pepper

Brown the garlic in the oil. Stir the onion slices into the oil and sauté for 1 minute. Add the escarole and capers; mix well. Cook over high heat for 3 or 4 minutes, stirring constantly. Season with salt and pepper. *Serves 4 to 6*

DAIKON

Daikon—also known as *Chinese* or *Japanese radish*—is a super vegetable for dieters because it speeds up the breakdown of fat in the body. If you ate enough, you would become very skinny. It tastes just like radish, although somewhat hotter, and it cooks wonderfully! Shaped like a carrot, daikon is pearly white, smooth and usually fairly large, between 1 and 2 pounds. It can grow up to 50 pounds, but I would be astonished if you ever encountered one that big on this continent.

The other day a man came to my cash register with a sack full of daikon. I guess I must have had a peculiar expression on my face because he laughed and said, "I only come to Pete's once every two weeks, and I can't get daikon anywhere else. I eat a lot of it." That was obvious. He had almost 15 pounds of the vegetable!

Daikon is available all year but is at its mildest and most tasty during the winter and fall; in the spring and summer it tends to be hotter in flavor. Look for smooth, clean, firm roots that should appear to be slightly shiny. Size has little effect on the taste, so look for a whole daikon or a piece that is the right size for you.

Contrary to its appearance, daikon does not keep particularly well. It tends to dry out, becoming spongy and losing most of its flavor if kept for too long. If you are going to eat it raw, don't keep it for any more than 2 or 3 days. If you are going to cook it, you can keep it for up to a week, wrapped lightly in plastic and placed in the refrigerator. Daikon is fantastically low in calories, with only 15 in 4 ounces. It is also an excellent source of vitamin C and a good source of folate.

Daikon is very versatile. In addition to all its raw possibilities, it is delicious in soups or stews, although it should be added only for the last few minutes of cooking. If you have an artist inside you, try carving daikon into an edible garnish. If daikon had been popular with Michelangelo, we would have eaten his work by now. Imagine finding a mini-David with your next tray of dipping vegetables!

Each serving contains: Cal-81, Prot-1g, Carb-5g, Fib-2g, Tot. Fat-7g, Sat. Fat-1g, Chol-0mg, Sdm-118mg

Use daikon as you would radish, but with more variety. It is delicious raw, with a dip, so include daikon sticks in your next tray of crudités. Grated, it is a tasty addition to coleslaw.

Daikon Soup

4 cups vegetable stock

1 clove garlic, minced

1 Tbsp soy sauce

1 tsp sesame oil

1/2 cup carrot, grated

1/2 cup daikon, thinly sliced

2 green onions, thinly sliced

2 Tbsp dill, finely chopped

Mix together the stock, garlic, soy sauce and sesame oil. Bring the mixture to a boil. Add the carrot and continue boiling for 2 minutes. Add the daikon, cover and turn the heat down. Simmer for 10 minutes, or until the daikon is tender. Garnish with green onions and dill. *Serves* 4

Each serving contains: Cal-53, Prot-2g, Carb-10g, Fib-3g, Tot. Fat-1g, Sat. Fat-0g, Chol-0mg, Sdm-350mg

Daikon, Zucchini and Red-Pepper Salad

2 small zucchini, thinly sliced (about 3/4 pound)

1/2 pound daikon, scrubbed, halved lengthwise and sliced

1 small red pepper, cut into strips

2 Tbsp white wine vinegar

2 Tbsp peanut oil

2 Tbsp sesame or walnut oil

Salt and sugar

1/4 cup freshly shelled walnuts

Mix the zucchini with the daikon and red pepper. Blend the vinegar and oils, and add a little salt and sugar to taste. Toss the vinaigrette with the vegetables and chill for about 1 hour.

Sprinkle with walnuts just before serving. *Serves* 4

Each serving contains: Cal-198, Prot-3g, Carb-8g, Fib-3g, Tot. Fat-18g, Sat. Fat-2g, Chol-0mg, Sdm-82mg

Daikon-and-Carrot Crunch

1 Tbsp sugar

1 Tbsp Dijon-style mustard

1/2 cup white wine vinegar

Salt

1/2 pound carrots, peeled and cut in fine julienne strips or coarsely grated

1/4 pound snow peas, trimmed and broken in half

1 pound daikon, peeled, cut in fine julienne strips or coarsely grated

1/2 cup sour cream or yogurt

3 green onions, thinly sliced

1 cup radish or alfalfa sprouts

Each serving contains: Cal-150, Prot-4g, Carb-20g, Fib-4g, Tot. Fat-7g, Sat. Fat-4g, Chol-13mg, Sdm-223mg

Stir the sugar, mustard and vinegar together; sprinkle with a little salt. Pour the mixture over the carrots, snow peas and daikon, and toss. Chill for 1 hour.

Drain the vegetables, squeezing them to get rid of the liquid. Blend in the sour cream or yogurt. Sprinkle with the green onions and sprouts. *Serves 4*

Sautéed Daikon

1 Tbsp peanut oil
3/4 pound daikon, scrubbed and thinly sliced
Salt and sugar
1 Tbsp parsley, minced
2 Tbsp fresh chives, minced
2 Tbsp toasted sesame seeds

Pour the oil into a frying pan or wok. Heat. Add the daikon and toss to cover with oil. Sprinkle with a little salt and sugar to taste. Toss over high heat until the daikon has mellowed a little, about 5 minutes. Remove from the heat; toss with parsley and chives. Sprinkle with sesame seeds and serve hot. *Serves 2*

Each serving contains: Cal-144, Prot-3g, Carb-10g, Fib-4g, Tot. Fat-11g, Sat. Fat-2g, Chol-0mg, Sdm-170mg

EGGPLANT

Eggplant has a wonderfully subtle flavor and a dense texture. It has a terrific ability to absorb the flavor of whatever it is cooked with, while adding a smooth, rich thickness.

If you are at all like me, you will be amazed to learn that eggplant is a berry. It belongs to the nightshade family, which includes tomatoes, potatoes, tobacco and petunias. No matter what it is, it is undeniably beautiful. Its shiny patent-leather skin is most often purple; but it can also be whitish, reddish, yellowish or striped. It can be anywhere from 2 to 10 inches in length, and anything from round to pear-shaped. More often than not our markets tend to stock the deep-purple, largish eggplants, although baby or Italian eggplants are becoming more popular and easier to find. They are used in the same way as the large eggplants, with some allowance made for their size.

Eggplant is available all year. The peak season is from July to the end of September. Whether you are buying the little European eggplant or the larger variety, look for fruit that is firm and heavy, with a smooth, glossy skin of uniform color. Avoid overly large eggplants, those with rough spongy spots or those with dark-brown signs of decay.

Eggplant is perishable, so don't plan on storing it for too long. If you must, keep it unwashed in a plastic bag in the refrigerator or in a dark, humid place. It can be kept up to 4 days, but the sooner you use it, the better.

Eggplant isn't going to make you fabulously healthy; it isn't a particularly rich source of vitamins or minerals. Four ounces of cooked eggplant have only 34 calories.

Eggplant tends to have a bitter taste that disappears after about 20 minutes of cooking. If you are going to cook it less than that, lightly salt the cut vegetable and let it stand for about 20 minutes. The salt will draw out the bitter juices. Salting the eggplant is also recommended in recipes for which the vegetable needs to be drier.

It is not unusual for a recipe to call for eggplant to be fried, but anyone who has fried the vegetable knows just how much fat this involves. Eggplant is very absorbent. If you wish to cut down on the fat, bake the eggplant in a 325F oven for 25 minutes on an oiled cookie sheet, or brush the slices with oil and broil them for 5 minutes on each side, until golden.

Sautéed Eggplant and Variations

1-1/2 pounds eggplant, trimmed and cut into 1/2-inch slices
Flour seasoned with salt and pepper
1/3 cup olive oil, or less, if you can get away with it
4 Tbsp butter

Dip the eggplant slices into the seasoned flour. Heat the olive oil and butter in a large frying pan. Sauté the eggplant until tender and golden on both sides. Drain the slices on a paper towel and keep warm in a low oven. *Serves 4*

With Parmesan cheese: simply sprinkle the sautéed slices with Parmesan cheese and broil for 2 or 3 minutes.

With tomato: top the sautéed eggplant with slices of fresh tomato, sprinkle with fresh oregano or basil and broil. For a real treat, sprinkle with grated Mozzarella cheese for the last 2 or 3 minutes of broiling.

With onion: top the cooked eggplant with sautéed onion.

Eggplant Casserole

1-1/2 pounds eggplant, trimmed and cut into 1/2-inch slices
Flour seasoned with salt and pepper
1/4 cup olive oil
1/2 medium onion, sliced
1/2 red or green bell pepper, sliced
1 medium tomato, sliced
1 Tbsp olive oil

Each serving contains: Cal-365, Prot-3g, Carb-23g, Fib-5g, Tot. Fat-30g, Sat. Fat-10g, Chol-31mg, Sdm-390mg

If you wish to cut down on the fat used when frying eggplant, bake the egg-plant in a 325F oven for 25 minutes on an oiled cookie sheet, or brush slices with oil and broil for 5 minutes on each side, until golden.

Each serving contains: Cal-382, Prot-6g, Carb-36g, Fib-6g, Tot. Fat-25g, Sat. Fat-7g, Chol-18mg, Sdm-566mg

Salt and pepper to taste
Minced garlic, if desired
1/2 cup breadcrumbs
2 Tbsp Parmesan cheese
2 Tbsp butter

Dip eggplant slices into the seasoned flour. Sauté the eggplant in 1/4 cup olive oil until almost tender. Arrange the eggplant slices in a well-buttered casserole dish, alternating with layers of onion, bell pepper and tomato. Drizzle a little olive oil on each layer. Season with salt, pepper and some garlic if you like. Cover with bread-crumbs mixed with Parmesan cheese and dot with butter. Bake at 350F until the vegetables are tender, about 40 minutes. *Serves 4*

Eggplant Parmigiana

3 eggplants, trimmed but not peeled, cut in 1/4-inch slices, salted and left to drain
All-purpose flour
2 eggs, beaten with
2 tsp olive oil
Fine dry breadcrumbs
2 Tbsp olive oil
2 or 3 large tomatoes, peeled and sliced
2 Tbsp fresh basil, minced
1 cup Mozzarella cheese, sliced
2/3 cup Parmesan cheese, grated

Each serving contains: Cal-347, Prot-15g, Carb-37g, Fib-8g, Tot. Fat-17g, Sat. Fat-6g, Chol-94mg, Sdm-386mg

Wipe the eggplant dry. Dip each slice into the flour and shake off the excess. Dip into beaten eggs, shake again and dip into bread-crumbs. Heat the oil in a large frying pan. Brown each slice until golden on both sides, turning only once. Drain on paper towels.

In a 2-quart casserole, arrange three layers of tomato, eggplant, basil, Mozzarella and Parmesan cheese. Bake at 350F for 20 or 30 minutes. For a lighter dish, bake or broil the eggplant as described above and omit the egg-and-flour coating when frying. *Serves 6*

Stuffed Eggplant

3 medium eggplants
1 cup onion, chopped
2 cloves garlic, crushed
1 bay leaf
2 medium tomatoes
1 Tbsp basil, minced

1/2 tsp tarragon, minced

1/2 tsp oregano, minced

2 cups ricotta or cottage cheese

1/4 cup Parmesan cheese, grated

1 cup fine breadcrumbs

Salt, pepper and nutmeg to taste

Slice the eggplants in half lengthwise and bake the halves face down on a oiled tray at 350F for 20 to 25 minutes. Scoop out the flesh and mince it.

Sauté the eggplant flesh with the onion, garlic and bay leaf until the onions are transparent. Combine with the tomatoes, basil, tarragon, oregano, ricotta cheese and half of the Parmesan. Let stand 20 minutes; drain off excess liquid, and remove bay leaf.

Stuff the shells with the eggplant mixture. Arrange the stuffed skins in a baking pan so that they are supported by one another. Top with the remaining Parmesan and breadcrumbs, and season with salt, pepper and nutmeg. Bake at 350F for 40 minutes. *Serves 6*

Each serving contains: Cal-323, Prot-16g, Carb-37g, Fib-8g, Tot. Fat-14g, Sat. Fat-8g, Chol-45mg, Sdm-347mg

Vegetarian Moussaka

3 medium eggplants, unpeeled, sliced into 1/2-inch slices

1 recipe Mushroom Sauce, below

1 recipe White Sauce, page 60

Breadcrumbs

Grated Parmesan or Chedder cheese

Salt the eggplant slices lightly and bake on an oiled baking tray at 350F for 15 minutes or until tender. Make Mushroom Sauce and White Sauce.

Cover the bottom of a large well-oiled casserole dish with eggplant slices and half of the mushroom sauce. Layer on the rest of the eggplant and the rest of the mushroom sauce. Top with white sauce. Sprinkle with breadcrumbs and a little extra grated cheese. Bake, covered, at 350F for 35 minutes. Uncover and bake for another 15 minutes. *Serves 8 hungry people*

Each serving contains: Cal-468, Prot-17g, Carb-40g, Fib-8g, Tot. Fat-28g, Sat. Fat-15g, Chol-273mg, Sdm-729mg

MUSHROOM SAUCE

2 cups mushrooms, sliced

3 Tbsp butter

1 large onion, chopped

2 cloves garlic, minced

3/4 cup tomato paste

2 Tbsp cilantro (coriander), chopped

2 tsp parsley

2 tsp basil, minced

1/4 cup dry red wine

Salt, pepper and cinnamon
1/2 cup dry breadcrumbs
1/2 cup Parmesan or Cheddar cheese, grated
4 eggs, beaten

Sauté the mushrooms in butter with the onion and the garlic. Add the tomato paste, cilantro, parsley, basil, red wine and spices. Simmer until the liquid is absorbed. Add the breadcrumbs, cheese and eggs, and remove from heat.

WHITE SAUCE
1/2 cup butter
1/2 cup flour
2-1/2 cups warm milk
4 egg yolks
1 tsp cinnamon

Melt the butter and blend in the flour. Whisk in the milk and simmer, stirring vigorously until thick. Beat in the egg yolks and cinnamon.

Baked Eggplant Italiana

4 small eggplants, about 6 inches long, trimmed, peeled and cut into 1/4-inch slices
Salt
2 hard-cooked eggs, sliced
3 large, firm, ripe tomatoes, cut into 1/4-inch slices
2 cups Mozzarella cheese, grated
2 Tbsp capers
Salt and pepper
1/4 cup cilantro (coriander)
1/4 cup fresh basil leaves
2 cloves garlic
1/4 cup olive oil

Lay the eggplant slices on a large tray and sprinkle with a little salt. Let stand at room temperature to dry off the excess moisture. Drain and dry between paper towels.

In a pie plate, make overlapping layers of eggplant, egg, tomato and Mozzarella. Top each layer with capers. Sprinkle with pepper and a little salt.

Mince the cilantro, basil, garlic and olive oil together. Sprinkle over the eggplant mixture. Cover with aluminum foil and bake at 350F for 20 minutes. Remove the foil and bake for another 10 minutes. This is good hot, lukewarm or cool, but not chilled. *Serves 4*

Each serving contains: Cal 177, Prot-9g, Carb-14g, Fib-2g, Tot. Fat-10g, Sat. Fat-5g, Chol-123mg, Sdm-476mg

Each serving contains: Cal-207, Prot-5g, Carb-10g, Fib-0g, Tot. Fat-17g, Sat. Fat-10g, Chol-148mg, Sdm-158mg

Each serving contains: Cal-461, Prot-19g, Carb-35g, Fib-12g, Tot. Fat-30g, Sat. Fat-10g, Chol-150mg, Sdm-491mg

Earthy Eggplant Soup

2 cups potato, chopped

1-1/2 cups onion, chopped

1 cup celery, chopped

1 tsp curry powder

1 tsp ginger root, grated

3 Tbsp butter

4 cups vegetable stock

2 eggplants, peeled and chopped

2 tsp thyme, minced

3 tsp basil, minced

1 cup thick tomato sauce

2 Tbsp tomato paste

Salt and pepper

1/4 cup cilantro (coriander), chopped or broken into sprigs

Sauté the potato, onion, celery, curry and ginger root in the butter for 15 minutes, stirring frequently. Add the stock and bring to a boil. Add the eggplant and herbs, and turn down the heat. Simmer for 30 minutes. Stir in the tomato sauce and tomato paste. Season with salt and pepper. Simmer until good and hot. Garnish with cilantro. *Serves 4 to 6*

<u>Each serving contains</u>: Cal-303, Prot-7g, Carb-53g, Fib-13g, Tot. Fat-10g, Sat. Fat-6g, Chol-23mg, Sdm-643mg

FENNEL

There was no doubt in Pete's mind that fennel and anise were the same thing, until I bet him $20 that they weren't. I won, sort of, but so did he, sort of. Fennel and anise *are* the same thing—fennel and the *vegetable* anise. But there is also the *herb* anise, and fennel and the herb anise are not the same thing. In England, fennel is usually called *anise*; on this side of the ocean, fennel is usually called *fennel* or sweet anise. Except at Pete's. This section is about the vegetable sometimes known as *anise*.

Fennel is a particularly beautiful vegetable, especially appealing as winter draws to a close because its dark feathery leaves are so reminiscent of spring. A fennel plant looks like celery that has had an accident. It's a bulbous vegetable with thick, broad leaf stalks that overlap one another at the bottom of their stems to form a firm, white, crisp bulb, 3 to 5 inches in diameter. The stalks end in feathery, bright-green leaves, which can grow up to 2 feet tall. It looks rather like dill growing from a celery stalk. Although fennel tastes vaguely like licorice, like the herb anise, they are related only by taste.

Fennel is one of those vegetables that was made to be braised. It's simple and delicious. It's also called sweet anise.

Fennel, called *finocchio* by the Italians, is a winter vegetable, available from October to the end of April. Look for firm, crisp, white bulbs with feathery bright-green leaves. The stalks should be at least 10 inches long, a length that guarantees juiciness. Avoid soft, coarse, discolored or cracked bulbs with brownish-edged bases or wilted stalks and tops. Wrap the bulbs and stalks in a plastic bag, and fennel will keep in your refrigerator for up to 4 days.

Fennel is a good source of potassium and iron and an excellent source of vitamins A and C. For a vegetable, it is also relatively high in calcium. Four ounces of raw fennel have 33 calories.

To trim fennel, simply cut off the feathery leaves close to the bulb and remove any tough or discolored outer leaves. Slice off the tough base. Do not trim the vegetable until just before you use it, to ensure that it stays fresh and crisp. To keep fennel tender, cut it *with* the grain, in quarters if it is large; in half if the bulbs are small. The leaves can be used as a garnish or to flavor soups, salads or stews.

The easiest way to use fennel is raw, as a salad ingredient. The first time I tasted fennel was at Pete's when he was trimming it for the stall. He handed me a piece of the vegetable and it was a wonderfully crunchy, refreshing little thing. It makes a delicious salad all by itself. Just slice it up and drizzle your favorite vinaigrette over it, or add slices of fennel to your next salad. It is especially good with romaine lettuce and a lemony dressing. It is also a tasty addition to a tray of crudités. Don't be afraid to explore with raw fennel. It tastes super in the most unlikely places!

Fennel-and-Celery Parmesan

4 large heads of fennel, trimmed and cut lengthwise in quarters

2 cups vegetable stock

4 ribs celery, sliced diagonally

1/4 tsp dried, crumbled oregano

2/3 cup melted butter

Salt and pepper

3/4 cup Parmesan cheese, grated

Paprika

Simmer the fennel in boiling vegetable stock with the celery for about 5 minutes, or until just tender. Drain thoroughly.

Stir the oregano into the butter. Put half the fennel and half the celery in a shallow, well-greased baking dish. Sprinkle with salt and pepper, brush with half the butter mixture and sprinkle with half the cheese. Top with the remaining fennel, celery, butter and cheese. Sprinkle with paprika. Bake at 400F for about 10 minutes or until it is golden brown. *Serves 4*

Each serving contains: Cal-450, Prot-12g, Carb-23g, Fib-11g, Tot. Fat-37g, Sat. Fat-23g, Chol-98mg, Sdm-891mg

Braised Fennel

2 heads of fennel, trimmed and cut lengthwise in quarters
4 Tbsp butter
1 cup vegetable stock
Salt and pepper
2 Tbsp fresh basil or dill, chopped

Lightly brown the fennel in the butter in a large frying pan. Add the stock and bring it to a boil. Turn down the heat and cover the pan. Simmer the fennel for about 30 minutes, or until tender. Season with salt and pepper.

Remove the fennel and keep it warm. Boil the liquid until it is reduced by half, and pour it over the fennel as a sauce. Sprinkle with the chopped herb. *Serves* 4

Each serving contains: Cal-145, Prot-2g, Carb-10g, Fib-5g, Tot. Fat-12g, Sat. Fat-7g, Chol-31mg, Sdm-248mg

Hellenic Fennel

1-1/2 cups dry white wine
1-1/2 cups vegetable stock
2 Tbsp olive oil
2 medium-size tomatoes, peeled and chopped
Rind of 1 lemon, grated
1 bay leaf
2 Tbsp fresh dill, chopped
Salt and pepper
4 large heads of fennel, trimmed and cut lengthwise
    in quarters

Combine the wine, vegetable stock, olive oil, tomatoes, lemon rind, bay leaf, dill, salt and pepper in a large saucepan and bring it to a boil. Turn down the heat and add the fennel. Simmer for 15 minutes or until the fennel is just tender.

Transfer the fennel to a deep serving dish. Cook the pan liquid over high heat, until it is reduced by one-third to intensify the flavor. Remove bay leaf. Pour the liquid over the fennel. Serve chilled. *Serves* 4

Each serving contains: Cal-216, Prot-4g, Carb-23g, Fib-11g, Tot. Fat-7g, Sat. Fat-1g, Chol-0mg, Sdm-203mg

FIDDLEHEADS

Fiddleheads are especially favored by New Brunswickers. During late spring, Pete's resounds with the question, "When will you be getting fiddleheads?" It is different every year because their arrival depends on the winter, on how high the river has flooded and on how early the snow melted. There are a lot of variables, but New Brunswickers wait for the first fiddleheads with great anticipation and can never seem to eat enough of them before the season is over.

If you frequent gourmet restaurants in any of North America's larger cities, you may have seen this exotic little item on the menu, accompanied by a hefty price tag. Many people with educated palates are more than willing to pay dearly for this delicate green, which has the flavor of an earthy asparagus. To many easterners, fiddleheads are the first sign of spring.

Fiddleheads are small green fern shoots, about 1 to 3 inches high, which before they have uncurled look remarkably like the heads of violins, hence the name. If Canada had provincial vegetables, fiddleheads would be New Brunswick's. Telling a Maritimer how to cook fiddleheads is like telling an Irishman how to cook potatoes.

However, this vegetable is not unique to New Brunswick. It grows throughout Canada, profusely in the east and in British Columbia, and sparsely in the Prairies. In the United States, fiddleheads grow in New England and in the central states and as far south as Virginia.

The season for fiddleheads is short—just before the ostrich ferns unfurl. If we are lucky enough to get a warm spring, the season is only a couple of weeks. But fiddleheads *are* spring, the first fresh Canadian green in the markets! No wonder their arrival is awaited with such impatience and greeted with such excitement.

Fiddleheads are available from early spring to mid-summer in some parts of the United States. Distributors may import them. You may find them frozen, because they freeze quite well, or you can freeze them yourself by blanching them for one minute in boiling water. They should then be drained, plunged into ice-cold water, and drained again. They can then be put on a baking sheet, placed in a freezer and bagged once they are frozen.

There is nothing quite like truly fresh fiddleheads. Look for deep-green fronds that are tight and springy, with short tails, no more than 1-1/2 inches in diameter. Fiddleheads don't keep particularly well. While they don't actually go bad, they're just so delicate that they lose that wonderful fresh, woodsy flavor and get a little tough if kept too long. However, if you must store them, put them in a plastic bag with water; change the water daily and you can keep them for up to a week.

Fiddleheads should be well washed before you eat them. Some of them will have a papery brown covering over the frond; this jacket does not affect the taste and comes off easily when rubbed between your hands under running water. Trim the tails very close to the curl of the fern.

Fiddleheads are a good source of vitamin C and provide some fiber. Contrary to some authorities, the delicate taste of fiddleheads is not conducive to heavy or strongly flavored sauces. If you like, you can make a Hollandaise sauce to go with them, or a white sauce flavored with nutmeg. But anyone who knows fiddleheads will tell you that the best way to enjoy them is to prepare them as simply as possible.

Fiddleheads only take about 5 to 10 minutes to steam or boil, and it is important to keep testing them because undercooked or overcooked fiddleheads are not at their best. Fiddleheads may be steamed, chilled and then sautéed in butter. You may also steam and chill them; then serve with your favorite vinaigrette. Try adding some hot mustard to the dressing: it complements the taste of the fiddleheads well.

One pound of fiddleheads will serve four if you have never tasted them before; two, if you are a devoted lover of the green fronds; and one, if it is your first feed of the season and you thought it would never come.

JERUSALEM ARTICHOKES

Jerusalem artichokes are delicious raw or cooked, hot or cold. Although they are not easy to find, they are rapidly becoming more popular and are no longer the specialty item they once were. If you have not yet introduced your body to Jerusalem artichokes, don't gorge yourself on them because they contain a starch that your body needs time to get accustomed to.

Jerusalem artichokes, sometimes called *sunchokes*, are available from November to February. Look for firm roots with no signs of mold. Steer clear of roots that are sprouting or blotched with green. You can keep them unwashed, in a plastic bag in the refrigerator, for up to a week. Artichokes are a good source of iron; they also contain some vitamin B and a small amount of vitamin C. Four ounces of the raw vegetable have about 60 calories.

Jerusalem artichokes should be peeled or given a hefty scrub before using. In order to prevent their white flesh from turning brown, it is a good idea to have a bowl of acidulated water on hand in which to plunge the cut vegetable. (Acidulated water consists of 3 tablespoons of vinegar or lemon juice in 1 quart of water.)

Sliced, raw artichokes are a great addition to a tray of crudités. Throw a handful into your next salad; or grate them, adding a mayonnaise dressing, a generous dose of black pepper, some chopped parsley and you'll have a delicious and unusual salad.

You can broil Jerusalem artichokes, roast them, steam them, boil them or toss them in a stir-fry. Boil them in about 1 inch of water for 15 minutes and eat them with butter, sprinkled with fresh, chopped tarragon. They are also tasty drizzled with a Hollandaise sauce.

These rather dull-looking vegetables are often called sunchokes, *and although that is really a brand name, it is perhaps more appropriate than Jerusalem artichokes. This North American native has absolutely nothing to do with artichokes, except in taste, and even less to do with Jerusalem. They are thin-skinned, knobby roots of a type of sunflower. Their resemblance to ginger root is unmistakable, but their taste is fresh and sweet, and their texture, crisp and slightly fleshy, like that of water chestnuts or jícama.*

Jerusalem Artichoke Soup

The delicate flavor of this vegetable makes the most wonderfully delicious soup. Rather a special-occasion creation.

- 1 large onion, sliced
- 1 small clove garlic, minced
- 2 pounds Jerusalem artichokes, peeled or scrubbed and chopped
- 4 Tbsp butter
- 3 cups vegetable stock
- Salt and pepper
- 2-1/2 cups milk
- 1/2 cup whipping cream
- 1 tsp fennel seeds, crushed
- 1/4 cup parsley, chopped

Sauté the onion, garlic and Jerusalem artichokes in the butter for 10 minutes, stirring frequently. Add the vegetable stock, salt and pepper to taste. Cook for another 10 minutes. Purée in a blender or food processor. Heat the milk and cream. Blend the cream mixture with the Jerusalem artichoke purée. Add the fennel seed. Heat the soup thoroughly. Sprinkle with parsley before serving. *Serves 4*

Each serving contains: Cal-507, Prot-12g, Carb-56g, Fib-6g, Tot. Fat-28g, Sat. Fat-17g, Chol-93mg, Sdm-290mg

Creamy Jerusalem Artichokes

- 1/2 cup whipping cream
- 1/2 cup cream or half-and-half
- 2 pounds Jerusalem artichokes, peeled or scrubbed, cooked and cut into 1/2-inch slices
- 2 Tbsp butter
- Salt and pepper
- 1/4 cup parsley, chopped

Mix the creams and heat slowly. Sauté the artichokes in the butter. Blend the cream and vegetable carefully. Season with salt and pepper and warm over the lowest heat. Sprinkle with parsley and serve when heated through. *Serves 4*

Each serving contains: Cal-365, Prot 6g, Carb42-g, Fib-4g, Tot. Fat-20g, Sat. Fat-13g, Chol-67mg, Sdm-158mg

JÍCAMA

This versatile vegetable is becoming more readily available due to the growing popularity of Asian and Latin cooking. Ranging in weight from 1 to 6 pounds, jícama are equally delicious cooked or raw and are very easy to use; all you need to do is peel off the dark beige skin and fibrous underlayer and slice the flesh.

Jícama is rather like a water chestnut in taste and texture but considerably less expensive. This tuberous vegetable is available off and on all year, its peak season being from December to June. Look for firm, smooth, nicely shaped jícama. The skin should be thin, the flesh very juicy.

Although size has little to do with the flavor, larger jícama tend to be fibrous and a little dry. Avoid blemished or scarred jícamas, or those with breaks in the skin. You may store jícama in the refrigerator for up to 3 weeks if it is uncut. Once you have cut it, wrap it tightly in plastic and use it within a week.

Jícama is an excellent source of vitamin C and folate and contains some potassium. One cup of shredded, raw jícama has about 50 calories.

Jícama can be used in almost anything. The more you experiment with it, the more useful you will find it. Toss a handful of cubed jícama into your next fruit salad, or add it to your next stir-fry. Add it in thin slices or julienne strips to a tray of crudités; it is particularly good with a chili dip. Try it as an appetizer with a little lime juice and your favorite seasoned salt.

There are only two things to remember about jícama: it must be peeled, because the skin is inedible, and it must be kept in acidulated water once it is cut or peeled, because it discolors quickly when exposed to air. (Acidulated water consists of 3 tablespoons of vinegar or lemon juice per quart of water.)

Jícama for Supper

1/4 cup low-sodium soy sauce

1/4 cup tahini

1 inch ginger root, peeled and grated

1 Tbsp brown sugar

5 to 8 ounces tofu, drained and cut into cubes

6 Tbsp butter or oil

1 pound jícama, peeled and sliced

1 large onion, thinly sliced and separated

1 pound russet potatoes, sliced into 1/4-inch slices

Salt and pepper

6 green onions, thinly sliced

2 Tbsp cilantro (coriander), chopped

1/4 cup sesame seeds

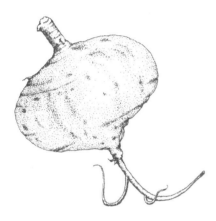

Jícama originated in Mexico, and from there spread to Asia and through the Pacific. It has a rather bland, slightly sweetish taste, which makes it a delicious addition to almost anything from a fruit salad to a stir-fry.

Each serving contains: Cal-566, Prot-19g, Carb-50g, Fib-11g, Tot. Fat-36g, Sat. Fat-13g, Chol-47mg, Sdm-773mg

Jícama can be used in almost anything. This is a salad with Indonesian origins. It is unusual and delicious in its difference.

Each serving contains: Cal-114, Prot-3g, Carb-15g, Fib-2g, Tot. Fat-6g, Sat. Fat-1g, Chol-0mg, Sdm-98mg

Each serving contains: Cal-85, Prot-3g, Carb-8g, Fib-1g, Tot. Fat-5g, Sat. Fat-1g, Chol-0mg, Sdm-96mg

In a medium-size bowl, blend the soy sauce, tahini, ginger and brown sugar. Add the tofu and leave it to marinate, stirring occasionally.

Melt the butter or heat the oil in a large frying pan over moderate heat. Sauté the jícama, onions and potatoes until the potatoes are golden brown, about 30 minutes. Season with salt and pepper. Add the tofu and any remaining marinade. Cook until the tofu is warmed through and the vegetables and tofu are well mixed. Stir in the green onions and sprinkle with cilantro (coriander) and sesame seeds. Stir to blend. Serve hot. *Serves 4*

Jícama Salad

1 cup small jícama, peeled and cut into cubes
1 cup fresh pineapple, cut into cubes
1 English cucumber, peeled and thinly sliced
1 cup alfalfa sprouts
Watercress
1 recipe Peanut Dressing, below

Lightly toss together the jícama, pineapple and cucumber. Chill and garnish with the sprouts and watercress. (I like to add a peeled mandarin orange and some of its grated rind just before serving.) Serve with Peanut Dressing. *Serves 6*

PEANUT DRESSING
2 Tbsp lime juice
2 Tbsp honey
1/4 cup peanut butter
1/4 cup water
1 Serrano or Jalapeño pepper, minced
Pinch of salt

Place the ingredients in a small saucepan and heat, stirring constantly until well blended. Chill before serving.

KALE

Kale, along with collards, most closely resembles wild cabbage. Like collards, kale does not come in a head; it is a bunch of leaves connected to a central stem. It has a sprightly taste. Its curly leaves look like sprigs of parsley, and this amazing "curly" texture remains even when the vegetable is cooked. Kale comes in the most wonderful colors: everything from dark green and lavender to an earthy, apple green.

The flavor is not unlike cabbage—although somewhat stronger—a surprise considering the texture. Like collards, kale improves with a frost; it can also withstand very high temperatures. Kale is good cut into strips and added to a stir-fry. Try it sautéed with onions, garlic or caraway seeds. Or braise kale in stock and add it to a soup.

Kale is available all year, but is most abundant—and most flavorful—from December to April. Look for small bunches of kale with a deep color in the leaves. It should be slightly moist and crisp. Avoid dry-looking kale with wilted, bruised, crushed or yellowed leaves, or with coarse stems. If you are buying it in the summer, make sure that the kale itself is not too warm as it deteriorates quickly if it is not kept cold. Kale does not like to be stored too long. Keep it in a plastic bag in the coldest part of the refrigerator, but for no more than 2 days.

Kale is an excellent source of vitamins A and C. One cup of the raw vegetable has about 20 calories.

If this vegetable is too strong for your taste, blanching it will moderate the flavor. Because the stems tend to be tough and very strongly flavored, it is generally recommended that you cut them out, although this is unnecessary when you are using tiny kale. Once you have the leaves free from the stems, wash them in a sink full of lukewarm water and rinse them under cold water several times.

In colder countries this vegetable has come into its own. The Scottish eat it puréed with potatoes, added to barley soup or cooked with oatmeal and cream to make a thick porridge.

Kalepota

Great as a main dish with a tomato salad.

> **2 Tbsp olive oil**
> **2 large cloves garlic, minced**
> **2 carrots, grated**
> **1 cup dry lentils**
> **1-1/2 pounds kale, stemmed, washed and cut in 1/2-inch strips**
> **1 cup vegetable stock**
> **1 or 2 Serrano or Jalapeño peppers, chopped**
> **28-ounce can tomatoes and juice**
> **Lemon juice**
> **1 Tbsp olive oil**
> **Pepper**

Heat the oil in a large saucepan and sauté the garlic until lightly browned. Add the carrots and lentils, and stir to coat with oil and garlic. Add the kale, vegetable stock and peppers. Cover and simmer over low heat until lentils are just tender, about 30 minutes, stirring occasionally. Add the tomatoes and juice, and cook for another 10 minutes. (Keep an eye on the liquid as it cooks and add more stock if it looks as though things might scorch.) Add lemon juice to taste. Toss with olive oil. Sprinkle with black pepper and serve. *Serves 4*

Each serving contains: Cal-374, Prot-19g, Carb-51g, Fib-13g, Tot. Fat-12g, Sat. Fat-2g, Chol-0mg, Sdm-384mg

Creamed Kale and Mushrooms

2 pounds kale, stemmed, washed and cut into bite-size pieces
4 Tbsp butter
4 Tbsp all-purpose flour
1 cup milk
1 cup cream or half-and-half
1/2 pound mushrooms, sliced
Salt, pepper and nutmeg

Put the kale in a saucepan, adding just enough salted water to cover. Bring to a boil and cook, covered, for 20 minutes or until tender. Drain well and chop.

Melt the butter, stir in the flour and cook for 2 minutes, stirring constantly. Stir in the milk and cream; it is a good idea to have them heated and ready to add. Cook over low heat, stirring constantly, for 10 minutes. Add the mushrooms for the last 5 minutes of cooking time. Season with salt, pepper and nutmeg. Add the kale and heat through. *Serves 4*

<u>Each serving contains:</u> Cal-333, Prot-10g, Carb-27g, Fib-6g, Tot. Fat-22g, Sat. Fat-13g, Chol-62mg, Sdm-293mg

KOHLRABI

The name of this little oddity means "cabbage turnip" in German. Unfortunately, kohlrabi has been underrated. It is a peculiar vegetable, but that is not to say that it is not delicious. It is one of those things that people either love or hate, and those who love it are beginning to outnumber those who don't. It is wonderful steamed and buttered; it is also delicious raw, as a dipper, and as an ingredient in salads. But be warned: as a rule, children are not fond of it.

If you have not tried kohlrabi in a while and are of two minds about it, or if you think you are a kohlrabi hater but would like to consider a change in camps, or if you are a kohlrabi devotee from way back, read on. If your mind is made up that you hate kohlrabi, or if you have no worries that you may be missing out on something special, shame on you!

Kohlrabi is available from late May to November, its peak months being June and July. Look for kohlrabi with small, smooth bulbs and a thin, crisp rind. If the tops have not been cut off, the leaves should be firm, fresh and green. Larger kohlrabi are not as sweet and tend to be woodier than the smaller ones.

If you get the leaves with the bulbs, cut them off and use them within a day or two as a soup seasoning. You may wrap the bulbs and keep them in the refrigerator for up to a week.

Kohlrabi is a wonderful source of vitamin C and a good source of potassium. It is low in calories, with only 40 calories in 1/2 cup of the raw vegetable.

If none of the recipes below appeal to you, don't give up on kohlrabi: peel them, parboil them and add them to a vegetable soup. Or simmer them in vegetable stock in a large frying pan and add a white sauce made with some of the liquid left over from the simmering. If this doesn't tickle your taste buds, give up; you have Pete's permission, you'll have done your best. Seriously, this delicious little vegetable deserves a couple of chances to prove itself to the unbeliever.

Marinated Kohlrabi

I first had something like this in Spain. This recipe is only a close imitation of the original.

The Spanish serve this dish with a bowl of black olives.

3 Tbsp olive oil

1 large clove garlic, minced

1 small onion, finely diced

1 Serrano or Jalapeño pepper, seeded and minced

1 tsp fresh thyme

3 Tbsp red wine vinegar

12 large black olives

6 whole capers

12 small kohlrabi, peeled, boiled for 3 minutes and chilled in ice water

1 Tbsp parsley, chopped

1/4 cup green onion, chopped

Heat the olive oil in a skillet and sauté the garlic, onion, pepper and thyme. Add the vinegar. Simmer to reduce the liquid, and allow the mixture to cool. Mix in the olives and capers. Pour the pepper mixture over the kohlrabi in a fairly narrow bowl. Marinate for about 1 hour, stirring frequently. Before serving, sprinkle with parsley and green onions. *Serves* 6

Each serving contains: Cal-128, Prot-3g, Carb-14g, Fib-4g, Tot. Fat-8g, Sat. Fat-1g, Chol-0mg, Sdm-167mg

Pete's Kohlrabi

1 pound small kohlrabi, peeled and grated

2 Tbsp butter or olive oil

Kohlrabi leaves, shredded and boiled

Salt and pepper

Sauté the kohlrabi for a few minutes in olive oil or butter, until tender. Add the kohlrabi leaves and sauté for an additional minute. Sprinkle with salt and freshly ground black pepper. For an interesting variation, sauté 1/2 pound of mushrooms with the kohlrabi. *Serves* 4

Each serving contains: Cal-84, Prot-2g, Carb-8g, Fib-2g, Tot. Fat-6g, Sat. Fat-4g, Chol-16mg, Sdm-149mg

The next time you are making up a tray of crudités, include some peeled and sliced kohlrabi. Or you might blanch, chill and marinate it in your favorite dressing and add it to your next salad. There is some dispute as to whether kohlrabi is better in the midst of an elaborate creation, or whether it is best simply steamed and seasoned. Pete says kohlrabi belongs in the column headed, "Best steamed with lots of butter and pepper."

Each serving contains: Cal-96, Prot-5g, Carb-16g, Fib-4g, Tot. Fat-3g, Sat. Fat-1g, Chol-106mg, Sdm-111mg

Greek Kohlrabi

2 cups vegetable stock

1 tsp ground fennel

1 tsp thyme, minced

8 small kohlrabi, trimmed, peeled and quartered

1-1/2 tsp cornstarch

2 egg yolks

Juice of 1/2 lemon

Salt and pepper

2 Tbsp chives, chopped

In a medium saucepan, combine the stock, fennel and thyme. Heat to the boiling point, add the kohlrabi, lower the heat and simmer partially covered, until tender, about 15 minutes. Drain, saving the liquid. Arrange the kohlrabi on a serving dish and place in a warm oven.

Mix the cornstarch with 1 tablespoon of the cooking liquid. Beat in the egg yolks. Add the lemon juice and another 1-1/4 cups of the stock. Cook over low heat, stirring constantly, but do not allow the mixture to boil. Season with salt and pepper. Add more stock if the sauce is too thick for your taste.

Pour the sauce over the warm kohlrabi. Sprinkle with chives and serve. *Serves 4*

LEEKS

Leeks are available in winter, from late autumn until the middle of spring. Buy leeks that are clean and white, are well blanched 2 to 3 inches from the base, and have crisp, fresh green tops. Avoid leeks with soft spots, fibrous bases, or yellowish, wilted or bruised tops with unduly loose leaves. Small leeks are the most tender. If you are serving leeks as a vegetable dish, cut off the limp green ends of the leaves. If you are making soup, don't cut anything off: use the entire vegetable.

To store leeks, cut off the rootlets and throw away the coarse outer leaves; trim off the tops of the leaves and place the remaining vegetable in a plastic bag in the refrigerator. Do not leave unwrapped leeks near any other foods because they will absorb some of the leeks' flavor.

Leeks are an excellent source of folate and vitamin C and a good source of iron. Four ounces of raw leek have about 75 calories.

Because sand and dirt always gets caught between the layers of leaves, leeks are a bother to clean. To make sure you get all of the dirt out, Pete recommends a good wash and a sharp knife. Cut the leeks lengthwise, halfway through, so that as you wash them you separate the layers of the leek, letting the water pour through them.

Pete says this gives him nice clean leeks every time—something he considers of utmost importance. "There is nothin' more 'orrible," says he, "than bitin' into a beautiful, soft, luscious-lookin' leek and gettin' grit in your mouth . . . So my darlin's, give those gorgeous leeks a good wash." If you're going to be using the leeks sliced, the easiest thing to do is to slice them, put them in a colander and wash them under running water.

Braised Leeks

A luxurious and delicious treat.

3 Tbsp oil

12 average-size leeks, trimmed and cleaned

Salt and pepper

2 tsp fresh thyme, finely chopped

1/2 cup vegetable stock

Lemon juice

Parsley, chopped

Put a little oil in a shallow baking dish, lay the leeks in the dish and bake in a 350F oven for 5 to 10 minutes, turning the leeks every few minutes.

Transfer the leeks to a large saucepan, cutting them in half if necessary. Season with salt, pepper and thyme. Add the stock, bring to a boil, reduce the heat, cover and simmer for 15 minutes.

Sprinkle with some lemon juice and the chopped parsley. *Serves 6*

Leeks au Gratin

1-1/4 cups vegetable stock

12 medium to large leeks, well washed, with all but the first 2 inches of the green cut off

1 cup mushrooms, sliced

4 Tbsp butter

4 Tbsp all-purpose flour

1 cup mild Cheddar cheese, grated

Salt and pepper

1/2 tsp Dijon-style mustard

Nutmeg

2 Tbsp dry sherry

1/4 cup parsley, coarsely chopped

Looking like overgrown green onions, leeks are readily available for most of the year. As a member of the onion family, they are versatile and delicious in combination or alone.

Each serving contains: Cal-213, Prot-4, Carb-36g, Fib-6g, Tot. Fat-7g, Sat. Fat-1g, Chol-0mg, Sdm-95mg

Put the stock in a medium saucepan and bring to a boil. Lower the temperature, and add the leeks and mushrooms. Simmer over low heat for 5 to 7 minutes, until the leeks are barely tender. Drain, reserving cooking liquid. Place the leeks and mushrooms in a buttered baking dish.

Melt the butter in a skillet and stir in the flour. Stir constantly for one or two minutes, taking care not to brown the mixture. Stir in 2 cups of the cooking liquid, adding more vegetable stock if required. Simmer the mixture, stirring constantly. Add 3/4 cup of the cheese. Taste and season with salt, pepper, mustard and nutmeg. Cook until the cheese is melted. Add the sherry.

Pour the sauce over the leeks and mushrooms. Sprinkle with the remaining cheese. Broil for a few minutes or bake at 425F until the top is golden brown.

Sprinkle with parsley just before serving. *Serves 4 to 6*

Each serving contains: Cal-500, Prot-15g, Carb-64g, Fib-11g, Tot. Fat-22g, Sat. Fat-13g, Chol-61mg, Sdm-457mg

Vichyssoise

No cookbook can possibly mention leeks and not give a recipe for vichyssoise, the soup invented by the French chef Louis Diat. Some credit this soup with introducing the leek into North American kitchens.

2 Tbsp oil

4 medium potatoes, thinly sliced

4 medium white onions, thinly sliced

4 leeks, white parts only, thinly sliced

1 clove garlic, mashed

4 cups vegetable stock

1-1/2 cups milk

1/2 cup yogurt

Salt and pepper, preferably white pepper

2 tsp fennel

1/2 tsp mace

2 Tbsp minced chives or parsley

Heat the oil in a saucepan. Add the potatoes, onions, leeks and garlic and 1 cup of the vegetable stock. Simmer, covered, over very low heat until the vegetables are very soft, stirring frequently.

Add the rest of the stock to the leek mixture. Simmer, covered, for 10 minutes. Add the milk, and bring to the boiling point, but do not boil. Cool the mixture, and stir in the yogurt. Season to taste with salt, pepper, fennel and mace.

Purée the soup in a blender. If it is too thick, thin with a little cold milk. Chill thoroughly. Sprinkle with chives or parsley before serving. *Serves 6*

Each serving contains: Cal-269, Prot-7g, Carb-45g, Fib-6g, Tot. Fat-8g, Sat. Fat-2g, Chol-11mg, Sdm-116mg

LETTUCE

There is more to lettuce than iceberg and romaine. Many delicious varieties await the adventurous salad lover.

Unfortunately, it seems that a lot of the wonderful world of lettuce slides right past most of us. We tend to stick to iceberg lettuce, or occasionally we will use romaine, but there are many other varieties of lettuce that are not used to full advantage.

I was surprised when I started asking the cooks and chefs who shop at Pete's what their favorite type of lettuce was. None of them said iceberg. This is not to put down this trusted North American standard but to encourage those who are not by nature adventurous to step out on a limb and try something different.

One day I noticed a woman examining the red and green peppers with a confused expression. I asked her if I could help her with anything. She said that she was having a salad party and wanted to know what else she could put in her salads. She put down her basket and displayed her choices. She had a wealth of wonderful additions, but all she had for lettuce were a few heads of iceberg and a couple of romaine. I grinned and said that I thought that all she needed was a little variety in her lettuce. When she looked a little surprised, I showed her the Bibb, Boston and green-leaf lettuces. "That's it!" she exclaimed. She added two of each and went home to her salad party, which she later told me was a great success. I can't help noticing that although she now buys lettuce every time she shops, it is rarely iceberg.

From the wonderfully delectable Bibb lettuce to the robust romaine, there is something in your market just waiting for you to taste. I am ashamed to admit that I had worked for Pete for 2 years before I bought anything but iceberg or romaine lettuce, and then it was only because someone else was making the salad for supper. I am jealous of all of you who discovered the diversity of the world of lettuce before I did.

Crisphead lettuce is more popularly known as *iceberg lettuce*, which technically is incorrect. This is the most common lettuce largely because it is perfectly suited to the rigors of long-distance travel and the stresses of harvesting and marketing. Crisphead lettuces have firm heads, usually about 6 inches in diameter with pale-green leaves and a crisp, juicy texture. The taste is very mild.

Butterhead lettuce has small loose-leaved heads with soft, delicate leaves and a subtle, wonderfully buttery taste. The chief commercial varieties are B*oston* and B*ibb* lettuce. Boston is medium-sized, with a firm, clearly defined head that tends to be a little pointed and has thick, broad, smooth, meaty leaves. Bibb lettuce is regarded by many as the ultimate lettuce, the lettuce to end all lettuces. It is small, with dark-green leaves that are perfectly tender and have a delicate buttery flavor. Bibb lettuce has five times the nutrients of iceberg lettuce.

Romaine lettuce has long, almost rectangular heads with broad, stiff upright leaves that are crisp, coarse and rather sweet. It is, of course, essential to Caesar salad and is particularly good in combination with other lettuce. It is beautifully suited to cooking.

Looseleaf lettuce is so called because rather than growing in a head, it grows from a stem. The leaves are curly, smooth, tender and a little more meaty than crisphead lettuce. Their color varies from a fresh to a rusty green. The flavor is clean and delicate.

Lettuce is available all year round. Bibb can be harder to find but the others are readily available. Look for fresh, crisp heads, bright green in color and free from blemishes. Lettuce should be refrigerated immediately after buying. It needs some moisture during storage but must not be kept wet. Rinse it with cold water, give it a little shake to get rid of the excess water, wrap it in paper towels and put it in a plastic bag in the refrigerator where it will keep for 3 to 5 days.

Darker-leaf lettuces are good sources of vitamin A, and some varieties are excellent sources of folate. Most are good sources of fiber and low in calories. Four ounces of raw lettuce have only 17 to 22 calories.

One of the most important things when making a salad is the preparation of the lettuce. It should be washed in a sink of ice-cold water and then dried. It is imperative that the lettuce be as dry as possible so that the dressing may be evenly distributed. A salad spinner gives good results, except for Bibb and Boston lettuce, which are so delicate that they should be drained on a clean cloth towel or paper towel.

Caesar Salad

2 cloves garlic, one minced

1 large head romaine, washed and dried

6 to 8 Tbsp olive oil

1 avocado, peeled, seeded

2 Tbsp lemon juice

Salt and pepper

1 egg, slightly warmed in boiling water, about 1 minute

1/2 cup grated Parmesan cheese

1/2 to 1 cup croutons

3 Tbsp bacon bits

Mash the whole clove of garlic against the inside of a glass, pottery or wooden salad bowl. Tear the romaine into bite-size pieces, and toss into the bowl. Pour the oil over the lettuce and toss well. Add the avocado, lemon juice, salt, pepper and minced garlic. Toss again. Break the egg over the salad, add the cheese and toss once more. Sprinkle with the croutons and bacon bits, and serve immediately. *Serves 4 to 6*

The key to a good Caesar is to serve it before it is made! The dressing should be tossed in, olive oil first, then served immediately. Never let your Caesar wait. It is a salad, not a marinade. Don't be afraid to add more lemon juice, oil, Parmesan or croutons, but be careful not to overdo any one thing.

Each serving contains: Cal-488, Prot-13g, Carb-16g, Fib-5g, Tot. Fat-43g, Sat. Fat-8g, Chol-63mg, Sdm-549mg

Bibb Lettuce in Cream

This recipe calls for fresh, young, tender lettuce.

3 small heads Bibb lettuce, trimmed and washed
1/4 cup sugar
1/4 cup white vinegar
3/4 cup cream or half-and-half
Salt and white pepper

Wrap the lettuce in a cloth towel and chill for 1 hour. Tear apart the lettuce and put into a salad bowl. Stir the sugar into the vinegar until it is dissolved. Stir in the cream. Pour the sauce over the lettuce and toss. Chill for 10 minutes. Before serving, pour off any excess dressing. Season with salt and pepper. *Serves 4*

Each serving contains: Cal-142, Prot-4g, Carb-21g, Fib-3g, Tot. Fat-6g, Sat. Fat-3g, Chol-17mg, Sdm-97mg

Bibb Lettuce, Pepper and Mushroom Salad

4 heads Bibb lettuce, washed, dried and broken up
1/2 pound fresh white button mushrooms, washed and thinly sliced
1 small red pepper, sliced
2 Tbsp chopped parsley
2 tsp fresh basil, chopped
1/4 cup vinaigrette, page 17

Place the lettuce, mushrooms and pepper in a salad bowl. Sprinkle with the herbs. Pour the vinaigrette over the lettuce just before serving and toss.

You may wish to toss in some thinly sliced hard-cooked eggs for a little more protein. *Serves 4 to 6*

Each serving contains: Cal-132, Prot-6g, Carb-13g, Fib-5g, Tot. Fat-8g, Sat. Fat-1g, Chol-0mg, Sdm-313mg

Stuffed Iceberg Lettuce

1 medium-size iceberg lettuce
1/2 pound cottage cheese, at room temperature
1/3 cup blue cheese, crumbled, at room temperature
1/4 cup mayonnaise
1 rib celery, finely chopped
3 Tbsp red pepper, minced
1 green onion, chopped
Chives
1/4 cup walnuts, finely chopped
1 tsp vegetarian Worcestershire sauce
Tabasco sauce
Sliced tomatoes
Sprigs of parsley

Core the lettuce and hollow out the center, leaving a shell about 1 inch thick. Wash and drain the lettuce carefully, drying it on a paper towel.

Mix the cottage cheese, blue cheese and mayonnaise. Blend in the celery, red pepper, onion, chives, walnuts, Worcestershire sauce and a dash of Tabasco. Mix thoroughly.

Fill the lettuce with the cheese mixture, wrap it in wet paper towels and foil and tie it with a string to keep its shape.

Chill for at least 2 hours. To serve, cut in wedges and garnish with sliced tomatoes and sprigs of parsley. *Serves 4 to 6*

Sautéed Lettuce

2 heads romaine, washed, shaken dry, and cut into quarters

1 large onion, sliced

1 large tomato, peeled and seeded

1/2 pound mushrooms, sliced

3 Tbsp olive oil

Basil, thyme or marjoram

Salt and pepper

Vegetable stock

Cook the lettuce in boiling water for 2 minutes, ensuring that it does not become soggy. Drain the lettuce and lay it in a strainer to allow any excess moisture to drip off. Dry between paper towels.

Sauté the onion, tomato and mushrooms in the olive oil, stirring constantly until the onion is tender. Add the lettuce. Season with a pinch of the herbs, salt and pepper. Sauté over low heat for 10 minutes. If there is any danger of scorching, add some vegetable stock. Serve very hot. *Serves 4 to 6*

Cape Cod Salad

A great salad, especially for lovers of red wine.

4 heads Bibb lettuce, washed and dried

1 small head romaine, washed and dried

1 bunch watercress, washed and dried

1/2 cup walnut halves

1/2 cup Mozzarella cheese, grated

1/2 cup olive oil

2 Tbsp red wine

1 Tbsp red wine vinegar

Salt and pepper

Tear the lettuces into a salad bowl; add the watercress, walnut halves and cheese. In a separate bowl, blend the oil, wine, vinegar, salt and pepper. Pour the vinaigrette over the salad just before serving and toss. *Serves 6*

Each serving contains: Cal-277, Prot-13g, Carb-10g, Fib-2g, Tot. Fat-22g, Sat. Fat-6g, Chol-25mg, Sdm-507mg

Each serving contains: Cal-164, Prot-6g, Carb-13g, Fib-5g, Tot. Fat-11g, Sat. Fat-2g, Chol-0mg, Sdm-92mg

My aunt and uncle picked up this recipe on Cape Cod and it quickly became a family favorite.

Each serving contains: Cal-282, Prot-7g, Carb-9g, Fib-4g, Tot. Fat-26g, Sat. Fat-4g, Chol-7mg, Sdm-96mg

MUSHROOMS

Pete's advice on storing mushrooms is clear: "Don't." When I asked him to expand a little he said: "Don't keep 'em, eat 'em!"

This odd little creation is a peculiarity in the vegetable world. It is really the fruiting body of a variety of fungus. Having no leaves, flowers, seeds or roots, this plant depends on non-living organic matter rather than photosynthesis for food. The mushroom has been thought of as exotic and slightly mysterious for thousands of years. The Pharaohs ate mushrooms, and today it is only the fabulously wealthy or the fabulously lucky who eat truffles, perhaps the most exotic, most rare, most expensive and most delicious fungus available.

Although button mushrooms are easy enough to find, they are not cheap; growing them is a precise and time-consuming process. Because of their perishable nature, mushrooms are picked, packed, and shipped to market in less than 24 hours.

Many types of mushrooms grow only in the wild and this makes them not only expensive, but also hard to find. Unless you make daily visits to your market, it is unlikely that you will be lucky enough to catch the rarer mushrooms as they arrive. But button mushrooms are widely cultivated and always in good supply. And all that you need to enjoy these little delights is a frying pan, some butter and black pepper. Right, Pete?

Button mushrooms are available all year round, having no peak season, and in most markets and produce departments of large grocery stores it is possible to bag your own mushrooms. Look for plump, smooth, white mushrooms with tightly closed caps. Avoid shriveled, wide-open or slimy mushrooms or any with blemishes or dark spots.

Mushrooms are not suited to storing. However, if you have no choice and must store these delicate little fungi, ensure that they are wrapped in paper towels or put in a paper bag before refrigerating. And do not forget that mushrooms are fragile and need to be handled carefully. Give them enough space; don't squash them up against anything. If you plan to use them raw, with a dip, or if you want to keep them perfect for a day or two, cover them with a paper towel that has been dipped in water and wrung half-dry. Store them on a shallow tray in a refrigerator.

Mushrooms are about 80% water so they can absorb a lot of fat or cream in cooking. But raw, 4 ounces of the delicate fungi have only 35 calories. Mushrooms are a fair source of minerals, especially potassium, and a good source of protein and a number of the B vitamins, including riboflavin and niacin.

When cooking mushrooms for a large number of people, bear in mind that they release a considerable amount of water and can make a dish watery. Mushrooms also shrink when cooked, so what looks like a good-sized serving of raw mushrooms may be too little when cooked. One pound will generously serve three mushroom devotees, or it will keep four ordinary mortals quite happy.

Another consideration is the best way to wash mushrooms: soaking them all but destroys their flavor; wiping them with a damp cloth is a time-consuming but effective way to clean mushrooms. A faster and easier option is to put them in a metal sieve and hold them under cold running water, swishing them constantly until they are clean. Then pat them dry with a paper towel.

However, when asked about washing mushrooms, Pete said that the only time he bothers to wash them is if he is using them in a dip. In stew, soup or even for pan-frying, Pete pointedly refuses to wash mushrooms. He likes to keep his mushrooms as dry as possible because, as he explains, his preference is for golden-brown fried mushrooms, which is all but impossible if there is too much moisture in the vegetable.

Mushroom Sauce for Pasta

1 cup onions, thinly sliced

3 cloves garlic, finely minced

4 Tbsp butter

2 pounds mushrooms, thinly sliced

1 cup yogurt

1/2 tsp nutmeg

2 Tbsp basil, finely chopped

Salt and pepper

1/4 cup parsley, chopped

Parmesan cheese, grated

Sauté the onions and garlic in half the butter for about 4 minutes, stirring constantly until the onions begin to turn transparent.

Meanwhile, sauté the mushrooms in the rest of the butter for about 4 minutes, until tender but still firm. Lower the temperature. Add the onion mixture. Sauté for about 15 minutes.

Add the yogurt, nutmeg, basil, salt and pepper. Heat through, stirring constantly and ensuring that the mixture does not boil. Pour the sauce over pasta and toss gently. Sprinkle with chopped parsley, and serve with grated Parmesan cheese. *This makes enough sauce for 1 pound of cooked pasta, or 6 servings*

Each serving contains: Cal-163, Prot-7g, Carb-12g, Fib-2g, Tot. Fat-11g, Sat. Fat-7g, Chol-29mg, Sdm-226mg

Stuffed Mushrooms

1 pound fresh spinach

1 pound large fresh mushrooms, cleaned and stemmed, the stems reserved

Melted butter

1/4 cup fine breadcrumbs

1/4 cup grated Parmesan cheese

1/3 cup Cheddar cheese, grated

1/3 cup blue cheese, crumbled

6 green onions, minced

1/2 cup parsley, chopped

1 Tbsp fresh basil, chopped

Sprinkle the spinach with water and steam in a large saucepan with a tightly fitting lid. Drain in a sieve, pressing out the excess water. Chop the spinach and set aside.

Mince the mushroom stems and sauté in a little butter. Combine all ingredients except the mushroom caps. Mix well.

Brush the outsides of the mushroom caps with butter and fill with the spinach mixture. Bake on a cookie sheet at 375F about 20 minutes or until mushrooms are soft. Serve immediately. *Serves* 8

Mushrooms and Cream

This combination is especially good on buttered rice.

3 Tbsp butter

1/2 cup onion, chopped

1 pound mushrooms, trimmed and sliced

2/3 cup cream or half-and-half

1/4 tsp nutmeg

Salt and pepper

3 Tbsp parsley, finely chopped

Melt the butter in a deep frying pan. Sauté the onion for about 2 minutes; then add the mushrooms and sauté for another 2 minutes. In the meantime, heat the cream, add it to the mushrooms and season with nutmeg, salt and pepper. Simmer, stirring constantly, for another 3 minutes or until the cream has thickened. Sprinkle with parsley before serving. *Serves* 4

Mushroom-and-Leek Soup

6 leeks, well washed and thinly sliced

1/2 cup butter

1/2 pound mushrooms, sliced

1/4 cup all-purpose flour

Salt and pepper

1 cup vegetable stock

3 cups milk

1 Tbsp sherry

Fresh chives, chopped

1 tsp fresh tarragon

Sauté the leeks until soft in 1/4 cup of the butter. Set aside.

Each serving contains: Cal-121, Prot-7g, Carb-8g, Fib-3g, Tot. Fat-8g, Sat. Fat-5g, Chol-19mg, Sdm-271mg

Each serving contains: Cal-165, Prot-4g, Carb-9g, Fib-2g, Tot. Fat-14g, Sat. Fat-8g, Chol-38mg, Sdm-176mg

Each serving contains: Cal-322, Prot-8g, Carb-31g, Fib-4g, Tot. Fat-20g, Sat. Fat-12g, Chol-58mg, Sdm-319mg

Okra is a favorite vegetable with people of the southern United States who specialize in Creole cooking. But despite its popularity with West Indian, Arabian and tropical-American cooks, it is not well known in North America and is virtually unheard of in Europe.

Each serving contains: Cal-36, Prot-2g, Carb-8g, Fib-3g, Tot. Fat-0g, Sat. Fat-0g, Chol-0mg, Sdm-6mg

Sauté the mushrooms in the remaining butter until soft. Blend in the flour, salt and pepper. Add the stock and milk and simmer, stirring until mixture is thick and creamy. Add the leeks and simmer for 10 minutes. Stir in the sherry and sprinkle with chives and tarragon. Serve immediately. *Serves 6*

OKRA

Okra is not on Pete's list of favorite vegetables. He is, nonetheless, full of information on how to select good okra and how to store it; he even has a few recipes. He claims that the best way to use it is as a thickener for soups, gumbos or Creole stews, where its gummy, gluey quality serves it well.

Okra, in good condition, is quite an attractive vegetable. Eight-sided, about 2 to 3 inches long, deep green in color with a cute little cap at one end and a nice neat point at the other, okra looks a bit like a Chinese knick-knack.

It is available all year round, with its peak season being from July to September. When buying okra, look for small to medium-size young pods; mature okra pods tend to be fibrous. Okra should be deep green, crisp and free from blemishes. Avoid dry, shriveled or discolored pods, or those that are stiff and woody. The pods should snap easily, but unless you are out to annoy your greengrocer, checking okra by snapping the pods should be done stealthily. If the pods are pliable, they are too old. You can keep okra for up to 4 days in an open plastic bag in the refrigerator.

Okra is a good source of potassium and an excellent source of vitamin C and folate. Four ounces of cooked okra have 35 calories.

Never cook okra in a tin or iron pan because the pods will turn black. They will still be edible but they will look unappetizing. And, unless you want to take full advantage of its gummy quality, do not cut the pods until after the vegetable is cooked; then you can safely remove the little caps and cut them any way you like. A drop of lemon juice or vinegar in the cooking water helps reduce the mucilaginous quality.

Steamed Okra and Variations

This is the simplest way of preparing okra and if you are unfamiliar with the vegetable, it gives you a chance to try it out.

Wash and trim 1 pound of okra, using pods as small and as young as you can find. Cook in a small amount of boiling water for 10 minutes, or until just tender. Drain well. *Serves 4*

With butter and lemon: pour about 1/4 cup melted butter and the juice of 1/4 lemon over the okra. Toss well.

With garlic and oil: pour a little olive oil over the okra and sprinkle with some very finely minced garlic. Toss well.

With garlic-basil butter: blend some butter with minced garlic and basil. Toss with hot okra.

In vinaigrette: chill the okra completely and pour your favorite vinaigrette over the pods. Toss well.

Okra, Tomatoes and Rice

1 cup onion, chopped

1/2 pound okra, washed, trimmed and sliced

2 Tbsp olive oil

1 cup uncooked rice

1 pound canned Italian plum tomatoes, or use fresh ones
   if they are available

Salt and pepper

1/4 tsp cloves

1 or 2 Serrano or Jalapeño peppers, minced

1/2 cup water

Chopped parsley

Sauté the onion and okra in the olive oil until the onion is soft. Add the rice, tomatoes, salt, pepper, cloves, peppers and water. Bring the mixture to a boil and pour into a greased 2-quart casserole. Bake at 350F for 1 hour or until the rice is tender. Sprinkle with chopped parsley before serving. *Serves* 6

Each serving contains: Cal-193, Prot-4g, Carb-33g, Fib-3g, Tot. Fat-5g, Sat. Fat-1g, Chol-0mg, Sdm-56mg

Okra Plus

If this looks as though it is becoming too dry, add a little warm vegetable stock.

2 medium onions, minced

2 potatoes, parboiled in boiling water, sliced

2 ribs celery, chopped

1 red pepper, cut into strips

5 Tbsp oil

1 pound young okra, trimmed and cut into 1/2-inch slices

1 cup corn kernels

6 plum tomatoes, peeled and chopped

4 Tbsp fresh basil, minced

2 or 3 Serrano or Jalapeño peppers, chopped

2 tsp celery seed

1/4 cup bacon bits

1/2 cup cilantro (coriander), minced

Salt and pepper

In a large frying pan, sauté the onions, potatoes, celery and red pepper in the oil. Stir constantly until the pepper is almost soft; then add the okra. Sauté the mixture, stirring constantly until the okra is golden. Add the corn, tomatoes, basil, peppers and celery seed. Simmer, covered, for 10 to 15 minutes or until okra is tender, taking care not to overcook the mixture. Sprinkle with bacon bits and cilantro; season with salt and pepper. Serve hot. *Serves 4*

Fried Okra

1 pound okra, trimmed and washed and cut into 1/2-inch slices (I prefer cooking it whole and cutting it once it's cooked.)
2 eggs, beaten with
1/2 tsp salt
1 cup cornmeal
Peanut oil
Dry mustard

One day at Pete's a man came up to my cash register with a sack of okra. "Now," he said, "I can go right home and have my favorite supper." When I asked him how he planned to prepare it, he gave me his recipe. "Eat it with lots of salt. You will love it, I know." I don't quite love it but it does taste good.

Put the okra in a bowl. Pour the beaten eggs and salt over the okra and toss until the pods are completely coated. With a slotted spoon, transfer the okra to a bowl filled with the cornmeal, and toss again until well coated.

Heat about 1/2 inch of peanut oil in a large frying pan. Add the okra and stir. Cover the frying pan and cook over medium heat, stirring frequently, until the okra is golden brown and crisp. Sprinkle with a pinch of dry mustard. Drain on a paper towel and serve immediately. *Serves 4*

Vegetable Gumbo Soup

Okra is traditionally used as a thickener in soups and stews in southern cuisine. Here is a typical recipe.

4 Tbsp butter
1 onion, finely chopped
4 cups vegetable stock
1 green pepper, finely chopped
1 cup okra, chopped
Pinch of cayenne pepper
2 cups canned tomatoes, chopped
Salt and pepper

Melt the butter in a large pot. Add the onion and sauté, stirring frequently, until transparent. Add the vegetable stock, green pepper, okra, cayenne and tomatoes. Simmer, partially covered, for 1 hour. Season with salt and pepper to taste before serving. *Serves 6 to 8*

ONIONS

Onions were so highly thought of in ancient Egypt that there was actually an onion cult. Although we do not esteem onions quite so highly these days, it would be hard to imagine a lot of our favorite dishes without the onion. Few of us would be willing to eat cooking onions whole and raw, but Spanish onions (of which there are many, many varieties) can really make a salad special or a sandwich extra delicious. From chives to the huge, sweet, eating onions is a world of taste and flavorings just waiting to excite our palates and enhance our meals.

The realm of the onion is enormous and confusing, so to make things a little clearer we'll explore them type by type.

Chives are usually regarded as an herb. These long, slender green shoots are available as fresh as fresh can be early in the summer. The green shoots are delicious finely chopped and sprinkled on sandwiches or salads or used as a garnish on vegetables. The plant should be clipped at least three times during the course of the summer; otherwise, the shoots develop beautiful, but inedible, purple flowers.

Green onions and **scallions** are not the same, although the two terms are used interchangeably. Scallions are the shoots of white onions, which are pulled before the bulb has formed. Green onions are harvested while they are still green, and the bulb is obvious. Nevertheless, the two can be substituted in recipes. Both scallions and green onions have a mild flavor and are delicious chopped and added to a salad, sprinkled on scrambled eggs or as a last-minute addition to a stir-fry.

Shallots are a key ingredient in many delicious and wonderful sauces and butters. Their delicate intriguing flavor is enhanced by cooking, blending superbly with rice and pasta. Shallots are superb in a vinaigrette or simply minced and added to a salad. They are usually dried and used like garlic.

Eating onions are sometimes called *short-day* or *early-maturing* onions. Their skin is thin and their moisture content high. Pete refers to them as eating onions because their exceptionally mild flavor and crisp juiciness make them delicious for eating when raw. They are also known as *sweet onions*, and while there are many varieties, the best known is the *Spanish onion*. Depending on the season, year and country of origin, Spanish onions are of varying strengths. Although they can be cooked, they are best eaten raw. Slice them paper-thin and toss a handful onto a green salad, slip a few slices into your next sandwich or try putting out a few chunks of these delicacies with your next tray of crudités.

Cooking onions, or *long-day* onions, are the main crop. They have several thin, dry layers of skin; their flesh has a strong flavor and is not as moist as the flesh of eating onions. Most of us are familiar with these onions; they are the yellow ones we buy in mesh bags and use all the time.

Whole onions may be stored unwrapped in a dry, cool, well-ventilated place for up to 2 months. Once cut, they should be wrapped in plastic and refrigerated for up to 4 days.

Onions are available all year. Chives, of course, are really only available if you grow them yourself or purchase small plants at nurseries or greenhouses. When buying green onions look for young, tender, clean shoots with firm, well-trimmed bulbs and fresh, bright green tops. Avoid withered or damaged green onions with broken or bruised leaves. Store them in your refrigerator, unwashed, for up to 5 days.

For shallots and the larger eating and cooking onions, look for hard, firm, dry onions with crackly, unblemished skin and small necks. As a rule, do not buy dry onions that have sprouted, but if they sprout while you are storing them, just cut off the green shoot. If the onion is not mushy, you can still use it.

Dry onions are a good source of vitamin C. Shallots and green onions provide some vitamin A. Although one would never consider eating a cup of chives, the number of calories contained in a cup of green onions is fairly close to that contained in a similar quantity of dry onions. Four ounces of raw onion have 40 calories.

Baked Onions

Put unpeeled medium or large onions in a single layer in a baking dish. Bake at 350F for about 30 minutes or until they are soft. Slip off the skins before serving. They will come off easily.

If you are eating the onions hot, serve them with salt, pepper and butter, like baked potatoes. If you eat them cold, drizzle them with a little olive oil and lemon juice.

Boiled Onions and Variations

Simply boil 1 pound of peeled, sliced onions in just enough salted water to cover them. Small onions need not be sliced and will take about 15 minutes to cook; larger onions will require about 20 minutes. Drain the onions well. *Serves 4*

Buttered onions: toss the onions with melted butter and black pepper.

With nutmeg: toss the onions with melted butter and nutmeg.

With tomato sauce: pour tomato sauce, seasoned with pepper and freshly chopped garlic, over the onions and garnish with chopped parsley.

Creamed onions, creamed onions in a cheese sauce: make a white sauce, or a cheese sauce by adding some grated Gruyère or Cheddar cheese to a white sauce, and pour it over the onions after they have been drained.

Each serving contains: Cal-43, Prot-1g, Carb-10g, Fib-2g, Tot. Fat-0g, Sat. Fat-0g, Chol-0mg, Sdm-3mg

Curried Onions

1/4 cup golden raisins

1/4 cup dry sherry

1 pound small white onions, peeled, or 1 pound sliced onions

4 Tbsp butter

2 tsp celery seed

Salt and pepper

1 cup water

1 Tbsp curry powder, more or less

Milk

1 Tbsp cornstarch

1/4 cup freshly grated coconut

Soak the raisins in the sherry for one hour.

Put the onions, 2 tablespoons of the butter, celery seed, salt, pepper and water into a saucepan. Bring to a boil and lower the temperature. Cover and simmer for 10 minutes, until the onions are tender but still firm. Remove the onions with a slotted spoon and set the liquid to one side.

In the top of a double boiler, melt the other 2 tablespoons of butter and blend in the curry powder. Add the onions and simmer over hot water for 10 minutes. Drain the onions into a bowl.

Measure the reserved liquid, add enough milk to make 1-1/4 cups and put into the top of the double boiler. Stir in the cornstarch and simmer, stirring frequently, until the liquid is thick and smooth. Add the onions, raisins and sherry, and cook over hot water until heated through. Sprinkle with fresh coconut. *Serves* 4

Each serving contains: Cal-254, Prot-4g, Carb-25g, Fib-3g, Tot. Fat-16g, Sat. Fat-10g, Chol-39mg, Sdm-222mg

Braised Onions and Variations

20 small onions, or 1 pound sliced onions

1/4 cup butter or oil

1/2 cup vegetable stock

Salt and pepper

Sauté the onions in butter until lightly browned. Add the stock, salt and pepper to taste. Cover the pan and cook the onions about 20 minutes, until tender-crisp. *Serves* 4

With Parmesan cheese: sprinkle the onions with lots of freshly grated Parmesan cheese just before serving.

With pasta: braised onions make a super pasta sauce. Just pour the onions over cooked pasta and sprinkle with Parmesan cheese.

Wine-braised onions: add 1/2 cup dry sherry, Madeira or bourbon to the braised onions, and simmer for about 3 minutes or until the liquid is reduced by half.

Each serving contains: Cal-238, Prot-4g, Carb-31g, Fib-6g, Tot. Fat-12g, Sat. Fat-7g, Chol-31mg, Sdm-196mg

A slightly more exciting way to prepare onions is to braise them. Easy and delicious!

Onion Frittata

2 Tbsp olive oil

2 large onions, sliced as thinly as possible

1/2 pound mushrooms, sliced

1 Tbsp all-purpose flour

2 Tbsp milk

6 eggs, beaten

1/2 tsp cayenne pepper

Salt, pepper and nutmeg

In a medium skillet, heat the oil and sauté the onions and mushrooms until the onions are soft and transparent.

In a bowl, mix the flour and milk together, and add the eggs and cayenne. Beat thoroughly. Season with salt, pepper and nutmeg. Pour the egg mixture over the onions and mushrooms, and fry the frittata until the bottom is set. Flip the frittata, using a plate, or broil the top until it is set. *Serves* 4

Each serving contains: Cal-226, Prot-12g, Carb-12g, Fib-2g, Tot. Fat-15g, Sat. Fat-3g, Chol-320mg, Sdm-169mg

PARSNIPS

Pastinaca sativa, the Latin name for parsnips, means "cultivated food." The poor parsnip! This odd-looking vegetable, which looks like an albino carrot, is often relegated to stews. But with a wonderful, sweet, nutty flavor, it is also delicious glazed, battered and deep-fried, puréed, or served in a soup.

Available all year, the peak season is from October to May. When buying parsnips, look for ones that are fat and round at the top, not less than 1-1/2 inches in diameter. Buy small to medium-sized parsnips that are firm, well-shaped and clean; the larger ones have a tendency to be woody.

To store parsnips, simply refrigerate them in a plastic bag. You can happily leave them there for up to two weeks.

Cooked parsnips are a good source of vitamin C and folate. When raw, they are a good source of potassium. Four ounces of raw parsnip contain about 85 calories.

Parsnips are easier to peel after they have been cooked. If you do happen to get some large parsnips, simply halve them lengthwise, core them and use them as though they were small.

The sweetest parsnips are those that have been left in the ground until after the first frost has turned some of the starch to sugar. Parsnips keep very well; in fact, some people claim that parsnips are better after they have been stored for a while.

Sautéed Parsnips and Variations

2-1/2 to 3 pounds parsnips, unpeeled
4 to 6 Tbsp butter
Salt and pepper

Steam or boil the parsnips in a small amount of water until they are easily pierced. This process may take from 20 to 45 minutes, depending on the size of the vegetable. Immerse the parsnips in cold water, and peel them when they are cool enough to handle. Cut off the tough ends, and slice the parsnips very thin. Sauté them in butter for 5 or 6 minutes. Season with salt and pepper. *Serves 4*

Glazed: sprinkle white sugar on the parsnips while they are sautéing. Stir well to make sure each piece of the vegetable is coated.

Nutty-glazed: combine 1/4 cup finely chopped walnuts with the white sugar and glaze as above.

With sour cream: blend 1-1/2 cups sour cream with some mace, ginger or cardamom. Stir the sour-cream mixture into the parsnips and heat through.

Each serving contains: Cal-408, Prot-4g, Carb-61g, Fib-17g, Tot. Fat-18g, Sat. Fat-11g, Chol-47mg, Sdm-277mg

Nutty Parsnip Fritters

2 pounds parsnips, cooked and peeled
6 Tbsp melted butter
1 Tbsp all-purpose flour
2 large eggs
3/4 cup milk
1/2 tsp cardamom or ginger
Salt and pepper
1/2 cup shelled nuts, almonds, hazelnuts or walnuts,
    coarsely chopped

Purée the parsnips in a food processor or blender. Add the butter, flour, eggs and milk, and make a smooth paste. Season with cardamom or ginger, salt and pepper. Stir in the nuts. Ease spoonfuls of the mixture onto a well-oiled cookie sheet. Bake at 350F for 15 to 20 minutes, or until golden brown. Drain the fritters on a paper towel. *Serves 6*

Parsnip fritters make wonderful hors d'oeuvres or are a delicious accompaniment to Mushroom-and-Leek Soup.

Each serving contains: Cal-328, Prot-7g, Carb-32g, Fib-9g, Tot. Fat-20g, Sat. Fat-9g, Chol-106mg, Sdm-214mg

Parsnip Soup

1/2 cup onion, chopped

1 cup carrots, thinly sliced

2 large parsnips, peeled, cored and diced

1 Serrano or Jalapeño pepper, minced

2 cloves garlic, minced

3 Tbsp oil

1 tsp curry powder

4 cups hot vegetable stock

1/2 cup sour cream

Chopped chives

Sauté the onion, carrots, parsnips, pepper and garlic in the oil for 10 minutes. If it appears that the vegetables might scorch, add some of the vegetable stock. Add the curry powder and gradually blend in the vegetable stock. Simmer until the parsnips are cooked. Purée the mixture in a blender or food processor. Return to the heat and adjust the seasoning. Add the sour cream and sprinkle with chives.

The parsnip taste becomes richer if this soup is set aside for a day or two. *Serves 6*

Each serving contains: Cal-189, Prot-3g, Carb-22g, Fib-6g, Tot. Fat-11g, Sat. Fat-3g, Chol-9mg, Sdm-43mg

Braised Parsnips

3 Tbsp butter

2 pounds parsnips, scrubbed and cut into chunks

1 Tbsp onion, grated

1/4 tsp sugar

Salt and pepper

6 large lettuce leaves

3 Tbsp minced parsley

Melt the butter in a large saucepan. Add the parsnips, onion, sugar, salt and pepper, and simmer the mixture, stirring occasionally. Wash the lettuce leaves and, leaving them wet, cover the parsnips with the lettuce. Put the lid on the saucepan and simmer over low heat for 15 minutes, or until the parsnips are tender. Shake the saucepan often to keep the parsnips from sticking. If the parsnip mixture seems too dry, add a little water, a tablespoon at a time. Sprinkle with parsley before serving. Serve with the lettuce leaves. *Serves 4 to 6*

Each serving contains: Cal-250, Prot-3g, Carb-42g, Fib-11g, Tot. Fat-9g, Sat. Fat-5g, Chol-23mg, Sdm-178mg

Parsnip French Fries

**8 medium-size parsnips, cooked, cored and cut into
    the shape of french fries, or cubed**
All-purpose flour
2 eggs, lightly beaten
Fresh breadcrumbs
Oil for frying

Dip the parsnips in the flour and the beaten eggs, and roll the pieces in the breadcrumbs. Fry the coated parsnips in oil at 400F until tender. Drain the fried parsnips on a paper towel, keeping the pieces warm until they are all cooked. *Serves 4*

Each serving contains: Cal-313, Prot-9g, Carb-63g, Fib-12g, Tot. Fat-4g, Sat. Fat-1g, Chol-107mg, Sdm-111mg

Midnight Parsnip Snack

Whenever I run out of popcorn, this is my favorite midnight snack. It's hopelessly easy.

Use your vegetable peeler to make thick strips of parsnip. Heat some peanut oil in a wok and drop in the parsnip strips. Stir-fry them for a moment or two. Drain on paper towels and voilà! Parsnip curls! Yum! *One parsnip makes 2 servings*

Each serving contains: Cal-172, Prot-1g, Carb-13g, Fib-3g, Tot. Fat-14g, Sat. Fat-2g, Chol-0mg, Sdm-7mg

PEAS

Peas have been around for more than 11,000 years, but until about 200 years ago they were usually dried and eaten in soups or porridge. Now, because they freeze and can so well, more than 80% of the North American pea crop is preserved in one of these two ways.

Garden peas are available from April to August. Edible-pod peas are available from February through June, except of course for snow peas, which are available all year round. Incidentally, for those of you who were wondering, there is little difference between sugar snap and snow peas, except that snap peas are smaller than snow peas and have a definite thread. They are, however, interchangeable in recipes.

When buying green or garden peas, look for fairly large, angular, bright-green pea pods packed with medium-sized peas. There is no way of telling by the outside how sweet and juicy they are inside, so—if you can be sneaky—snap a pod open and pop one of those little round green things into your mouth and test them for yourself. When buying edible-pod peas look for bright-green, glossy, crisp pods. In both cases, avoid peas with marks, soft spots or yellowish, swollen pods.

Like mushrooms, fresh peas are not meant to be kept unbagged in your refrigerator for more than a few hours. If you simply have to store your peas, put them in a plastic bag to retain their juiciness, but for no more than 2 days.

Pete points out that peas are one of the few vegetables that are not available fresh all year, imported from somewhere or another, but adds with great enthusiasm that, thanks to 20th-century technology, frozen peas are only a hair's breadth away from being every bit as wonderful as fresh peas. So next time you go shopping, if it's not fresh-pea season, buy a bag of frozen ones with Pete's blessing.

Don't bother washing garden peas after shelling; they stay nice and clean in their shells. Give edible-pod peas a quick rinse just before trimming them, then just snap off both ends and remove the string if there is one. Try not to keep them for more than 2 days.

Peas are a good source of fiber, potassium and niacin and an excellent source of vitamin C, folate and thiamin. They are a good source of potassium, and contain higher than average amounts of protein and iron. Four ounces of fresh garden peas, raw and shelled, have 95 calories. Four ounces of edible-pod peas contain 60 calories.

Each serving contains: Cal-195, Prot-9g, Carb-26g, Fib-9g, Tot. Fat-6g, Sat. Fat-4g, Chol-16mg, Sdm-134mg

Boiled Peas and Variations

3 to 4 pounds unshelled peas
1 tsp sugar
Butter
Salt and pepper

Shell the peas seconds before they are to be cooked. Cook them as briefly and gently as possible in boiling water with a little sugar . . . until just tender. Drain well and toss with butter, salt and freshly ground pepper. *Serves 4*

With herbs: after tossing the cooked peas with the butter, sprinkle them with freshly chopped parsley, tarragon, savory or mint.

With mushrooms: combine the peas with an equal quantity of sautéed mushrooms and a sprig of chopped, fresh tarragon.

With shallots: slice 2 or 3 shallots as thinly as possible. Sauté them in a little butter and toss them with the cooked peas.

With green onions: thinly slice green onions or scallions. Heat them in butter and toss with the peas.

With yogurt or sour cream: heat some yogurt or sour cream and a little minced dill. Stir the yogurt into the buttered peas.

Snow Peas, Red Pepper and Almond Salad

1/2 pound snow peas

2 cloves garlic, finely chopped

1 Tbsp white wine vinegar

1 Tbsp lemon juice

1 tsp sugar

Salt and pepper

1/3 cup salad oil

1/2 pound fresh mushrooms, sliced

1 large red pepper, in thin strips

1/2 green pepper, in thin strips

1/4 cup slivered almonds, toasted

4 hard-cooked eggs, sliced or cut in quarters

Trim the peas, and remove the strings. Blanch for one minute in boiling water. Drain the peas and plunge them into ice water to chill. Dry on paper towels.

In a small bowl, combine the garlic, vinegar, lemon juice, sugar, salt and pepper. Beat well. Continue beating and slowly drizzle in the oil to make a smooth dressing.

In a large bowl, toss the peas, mushrooms and peppers together. Add the dressing and almonds just before serving and toss once again. Garnish with the eggs. *Serves 6*

Each serving contains: Cal-227, Prot-7g, Carb-9g, Fib-2g, Tot. Fat-19g, Sat. Fat-3g, Chol-141mg, Sdm-90mg

Cold Dilled-Pea Soup

Most peas are picked when immature because this is when they are at their sweetest. As they mature, the sugar turns to starch and their protein content increases. The more-mature peas are picked to be dried. And we get to eat the immature peas as sprouts! Versatile little things, peas!

3 pounds peas, freshly shelled

1 small onion, chopped

1 clove garlic, minced

1 tsp tarragon, chopped

2 or 3 whole cloves

6 cups vegetable stock

Salt and pepper

3 cups sour cream or yogurt

Fresh dill

Boil the peas, onions, garlic, tarragon and cloves in the vegetable stock, just until the peas are tender. Remove the cloves. Season with salt and pepper. Purée the mixture. Blend in the sour cream or yogurt. Chill for at least 4 hours. Sprinkle with dill before serving. *Serves 8*

Each serving contains: Cal-263, Prot-7g, Carb-19g, Fib-5g, Tot. Fat-18g, Sat. Fat-11g, Chol-38mg, Sdm-93mg

Basted Eggs in Peas

3 shallots, very thinly sliced

2 Tbsp melted butter

2 pounds unshelled peas, shelled

1/4 cup water

Salt, pepper, mace, nutmeg and sugar

5 eggs

6 Tbsp yogurt

In an ovenproof skillet, sauté the shallots briefly in the butter. Add the peas, water and a pinch each of salt, pepper, mace, nutmeg and sugar, and continue to cook, covered, for a few minutes. Season the peas with a little more salt and/or sugar. When the peas are half-cooked, make 4 depressions in the peas with the back of a spoon, and slide an egg into each of the holes. Cover the skillet, and let the eggs and peas simmer for 5 minutes, or until the peas are done and the eggs are set but not hard. Beat the 5th egg into the yogurt and pour the mixture over the peas. Broil for a moment or two. Serve immediately. *Serves 4*

Each serving contains: Cal-234, Prot-14g, Carb-16g, Fib-4g, Tot. Fat-13g, Sat. Fat-6g, Chol-284mg, Sdm-220mg

Snow or Sugar Snap Peas

The best way to cook edible-pod peas is to stir-fry them in peanut or olive oil no more than 2 minutes so that they keep their wonderfully crisp nature. Sugar snaps are a delicious addition to any stir-fry or as a dish all on their own. Serve them with melted butter and a little lemon juice. *One pound of peas will serve 3 people*

Each serving contains: Cal-240, Prot-4g, Carb-12g, Fib-4g, Tot. Fat-20g, Sat. Fat-10g, Chol-41mg, Sdm-164mg

Peas and Lettuce

2 Tbsp butter

6 green onions, thinly sliced

1 head Boston or Bibb lettuce, finely shredded

1/2 small red pepper, sliced or cut into cubes

4 pounds peas, shelled

4 Tbsp vegetable stock

Fresh thyme

Salt, pepper and nutmeg

1/4 cup parsley, minced

Melt the butter in a skillet. Stir in the green onions, lettuce and red pepper. Add the peas, vegetable stock, thyme, salt, pepper and nutmeg. Cover tightly and simmer for no more than 10 minutes, or until the peas are tender. Sprinkle with parsley before serving. *Serves 4*

Each serving contains: Cal-213, Prot-11g, Carb-30g, Fib-11g, Tot. Fat-7g, Sat. Fat-4g, Chol-16mg, Sdm-144mg

Peas Italiana

1 small onion, minced

2 cloves garlic, minced

2 Tbsp butter

4 pounds peas, shelled

1/2 cup vegetable stock

Salt, pepper and sage

4 eggs, beaten

1/2 cup Mozzarella cheese, grated

Sauté the onion and garlic in butter until soft and golden. Add the peas, stock and seasonings. Cover tightly and cook over low heat for 10 minutes or until the peas are just tender, stirring frequently.

Beat the eggs and Mozzarella together, stir the mixture into the peas and remove it from the heat. Let stand, covered, 5 minutes. Sprinkle with additional Mozzarella before serving. *Serves 4*

North Americans are especially lucky because we have access to sugar snap peas, garden peas and the lovely little snow peas, which we get all year round.

Each serving contains: Cal-317, Prot-19g, Carb-29g, Fib-9g, Tot. Fat-15g, Sat. Fat-7g, Chol-239mg, Sdm-252mg

PEPPERS

There is something about peppers that is aesthetically pleasing: they look beautiful, feel gorgeous and taste heavenly. At Pete's, where everything looks superb anyway, some of the most attractive displays are the mountains of red and green peppers.

Bell peppers are available all year in green and red and, during the summer months, in purple and yellow. (Red peppers, incidentally, are simply riper green peppers.) Their peak season is from July to November. Look for bright, glossy, firm peppers, well-shaped and thick-fleshed. Avoid shriveled, bruised peppers and those with soft spots. Refrigerate your peppers, unwashed, in a plastic bag, where they will keep well for up to 5 days.

All peppers are excellent sources of vitamin C, and red peppers are particularly high in vitamin A. Four ounces of raw green pepper have only 30 calories; four ounces of raw red pepper have 35 calories.

When recipes call for peeled peppers, simply broil them in the oven, turning frequently until the skin is black and blistered. Let the peppers cool until you can handle them and slip the skins off.

Nothing perks up a salad like a handful of long, thin slices of red or yellow pepper; their sweet flavor sets off the rather nonchalant taste of lettuce. If you are feeling especially extravagant the next time you go shopping, pick up a couple of peppers and eat them like an apple, or cut them into strips to munch on while you're watching TV. They are a refreshing, delicious change from junk food, and they're good for you, too.

Peppers Mexicana

1-1/2 cups onion, thinly sliced

3 cloves garlic, crushed

Salt, pepper and paprika

4 Tbsp olive oil

6 medium bell peppers, red and/or green, cut in thin strips

2 Tbsp all-purpose flour

8 ounces Cheddar cheese, grated

4 large eggs

1-1/2 cups sour cream (or part yogurt)

1/2 tsp dry mustard

1 tsp cumin

1 tsp coriander

Sauté the onions and garlic with the salt, pepper and paprika in the olive oil. When the onions are transparent, add the peppers. Sauté over low heat for another 10 minutes. Sprinkle the pepper mixture with the flour. Mix well and continue cooking until there is no extra liquid. Spread a layer of sautéed vegetables in a well-oiled 2-quart casserole; cover with a layer of cheese and continue the layers until everything is in the casserole.

Beat the eggs and sour cream together and mix in the mustard, cumin and coriander. Pour the egg mixture over the cheese and vegetable layers. Sprinkle with paprika. Bake, covered, at 375F for 30 to 35 minutes and, uncovered, for an additional 15 minutes. *Serves 6*

Each serving contains: Cal-447, Prot-17g, Carb-13g, Fib-2g, Tot. Fat-37g, Sat. Fat-18g, Chol-207mg, Sdm-354mg

Stuffed Peppers

I asked Terry, a chef who is a regular at Pete's, for a recipe for stuffed peppers. He said, "No one eats stuffed peppers!" This delicious concoction is for you, Terry.

4 tomatoes, peeled and chopped

1 onion, finely chopped

1/2 cup pine nuts, lightly toasted

3 Tbsp raisins

1 cup brown rice, cooked

1-1/2 cups Cheddar cheese, grated

1/4 cup Italian parsley, chopped

1/2 tsp cinnamon

Salt and pepper to taste

4 green peppers, cored and seeded, with the tops reserved

1/3 cup vegetable stock

Mix the tomatoes, onion, pine nuts and raisins with cooked rice. Stir in the cheese, saving a little for the topping. Add the parsley, cinnamon, salt and pepper.

Stand the peppers upright in a baking dish, cutting a little slice off the bottoms, if necessary, to give them a firm base. Fill the peppers with the rice mixture. Sprinkle with the reserved cheese and pop on the lids. Pour the stock into the casserole and cover with foil. Bake at 375F for 30 to 45 minutes or until the peppers are tender. Serve hot or cold. *Serves* 4

Pepper Frittata

1 medium onion, sliced very thin

1 large clove garlic, minced

3 Tbsp olive oil

2 large green or red bell peppers, cut in strips

1/2 cup cooked asparagus tips

2 large tomatoes, chopped

Salt and pepper

2 Tbsp water

8 large eggs, slightly beaten

Sauté the onion and garlic in the olive oil over medium heat for 5 minutes or until the onions are soft. Add the peppers and asparagus tips, and cook for another 3 minutes or until the peppers are soft. Add the tomatoes and simmer gently for 10 minutes. Season with salt and pepper.

Beat the water into the eggs. Pour the egg mixture around the vegetables in the frying pan. Cook over low heat until the bottom of the frittata is set. If you think you can manage to flip the frittata without spilling it, go ahead. If you are not so daring, simply pop the whole thing under the broiler for 2 or 3 minutes, until the top is set. Serve hot or at room temperature. *Serves* 4

Variation: add 2 cups of cooked, peeled, thinly sliced potatoes to the frittata. Just add the potatoes with the onions, using 1 additional tablespoon of olive oil.

HOT PEPPERS

Hot peppers can be used interchange-ably, as long as you taste test to deter-mine the quantity required for the degree of "heat" you want.

Unless you have grown up eating hot peppers or are a very dedicated culinary explorer, you have probably limited your exposure to hot peppers, adding a pepper here or there as called for in a recipe. Yet, once you've become accustomed to fiery dishes made with chile peppers, they quickly become an addiction.

There is an enormous variety of spicy peppers, varying from the rather mild Anaheim to the Scotch Bonnet, which is only eaten by extreme enthusiasts. Surprisingly enough, the heat of a chile pepper is in the ribs inside the pepper, not in the seeds or the skin. To lessen the bite of a hot pepper, carefully slice out the ribs.

It is wise to wear rubber gloves when dealing with hot peppers; the juice can give you a painful and lasting burn. Pete learned a handy trick from a wise Jamaican friend: if you get a pepper burn, peel a banana and lay the inside of the peel on the afflicted area. The banana peel soothes the burn immediately.

To ward off nasty surprises, you should also make sure you give anything that comes in contact with the peppers a good wash, the knife and cutting board especially, because the heat of the peppers will last on almost anything. If you use the same knife to cut an apple that you have just used to cut a pepper, you will probably get a burn from the apple. So cut your peppers and then wash every-thing, including your cutting board. Be careful not to touch your face until you've washed your hands!

If you're not accustomed to cooking with hot peppers, then practice moderation and be wary; too many chile peppers can spoil a dish. Sample each pepper and the mixture to ensure that you're creating the desired effect. The best way to test a hot pepper is to cut off a slice, remove the ribs and enjoy the flavor without suffer-ing the burn, unless you're a masochist or have an asbestos tongue. In either instance, don't bother with the rib. You can also add chilies at the end of the cooking, a little at a time, until you reach a comfortable amount. Don't forget that many people will not be as tolerant of the heat as you. If you make a dish too hot, provide salt for cooling down. Putting a little salt on your tongue takes away the heat. Water won't help.

Some authorities feel that hot peppers should be peeled before they are added to a dish. Pete argues that he can't see the point. He chops his peppers so small that peeling them is unnecessary.

Hot peppers are available all year. Look for smooth, glossy, firm peppers. Certain types of peppers may look as though they have cracks that have healed over; but don't worry about their appear-ance. The healed cracks will not affect the taste. Hot peppers can also be blanched and frozen with little loss of piquancy, or refriger-ated in a paper bag for a week to 10 days.

Although most of the recipes in this book call for Serrano or Jalapeño peppers, any hot pepper will do.

Pete's Pickled Peppers

2 cups hot peppers, large peppers cut into 2-inch pieces (for small peppers, simply cut 2 slits in the skin)
1/4 cup granulated sugar
1/2 cup distilled white vinegar
Salt
1 clove garlic, minced

Cook the peppers for 5 minutes in boiling water, until just tender. Place the peppers in a colander, drain well and transfer to a bowl.

Stir the sugar and vinegar together until the sugar is dissolved. Add a pinch of salt and the minced garlic. Pour the liquid over the peppers, stir well and place the peppers with the liquid in a pint jar. *Makes 1 pint*

<u>1/3-cup serving contains</u>: Cal-60, Prot-1g, Carb-15g, Fib-1g, Tot. Fat-0g, Sat. Fat-0g, Chol-0mg, Sdm-92mg

PLANTAINS

This first cousin of the banana is in fact a vegetable and it must be cooked to be edible. I remember being intrigued by huge boxes of what looked like enormous rotten bananas every Saturday morning at the market. Not until I began working for Pete did I discover what they were or how to use them. They can be baked, boiled or fried. A tasty addition to any diet, they can be eaten alone or mixed with other things.

Plaintains are much larger than bananas, weighing up to 3 pounds. They are sold separately rather than in bunches and can be dark green, yellow or black in color, often appearing rather moldy. The flavor varies at each stage of ripening, but they are considered ripe when they are black and vaguely soft. When green, they are quite starchy and they taste rather bland. As the skin darkens, the vegetable takes on the sweetness and the aroma of a banana, yet will keep its shape when cooked. Whether you prefer plantains green or black is a matter of taste. Experience is about the only thing that will serve you there.

Plantains are available all year. If you want to buy the fruit green and ripen it at home, it will go through all the stages—from green to black—and will keep for quite a while. Do not refrigerate plantains unless you wish to stop them from ripening.

Plantains are high in carbohydrates and an excellent source of potassium and vitamin C. For a vegetable, they are relatively high in calories: four ounces of raw plantain have about 150 calories.

If you need to peel a green or yellow plantain, cut off the tips. Slit the skin several times from top to bottom, taking care not to cut so deeply that you cut the flesh, and remove the skin with a knife. If the plantain is ripe, that is, black, you may be able to peel it like a banana, but a knife definitely speeds up the process.

Plantain is a kind of tropical potato, as common in the tropics as potatoes are here and serving the same purpose. It is especially versatile because it can also be sweetened and used in desserts.

Baked Plantains

Choose plantains that are between dark brown and black if you want them to be full flavored and soft.

Allow about 1 medium plantain per person. Rinse each vegetable and trim off the tips. Make a lengthwise slit in each plantain and place them in a pan, slit side up. Bake at 375F for about 40 minutes or until soft, but not mushy.

Because it keeps its shape so well, you can remove the plaintain from its skin, slice it in diagonal strips and either sprinkle it with lime or lemon juice, or drizzle it with some melted butter. Once baked, plantains can be reheated in a frying pan and served with your favorite sweet or savory sauce.

Each serving contains: Cal-378, Prot-3g, Carb-72g, Fib-5g, Tot. Fat-12g, Sat. Fat-8g, Chol-31mg, Sdm-126mg

Dessert Plantains

2 large plantains, at the black-ripe stage, halved, peeled and slit lengthwise

1 cinnamon stick, broken up

3 cloves

3 Tbsp lime juice

1 Tbsp cold butter, cut into small cubes

2 Tbsp brown sugar

3 Tbsp rum

Freshly grated coconut

Arrange the plaintains in a buttered 1-quart casserole. Scatter with the spices and lime juice and dot with butter. Bake for 10 minutes at 450F. Sprinkle with half the brown sugar. Flip the pieces carefully and sprinkle with the rest of the sugar. Bake another 10 minutes, or until the plantains are tender and warm. Baste with the rum and bake for another 5 minutes. Sprinkle with coconut and serve hot.

This dessert is truly decadent with yogurt, ice cream or sour cream! *Serves* 4

Each serving contains: Cal-188, Prot-1g, Carb-32g, Fib-2g, Tot. Fat-5g, Sat. Fat-3g, Chol-8mg, Sdm-36mg

Sautéed Plantains

2 Tbsp peanut oil

2 Tbsp butter

2 half-ripe plaintains, peeled and cut into 1/4-inch diagonal slices

Salt and pepper

Heat the peanut oil and butter in a large frying pan. Sauté the plantain slices for 4 minutes on each side, until golden brown. Sprinkle with salt and pepper; serve as you would fried potatoes. *Serves* 4

Each serving contains: Cal-214, Prot-1g, Carb-27g, Fib-2g, Tot. Fat-13g, Sat. Fat-5g, Chol-16mg, Sdm-129mg

POTATOES

Whether boiled, mashed, scalloped or French-fried, the potato is one of the most popular vegetables in North America. We eat potatoes all year, every season, in a multitude of different ways. And at Pete's, when the new potatoes arrive from Florida, they sell like proverbial hot cakes at three times the price of winter potatoes. But who can blame us? The taste of the small thin-skinned new potato is one of the first tastes of spring.

Because they store well, potatoes are available all year round, with the new potatoes having a peak season from mid-March to July. For baking, buy firm, well-shaped potatoes that are clean and relatively smooth. Avoid shriveled, bruised or blemished potatoes. Don't purchase potatoes that have frostbite, signs of decay or sprouts. If you're buying new potatoes, look for well-shaped, firm, clean potatoes with thin skins that break easily. Cracked or green-tinged potatoes should generally be avoided.

It is wise to buy your potatoes only two to three weeks ahead of time. If you have no choice but to buy them in bulk, you can store the potatoes in a cool, dry, well-ventilated place for up to 2 months. Don't keep your potatoes in the refrigerator; the low temperature will cause some of the starch to turn into sugar.

Like most fruit and vegetables, potatoes are low in fat and sodium; they are a good source of potassium, iron and vitamin C, most of which is found in the skin. One large potato has about 140 calories.

Because so much of the potato's nutrition is in or near the skin, it is preferable to cook potatoes with the skins on, whenever possible. Moreover, if peeled potatoes are not used immediately after peeling, they should be kept in cool water to prevent them from turning gray. I remember once making a chowder full of gray potatoes because I did not know enough to keep them in water after peeling and cutting them. They tasted fine; they just looked horrible! Do remember that soaking potatoes in cold water will remove some of the starch, but you also lose some nutrients.

To bake: scrub the potato and dry it with a paper towel. Pierce the skin to let the steam escape. Inserting a nail or an aluminum or stainless-steel skewer into each potato will ensure even baking. If you are only baking potatoes, a 450F oven will take 40 minutes. If you are baking the potatoes with a casserole, they may take about 1-1/2 hours at 350F. Potatoes can be baked at almost any temperature; all that varies is cooking time.

To pan roast: cut up large peeled potatoes, or use new ones that have been scraped. Brush the potatoes with olive oil and place them cut side down in a pan. Roast at 325F for about 1 hour, turning the potatoes several times to make sure they are evenly roasted. Brush frequently with more oil to keep potatoes soft and moist. If you are short of time, boiling potatoes until they are almost done will shorten their roasting time and yield almost the same result.

For mashed potatoes: cut peeled potatoes into even-sized chunks; wash and drain. Cook the potatoes in boiling salted water until tender. Drain and shake them dry over medium heat to make the potatoes mealy. Mash, adding butter, salt, pepper and hot milk or potato water. Mashing over low heat will ensure that the potatoes stay hot and fluffy. Mashed potatoes should be served at once. Do not let them stand at room temperature; if necessary, keep them warm in a 275F oven.

To boil new potatoes: new potatoes are the only potatoes that should be boiled, and boiling is the only way new potatoes should be cooked. If you don't buy your new potatoes bagged but choose them individually, choose small ones, for these boil fastest. Bring a pot of salted water to a boil and add the potatoes and a sprig of fresh mint or dill. Boil just until the potatoes are tender when pierced with a fork. Remove the potatoes from the water and sprinkle them with fresh mint or dill and lots of black pepper and some butter.

Danish New Potatoes

2 pounds new potatoes

2 Tbsp butter

2 Tbsp sugar

1 tsp salt

Sprig of fresh mint, chopped

Cook the potatoes in boiling salted water until tender. Drain and peel. (If you want to be a genuine Dane, peel the potatoes; if you want the extra fiber and vitamins, don't.) Heat the butter in a skillet, and stir in the sugar and salt. Cook over low heat, stirring constantly, just until the sugar is golden-brown. Add the potatoes. Sauté over low heat until the potatoes are browned on all sides. Stir gently or shake the pan frequently to avoid sticking. Sprinkle with fresh mint. *Serves 4 to 6*

Each serving contains: Cal-220, Prot-5g, Carb-35g, Fib-4g, Tot. Fat-6g, Sat. Fat-4g, Chol-16mg, Sdm-598mg

Potato Soup à la Pete

This is a great soup, and it's quick to make. Perfect for those cold winter days. It's filling and will warm you from the top of your head to the soles of your feet. If you don't mind the extra calories, you can make the soup richer by adding a cup of half-and-half.

2 Tbsp butter

2 cups potatoes, peeled and cut into 1/4-inch cubes

3 medium onions, thinly sliced

6 cups vegetable stock

Salt and pepper

1 tsp mace

1 tsp nutmeg

3 Tbsp chopped roasted green chile peppers

Fresh parsley, chives or dill, chopped

Melt the butter in a medium-size saucepan and add the potatoes and onions. Cook, covered, over low heat, for about 5 minutes or until the potatoes are almost tender. Stir frequently. If there appears to be some danger of scorching, add a couple of tablespoons of the stock. Add the remaining stock and season with salt and pepper. Simmer, covered, for 5 or 10 minutes or until the potatoes are very tender.

Stir in the mace and nutmeg. You can purée this mixture in a blender or food processor. Return the mixture to the saucepan and heat gently until the soup is good and hot. Sprinkle with the chiles and parsley, chives or dill. *Serves* 4

Each serving contains: Cal-196, Prot-4g, Carb-34g, Fib-6g, Tot. Fat-6g, Sat. Fat-4g, Chol-16mg, Sdm-84mg

Potato Pancakes

I had a discussion with a friend who considers himself to be a potato pancake specialist. He claimed that the best potato pancakes were made in a little restaurant in Winnipeg. But he ate his words when he tried this version!

3 eggs, separated

4 cups grated potatoes, well drained

6 Tbsp grated onion

3 Tbsp very fine breadcrumbs

Dash of cayenne pepper

Salt and pepper

Peanut oil

Sour cream

Beat together the egg yolks, potatoes, onion, breadcrumbs, cayenne, salt and pepper. In a separate bowl, beat the egg whites until stiff, and fold them into potato mixture. Heat 1/2 inch of oil in a skillet. Use a heaping teaspoon of the batter for each pancake. Flip the pancakes when the edges are golden brown.

Keep the pancakes warm in an oven until all of pancakes are cooked. Serve with sour cream. *Serves* 6

Winter potatoes have more starch than new ones, and because the starch content determines the cooking quality of the potato, new potatoes and stored potatoes should be cooked in different ways. Starchy potatoes are well-suited for mashing and for making French fries. Potatoes low in starch tend to be dry when baked; they are also excellent pan-fried and good in salads and casseroles.

Each serving contains: Cal-322, Prot-7g, Carb-24g, Fib-2g, Tot. Fat-23g, Sat. Fat-8g, Chol-123mg, Sdm-108mg

Pete's Perfectly Exquisite Creamed Potatoes

4 big potatoes, peeled and cut into 1/2-inch chunks

2 Tbsp onion, minced

1/8 tsp mace

1/4 tsp nutmeg

1 cup cream or half-and-half

Salt and pepper

Paprika

2 or 3 green onions, chopped

Soak the potatoes in cold water for half an hour. Drain the potatoes and dry with a paper towel. Place the potatoes, onion, mace, nutmeg, cream, salt and pepper in the top of a double boiler. Steam, covered, over boiling water for 45 minutes or until the potatoes are tender and the sauce is thick. If the potatoes are too dry, add a little more cream or hot water, 2 or 3 tablespoons at a time. Sprinkle with paprika and green onions just before serving. *Serves 4*

Each serving contains: Cal-199, Prot-4g, Carb-31g, Fib-2g, Tot. Fat-7g, Sat. Fat-4g, Chol-22mg, Sdm-99mg

Potato Scallop au Gratin

2 pounds potatoes, peeled and cut in 1/2-inch slices

2 cups carrots, sliced

8 to 12 ounces Gruyère cheese, grated

2 eggs

2 cups milk

2 Tbsp dry sherry

1/2 tsp grated nutmeg

1 tsp Dijon-style mustard

Salt and pepper

In a well-buttered casserole, layer potatoes and carrots alternately with cheese.

Beat the eggs, milk, sherry, nutmeg, mustard, salt and pepper, and pour over the potatoes. Bake in a 1-quart casserole at 350F for 1-1/2 hours, or until liquid is absorbed and potatoes soft. *Serves 6*

Each serving contains: Cal-467, Prot-25g, Carb-40g, Fib-3g, Tot. Fat-23g, Sat. Fat-13g, Chol-144mg, Sdm-359mg

Potato Salad

I am not sure where this recipe came from, but I have been eating it for 25 summers. I remember watching my grandmother make it. Although there are lots of potato salads around, I think this one is something special.

DRESSING
1/4 cup sugar
1/4 cup flour
1-1/2 tsp Dijon-style mustard
Salt
4 egg yolks
1 cup milk
1/2 cup cider vinegar
1/2 cup yogurt

Mix the sugar, flour, mustard and some salt in the top of a double boiler. Stir in the egg yolks and milk; cook until thickened, stirring constantly. Add the vinegar, stir it in and then add the yogurt. Blend well and cool.

SALAD
6 potatoes, cooked and cut into chunks
6 hard-cooked eggs, sliced
1 cup chopped parsley, preferably Italian
2 ribs celery, chopped
1/2 cup chives or green onions, chopped
1/2 cup red and/or green pepper, chopped
1/2 cup chopped radishes
1/4 cup chopped red onion
Paprika

Put all the ingredients except the paprika in a large bowl and toss with the cooled dressing. Sprinkle with the paprika and chill. *Serves at least 8*

Each serving contains: Cal-253, Prot-10g, Carb-35g, Fib-2g, Tot. Fat-8g, Sat. Fat-3g, Chol-271mg, Sdm-148mg

Potato Soufflé

1/2 cup hot milk

1/2 cup Mozzarella cheese, grated

2 or 3 Tbsp butter, at room temperature

1 tsp nutmeg

1 tsp cayenne pepper

3 Tbsp minced parsley

2 cups fresh hot mashed potatoes

4 eggs, separated

Salt and pepper

Beat the milk, grated cheese, butter, nutmeg, cayenne and parsley into the potatoes while they are still hot.

Beat the egg yolks until thick. Beat the egg whites until stiff.

Add the egg yolks to the potato mixture. Check the seasoning and add salt and pepper to taste.

Fold in the beaten egg whites, and spoon the mixture into a well-buttered 1-quart baking dish. Bake at 400F for about 15 minutes or until puffed and golden. Serve immediately. *Serves 4*

<u>Each serving contains:</u> Cal-277, Prot-12g, Carb-18g, Fib-1g, Tot. Fat-18g, Sat. Fat-9g, Chol-251mg, Sdm-288mg

RADICCHIO

This gorgeous red-and-white vegetable has wormed its way into North American kitchens with surprising speed and ease. Ten years ago it was virtually unheard of, but today it is not that hard to find. It is no great wonder, for this little beauty is one of the most decorative vegetables on the market. The name, *radicchio*, is Italian for *chicory*. Indeed, this leafy creation has been a favorite in European kitchens for a long time.

The Italians have many different varieties of radicchio and use it a hundred different ways. (Pete would argue that the Italians produce the best radicchio.) The type that North Americans usually have access to is the *radicchio rosso* or *radicchio di Verona*. It is shaped like a cabbage rose and has reddish leaves with white ribs. It tends to be on the small side, similar to Bibb lettuce. It also comes in shades of red or green, with solid or variegated leaves. One wonderful thing about radicchio's growing popularity is that eventually it will be easier to find and less expensive to purchase.

Radicchio is available all year. If you look carefully, you should be able to find a virtually perfect head. Look for a pure, clean white base, a firm head with bright color and crisp leaves. Radicchio packs a lot more into a head than lettuce, so choose accordingly. And, because you use much less radicchio than you would lettuce, you will probably not need as much as you might expect. Avoid radicchio with brown edges, leaves with holes, or tired-looking heads.

Radicchio is one of the best garnish vegetables available to the cook, and for taste and texture it's wonderful too. It is deliciously crunchy and has a taste rather like an intense lettuce with a hint of radishy warmth. You can use it in any recipe that calls for Belgian endive or escarole.

Radicchio stands up to storing much better than you might think. You can keep it in the refrigerator, loosely wrapped, for up to a week. Don't bother washing it until about an hour before using. Then trim the bottom, separate the leaves, hold them under running water and either spin them dry or lay them between layers of paper towels. The leaves may be wrapped in a damp paper or cloth towel and chilled for about an hour before using.

Radicchio is an excellent source of vitamins A and C, and is high in fiber. One cup of raw radicchio has only 10 calories.

If you are using radicchio di Verona, the leaves make excellent little dishes; they keep their cup shape well and will hold in the juices from moist salads. Radicchio also grills and bakes wonderfully; just brush on a little melted butter or olive oil. Unfortunately, it loses its ruby color once cooked. Of course, when raw, it looks tremendous with whatever you put it next to. If you are including it in a salad or serving it with a dressing, keep the vinaigrette light; enhance the flavor, don't drown it. Try making a brilliant-looking salad with avocados, red peppers and radicchio; include a lime-juice vinaigrette and you'll have a treat you won't soon forget!

Radicchio is delicious warmed up by a quick sauté. Try it warm with sliced olives and julienne strips of a mild cheese, such as Mozzarella. Sprinkle on a few toasted pine nuts or walnuts for a little more crunch.

Radicchio, Peppers, Mushrooms and Fennel

5 large shiitake mushrooms (you can use button mushrooms if the Oriental ones are not available)

1-2 Tbsp olive oil

1 pound fennel

1/2 pound radicchio

2 Tbsp butter

1/2 green pepper, cut in strips

1/2 red pepper, cut in strips

Salt and pepper

1/4 cup toasted pine nuts

If you are using dried shiitake mushrooms, pour 1 cup of very hot water and 1 tablespoon of the olive oil over them, letting the mushrooms stand for at least 30 minutes. Remove the mushrooms from the water, dry them and slice the caps into strips.

If you are using fresh mushrooms, slice the caps into strips.

Cut the fennel into pieces the size of baby carrots. Core the radicchio and cut it into thin slivers.

Heat the butter and 1 tablespoon of olive oil. Add the fennel and peppers and toss over medium heat for about 5 minutes until tender. Add the radicchio, mushrooms, salt and pepper to taste. Toss for about 3 minutes, until the radicchio is wilted and tender. Stir in the pine nuts and serve at once. *Serves 4*

Each serving contains: Cal-249, Prot-6g, Carb-17g, Fib-6g, Tot. Fat-20g, Sat. Fat-6g, Chol-16mg, Sdm-199mg

Broiled Radicchio

Despite the fact that cooked radicchio is not as eye-appealing as raw radicchio, it tastes just as delicious.

1 radicchio, cut in half or quarters
Olive oil or melted butter
1 garlic clove, minced
Freshly ground black pepper

Brush the radicchio with lots of olive oil or melted butter and broil, turning only once, until softened but not limp. How long this takes depends on the thickness of the leaves and the size of the cut pieces. Check it frequently.

Meanwhile, heat a little minced garlic in some olive oil or butter and drizzle the mixture over the cooked radicchio. Sprinkle with freshly ground black pepper and serve immediately. *Serves 2*

Each serving contains: Cal-75, Prot-1g, Carb-3g, Fib-0g, Tot. Fat-7g, Sat. Fat-1g, Chol-0mg, Sdm-13mg

RAPINI

Rapini, also known as *broccoli raab*, is a type of broccoli, as its alias implies. You have probably seen it without knowing what it was. It is easy enough to recognize once you know what it is, or once you know that it is related to broccoli, but it is also easy to overlook. It resembles tiny bunches of broccoli on long stems among lots of large, spiky leaves. There may also be a yellow flower or two brightening up this beautiful deep-green vegetable.

Rapini is available off and on all year but is most easily found from November to mid-May. Look for rapini with good bright color, fresh-looking leaves, firm, smallish stems and relatively few opened buds. Refrigerate the vegetable, wrapped, for up to 3 days.

Rapini is a good source of potassium and vitamins A and C. It is very low in calories with only about 45 per cup.

How you cook rapini is very much a matter of personal taste. Its aggressiveness can be moderated if you blanch it in boiling salted water for a minute or two, drying it before preparing it for a recipe. But even blanched, some people still find it too strong. It is particularly good in dishes with lots of garlic or spices. The flavor can also be mellowed somewhat by blending the vegetable with cream.

Rapini can be cooked the same way as broccoli, but more quickly because it is essentially a green. It seems that most North Americans prefer it cooked quickly, for about 5 minutes or so; however, many people cook it longer. Pete enjoys it steamed for about 5 minutes. He then adds some coarsely grated carrot, some sliced tomatoes and a vinaigrette made with olive oil. It is delicious hot or cool.

If you have never tasted rapini, try it in the following recipe. It is an unusual addition to any diet.

Rapini Fried Rice

Some people prefer this dish with half white rice and half long-grain brown. Try the recipe first with the short-grain brown rice. If it is too crunchy or nutty, change to a blend you are more comfortable with.

3 Tbsp low-sodium soy sauce

1-1/2 tsp honey

3 Tbsp water

6 ounces tofu, drained and cubed

5 Tbsp peanut oil

1/2 cup pine nuts, almonds or cashews, toasted

1 pound rapini, washed and cut into bite-size pieces

2 carrots, coarsely grated

3 large cloves garlic, minced

1 Serrano or Jalapeño pepper, seeded and finely chopped

**1-1/2 cups short-grain brown rice, cooked and cooled
for a day or two**

1/2 cup green onions, thinly sliced

In a small bottle, mix 2 tablespoons of the soy sauce with the honey and water. Shake well and set aside.

Sauté the tofu with the remaining 1 tablespoon soy sauce and 1 tablespoon of the peanut oil in a wok for about 2 minutes; remove from the wok and set aside.

Sauté the nuts in 1 tablespoon of the peanut oil until lightly browned. Set aside.

Sauté the rapini and carrots with the garlic and pepper in 2 tablespoons of oil for 3 minutes until slightly softened. Set aside.

Heat the remaining oil in the wok. Add the rice and toss in the hot oil until heated through. Add the rapini, carrots, nuts and tofu. Toss for 1 minute.

Pour the soy sauce-honey mixture over the vegetables and stir over high heat until well-blended. Sprinkle with sliced green onions and serve. *Serves* 4

If you are a fan of aggressive vegetables, you should try rapini. Its strong bitter flavor is wonderful in combination with the right things, but it can be overwhelming with ingredients that are unable to hold their own next to its particular brand of enthusiasm.
It is a favorite with Italians and the Chinese, whose cuisines delight in aggressive ingredients.

Each serving contains: Cal-485, Prot-17g, Carb-37g, Fib-8g, Tot. Fat-34g, Sat. Fat-5g, Chol-0mg, Sdm-430mg

SPINACH

Spinach is available all year, though its peak months are April and May. Most of the time you can buy spinach prewashed and nicely packaged in cellophane bags.

If, however, you are buying spinach that needs to be washed, fill the sink with lukewarm water and swish the spinach around. Then lift the spinach out, clean the sink, fill it with cold water and wash the spinach once again. Repeatedly wash with cold water until there is no sand left. Drain the spinach. By not washing the spinach until you use it, you will save yourself the trouble of drying it. Let it cook in the water that clings to the leaves.

Look for spinach with a nice dark-green color and crisp leaves. Avoid spinach with yellow or soggy leaves. Spinach is extremely perishable so do not buy it and expect to store it for a while before using it. In fact, you should not expect spinach to keep in the refrigerator for more than 2 or 3 days, whether you buy it prepackaged or loose.

Dieters should delight in spinach because it has very few calories, about 30 in 4 ounces of the raw vegetable. And as all of us know, spinach is very good for us; it is an excellent source of vitamin A, a good source of vitamin C, and a fair source of minerals—especially iron—when cooked. So the next time you go shopping, pick up some extra spinach and try some of following treats.

Italian Spinach

3 pounds spinach, trimmed and washed

2 Tbsp olive oil

1/2 cup almonds, slivered

2 cloves garlic, crushed

2 tsp vinegar

1 tsp fresh basil, chopped

1 Tbsp fresh parsley, chopped

Salt and pepper

Tear the large spinach leaves into smaller pieces. Heat the olive oil in a deep pan. Toast the nuts in the oil, stirring constantly until golden. Add the spinach, garlic, vinegar, herbs and seasonings to taste. Simmer, covered, for 4 minutes, or until tender, shaking the pan to prevent the spinach mixture from sticking. Serve hot. *Serves 4*

Each serving contains: Cal-237, Prot-13g, Carb-16g, Fib-11g, Tot. Fat-17g, Sat. Fat-2g, Chol-0mg, Sdm-337mg

This beautiful, dark-green vegetable could be every cook's dream. It is delicious steamed, creamed, puréed, in a salad and as soup; and it is wonderful in combination with other foods—especially cheese, eggs and pasta.

Each serving contains: Cal-289, Prot-9g, Carb-26g, Fib-7g, Tot. Fat-18g, Sat. Fat-11g, Chol-41mg, Sdm-190mg

Spinach Soup

1 medium onion, finely chopped

2 cloves garlic, finely chopped

2 Tbsp butter

1 pound spinach, chopped

1 cup peas

2 cups vegetable stock

1 tsp fresh dill, chopped

1 cup mashed potatoes

1 cup sour cream

Fresh basil or chives, chopped

Sauté the onion and garlic in the butter until soft. Add the spinach and peas, and sauté them gently for 3 minutes. Add the vegetable stock and dill, and simmer for an additional 4 minutes. Add the potatoes and blend well. You might wish to give this mixture a quick zip in the food processor to ensure that the ingredients are well blended. Mix in the sour cream just before serving. Sprinkle with fresh basil or chives.

This soup can be served hot or cold. *Serves* 4

Spinach Frittata

The perfect solution for hungry, disorganized cooks.

3 Tbsp butter

2 cloves garlic, minced

1 small onion, diced

10 ounces spinach (1 package), chopped

1/4 cup wheat germ

1 tsp fresh basil, chopped

1 cup Cheddar cheese, grated

1 tsp Dijon-style mustard

6 eggs, beaten

Salt, pepper and nutmeg

Heat 1 tablespoon of the butter in a large saucepan. Sauté the garlic and onions for 5 minutes, until the onions are transparent. Add the spinach and stir until wilted. Remove from the heat and keep warm.

Mix the wheat germ, basil, cheese, mustard and eggs. Blend with the spinach mixture, and season with salt, pepper and nutmeg.

Put the rest of the butter in a frying pan. Pour in the spinach-egg batter. Cook over low heat until the bottom is set. Then either turn the frittata over (using a plate) or broil the top until it is set.

This fritatta is exquisite with cheese sauce. *Serves 4 to 6*

Each serving contains: Cal-355, Prot-21g, Carb-9g, Fib-3g, Tot. Fat-27g, Sat. Fat-14g, Chol-372mg, Sdm-513mg

Spinach-and-Ricotta Pie

10 ounces spinach (1 package)

1 small onion, diced

2 Tbsp butter

Salt and pepper

1 tsp fresh basil, chopped

1 pound ricotta cheese

3 eggs, beaten

3 Tbsp all-purpose flour

1/2 cup Cheddar cheese, grated

Pastry for a 9-inch pie

1/2 cup sour cream

1/2 cup yogurt

Paprika

Sauté the spinach and onion in the butter with the salt, pepper and basil. Mix the spinach mixture with the ricotta, eggs, flour and Cheddar in a small bowl. Spread the mixture in the pie shell. Blend the sour cream and yogurt, and spoon it over the top of the spinach, spreading it to the edges. Dust with paprika. Bake at 375F for 40 to 45 minutes. *Serves 4*

Each serving contains: Cal-501, Prot-26g, Carb-17g, Fib-2g, Tot. Fat-37g, Sat. Fat-22g, Chol-264mg, Sdm-462mg

Deciding which of the many ways to enjoy spinach can be a problem. The inventive French even have a dessert they make with spinach—a custard into which they blend dried apricots.

Spinach Salad

1 pound spinach, washed and dried

1/2 Spanish onion, sliced

1 cup mushrooms, thinly sliced

6 Tbsp olive oil

1 Tbsp soy sauce

2 tsp Dijon-style mustard

1 tsp lemon juice

Salt and pepper

4 hard-cooked eggs, sliced

2 Tbsp bacon bits

Parmesan cheese

Croutons or a generous handful of toasted pine nuts

Removing the stems, tear the spinach into bite-size pieces. Put them in a salad bowl with the onion and mushrooms.

Combine the oil, soy sauce, mustard, lemon juice, salt and pepper in a small bowl and mix well.

Just before serving, pour the vinaigrette over the spinach, mushrooms and onion. Toss lightly and arrange the egg slices on the top. Sprinkle the salad with bacon bits, a generous amount of Parmesan cheese and some croutons or toasted pine nuts. *Serves 4*

Each serving contains: Cal-424, Prot-18g, Carb-12g, Fib-5g, Tot. Fat-37g, Sat. Fat-7g, Chol-217mg, Sdm-793mg

Super Spinach

2 pounds spinach, washed, trimmed and coarsely chopped
2 medium onions, minced
2 Tbsp olive oil
1 tsp nutmeg
4 Tbsp pine nuts
Salt and pepper
1/2 cup raisins
1 cup yogurt, more or less
1 Tbsp fresh parsley, chopped

Sprinkle the spinach leaves with water and place them in a medium-size saucepan with the onions. Simmer, covered, for 5 minutes, shaking the pan frequently to prevent the spinach from sticking.

Add the olive oil and continue cooking for a few minutes. Add the nutmeg, pine nuts and seasoning. Remove from heat and add the raisins and yogurt. Sprinkle with parsley before serving. *Serves* 4

Each serving contains: Cal-295, Prot-13g, Carb-32g, Fib-8g, Tot. Fat-17g, Sat. Fat-3g, Chol-8mg, Sdm-279mg

SPROUTS

During the past ten years, these crunchy little delights have sprung from relative obscurity onto almost every market shelf and restaurant menu in North America. They add a little crispness to sandwiches or salads, and the sprouts from larger grains, such as mung beans, chickpeas and lentils, are good in soups and casseroles. Because of their versatility, it never hurts to have sprouts on hand.

One day I bought a bag of mung-bean sprouts at Pete's, and as I was walking home with a friend, I opened the bag and offered him some. I live very close to the City Market, but by the time we got home, we'd eaten them all. I had to turn around and go back for more so I could make dinner. Ever since, sprouts have become a regular snack for me. The next time you are tempted to buy junk food, reach instead for a bag of sprouts. You won't regret it. Besides being healthful, they are tasty and versatile.

The length of time you can store sprouts depends on how fresh they are when you buy them, and determining their freshness is quite easy. Look at the sprouts: they should be crisp and appear fresh, small with bright color. Mung beans should be white and crisp, with the bean still attached. When the sprouts begin to get old they get slimy and will leave a film on the plastic in which they are packaged.

Sprouts are an excellent source of protein and a good source of vitamin C. One cup of raw mung-bean sprouts has 37 calories. Four ounces of alfalfa sprouts contain 35 calories.

The best way to tell whether or not your sprouts are fresh is to take a good sniff; sprouts are young and delicate and their life is not particularly long. When they begin to "go," they smell like it.

Because alfalfa, clover and radish sprouts are so delicate, they do not stand up particularly well in a salad, but tend to get rather squashed.

Alfalfa sprouts are tiny alfalfa seeds, about twice the size of a pin head, with tails on them, 2-1/2 to 3-1/2 inches long. They are wonderfully tender, having a delicate crunch and a taste rather like immature lettuce. They are especially nice in sandwiches because they add a taste of something different and they add moisture without making your bread damp. Never use alfalfa sprouts for cooking.

Clover sprouts are probably the most beautiful of all the delicate sprouts. They have tiny bright-green clover leaves with shiny white tails anywhere from 3 to 5 inches long. The leaves themselves taste like clover and are thick and fleshy. Though they are not as moist as alfalfa sprouts, clover sprouts have more flavor; they are vaguely bitter, reminiscent of sweet grass and clover. And Pete's comment for these little treats is that you don't have to be a cow to eat them. These sprouts are also not recommended for cooking.

Spicy sprouts are a combination of alfalfa and radish sprouts, mixed together at a ratio of about 1/3 radish to 2/3 alfalfa sprouts. I imagine you could find radish sprouts solo if you really wanted to: just find out where your neighborhood dragon shops! Radish sprouts alone are very, very peppery. They are far hotter than any radish could ever be, but mix them with alfalfa sprouts and you have spicy sprouts—a well-named combination. Radish sprouts are more robust-looking than either the alfalfa or clover sprouts. Their leaves resemble an unopened four-leaf clover, and their color is a slightly dull green. They have short thick, white tails, and are especially good with eggs, in sandwiches or sprinkled on an omelet. And no, I wouldn't bother cooking with these sprouts.

Crispy sprouts are for hard-core sprout fans—lots of big, crunchy, nutty-flavored sprouts. These sprouts consist of a mixture of sprouted green beans, yellow peas, adzukis and lentils, sometimes in combination with garbanzo beans or chickpeas. Because this combination of beans does not sprout with the enthusiasm of the smaller seeds, you get a delicious mix of the beans themselves and the delicately flavored sprouts. Because these sprouts are not as fine in taste or texture as the ones mentioned above, they are well-suited to cooking. You can steam them for a few seconds and serve them with lemon juice or butter and pepper. Toss a handful into a soup, a casserole or the next stir-fry you concoct, where they'll make a tasty addition. They are also delicious piled onto sandwiches. If you are going to use crispy sprouts in a salad, chill them in ice water for half an hour to enhance their crispness.

Mung-bean sprouts are the granddaddy of all sprouts, having been used in Chinese cooking for thousands of years. In fact, it is the reintroduction of mung-bean sprouts that is largely responsible for the wide variety of sprouts we can now find. There are few corner grocery stores in North America where you will not find them. These sprouts have a crisp, moist texture and a bland, vaguely nutlike flavor that makes them a natural addition to salads and main dishes. Because they are slightly more robust than a lot of the other sprouts, they can easily withstand cooking.

Bean Sprouts au Gratin

2 Tbsp butter
2 Tbsp all-purpose flour
1 cup milk or cream, heated
1 cup Swiss cheese, grated
1 tsp dry mustard
Salt, pepper and nutmeg
6 cups mung-bean sprouts
1 cup fine breadcrumbs

Heat the butter in a skillet and stir in the flour. Cook for 1 minute, stirring constantly. Add the hot milk or cream and continue to stir the mixture. Simmer until the sauce is thick and smooth. Add 3/4 cup of the cheese and the mustard. Stir until the cheese is melted and season with salt, pepper and nutmeg.

Add the sprouts to the sauce. Put the entire mixture into a buttered 1-quart casserole dish and sprinkle with breadcrumbs and the remaining 1/4 cup grated cheese. Bake at 400F for 10 to 15 minutes or until golden. *Serves* 4

Each serving contains: Cal-391, Prot-18g, Carb-34g, Fib-4g, Tot. Fat-22g, Sat. Fat-13g, Chol-63mg, Sdm-378mg

Sprout Salad

1 English cucumber, sliced
1 small zucchini, sliced
3 medium-size tomatoes, sliced
1/2 red pepper, sliced
1/2 green pepper, sliced
1/4 cup sunflower seeds
2 tsp fresh basil, chopped
2 tsp fresh dill, chopped
1/4 cup yogurt
1 Tbsp mayonnaise
1 cup cottage cheese
Paprika

Each serving contains: Cal-218, Prot-14g, Carb-21g, Fib-5g, Tot. Fat-11g, Sat. Fat-3g, Chol-12mg, Sdm-250mg

Mix all the ingredients together in a large bowl and toss gently. Serve with a huge bowl of your favorite sprouts. *Serves* 4

Egg Foo Yung

2 cups mung-bean sprouts

6 eggs, beaten

2 Tbsp onion, grated

2 green onions, thinly sliced

1/2 cup snow peas, trimmed and cut in half

1/4 small red pepper, diced

Salad oil

Soy sauce

Salt and pepper

Cook the sprouts in boiling water for 1-1/2 to 2 minutes, until they are just tender but still firm. Drain well.

Put the eggs, onion, green onions, snow peas and red pepper in a wok or a large frying pan, and sauté the mixture, adding oil, soy sauce, salt and pepper to season. Stir constantly until the egg is cooked and everything is heated through. *Serves 4*

Each serving contains: Cal-202, Prot-12g, Carb-7g, Fib-2g, Tot. Fat-14g, Sat. Fat-3g, Chol-319mg, Sdm-495mg

SWEET POTATOES, YAMS AND BONIATO

Sweet potatoes and yams are completely different vegetables, although not everyone knows this. If you have the opportunity to see the two side by side, this confusion would surprise you because they look entirely different. Sweet potatoes are a familiar sight to all of us, but yams, or *ñame*, as they are called by everyone except North Americans, tend to be large, vaguely round in shape and covered with a thick, dark-brown skin, almost like a bark. The flesh inside may be white, yellow, red or purple or something in between. Although you would never mistake one for the other when you are buying them, sweet potatoes and yams are generally interchangeable in recipes.

Both yams and sweet potatoes are available all year, with sweet potatoes having a peak season from September to March.

Look for well-shaped, clean roots with evenly colored skins. Choose thick, chunky potatoes of medium size that taper toward the end. Do not buy sweet potatoes with signs of decay or bruises, because they spoil quickly.

As for yams, buy them with unwrinkled skins and weighing 1 pound or less. Avoid soft yams and those with blemishes or sunken areas. Sweet potatoes may be stored in a cool, well-ventilated place, but not in the refrigerator, for up to 2 weeks. Yams will tolerate the same conditions, but for no more than 1 week.

Sweet potatoes and yams are an excellent source of vitamins A and C and a fair source of potassium. Both have about 150 calories in 4 ounces of boiled flesh.

The simplest way to cook sweet potatoes and yams is to boil or bake them like white potatoes, except they cook faster and reheat better. Pete recommends a sprinkle of nutmeg on sweet potatoes and yams, along with the usual salt and pepper.

At the risk of totally and completely confusing you, I will tell you that the name *boniato* is Cuban for sweet potato, and that the boniato is the real sweet potato. Irregularly shaped, its skin may be creamy, purple or vaguely red in color. You may cook it as you would any sweet potato. It is superbly delicate in flavor, fluffy and less sugary than our orange-fleshed sweet potatoes.

Boniato is available all year round, becoming somewhat scarce in late winter. When you buy boniatos, ensure that they are rock-hard without any soft spots. Store them as you would sweet potatoes, in a cool well-ventilated spot and for as brief a time as possible, no more than 2 days.

If you are going to cook boniatos peeled, in a stew or boiled, keep them in a salt solution (1 teaspoon of salt in 1 cup of water), for they discolor quickly. When you cook boniatos, you'll want about half a pound for each person. My own personal advice is to first try them baked. Wash them off and cook them like sweet potatoes in a 400F oven for 1 hour. The skin gets wonderfully crunchy and the flesh becomes superbly creamy.

Half a cup of baked boniato has 115 calories and lots of vitamin A.

Sweet Potatoes with Orange

3 pounds sweet potatoes, washed

1/4 cup toasted cashews

1/4 cup light-brown sugar

2 Tbsp lime juice

1/2 cup freshly squeezed orange juice

Rind of 1 orange, grated

Salt

1/4 tsp cinnamon

4 Tbsp butter, cut up

Cook the sweet potatoes in boiling salted water for 15 minutes or until tender but still firm. Drain the water; cool the potatoes, peel and cut them into 1/4-inch slices.

Arrange the potatoes in layers in a shallow, buttered baking dish. Distribute the cashews though the layers and sprinkle with the sugar. Mix the fruit juices and rind, adding a pinch of salt and the cinnamon. Sprinkle over the potatoes and dot with the butter. Bake at 325F for 25 minutes or until golden. *Serves 4 to 6*

Each serving contains: Cal-559, Prot-7g, Carb-98g, Fib-8g, Tot. Fat-17g, Sat. Fat-8g, Chol-31mg, Sdm-288mg

Curried Sweet Potatoes

This spicy dish is great with yogurt.

> **2 pounds sweet potatoes**
> **2 Tbsp butter**
> **1 medium onion, minced**
> **1/4 tsp cumin**
> **1/4 tsp turmeric**
> **1/4 tsp ginger**
> **1/4 tsp cinnamon**
> **1 cup vegetable stock**
> **Salt and pepper**
> **Juice of 1 lemon**
> **1/4 cup freshly grated coconut**

Boil the sweet potatoes in their skins until almost done. Drain and rinse the potatoes in cold water, then peel and slice them.

Melt the butter in a saucepan and sauté the onions, stirring constantly, for 2 or 3 minutes. Add the spices and cook another 2 minutes. Add the stock, bring to a boil and reduce the heat. Cook, stirring occasionally, for 3 minutes. Season with salt and pepper.

Add the sliced sweet potatoes to the liquid and simmer, covered, for 10 minutes or until the sweet potatoes are tender. Sprinkle with the lemon juice and coconut just before serving. *Serves 4*

Each serving contains: Cal-324, Prot-5g, Carb-60g, Fib-7g, Tot. Fat-8g, Sat. Fat-5g, Chol-16mg, Sdm-160mg

Sweet-Potato Pancakes

If you are a fan of potato pancakes, you'll become addicted to this version in no time. And if you are not a fan, just try them . . . I bet you'll change your mind.

> **2 sweet potatoes, grated**
> **2 white potatoes, grated**
> **Salt**
> **2 carrots, grated**
> **1 Tbsp onion, chopped**
> **1 clove garlic, minced**
> **1/4 cup parsley, chopped**
> **4 eggs, beaten**
> **1/3 cup flour**
> **Juice of 1 lemon**
> **Salt, pepper, nutmeg and cinnamon**
> **Melted butter**
> **Sour cream or yogurt**
> **Chives, chopped**

There is an island in the Pacific called Ponape where yams are described as being 2, 4, or 6-man yams, indicating how many men it takes to lift the vegetables. It may be hard to believe, but there are records indicating that yams have grown up to 6 feet long and 600 pounds in weight!

Put both types of potatoes in a colander over a bowl. Sprinkle with salt and let stand for 15 minutes. Rinse and squeeze the potatoes to remove all the liquid.

Mix the potatoes with the carrots, onion, garlic, parsley, eggs, flour, lemon juice and seasonings. Thin the mixture with milk, if necessary. Melt the butter in a large frying pan. Drop in large tablespoonfuls of the batter and fry the pancakes until brown and crisp. Serve with a dollop of sour cream or yogurt and a sprinkle of chopped fresh chives. *Serves 4*

Each serving contains: Cal-327, Prot-11g, Carb-46g, Fib-4g, Tot. Fat-12g, Sat. Fat-5g, Chol-229mg, Sdm-220mg

Sweet-Potato Quiche

This is heavier than the average quiche. With a green salad, it makes a perfect winter meal.

2 pounds sweet potatoes

3 eggs, beaten

1/4 cup half-and-half

1 Tbsp all-purpose flour

1 cup Mozzarella cheese, grated

1 Tbsp soy sauce

1/2 tsp cinnamon

1/4 tsp mace

Salt and pepper

Pastry for a 9-inch pie

Boil the sweet potatoes until soft. Cool, peel and mash them.

In a medium-size bowl, mix the eggs and half-and-half; blend with the sweet potatoes.

Mix the flour with the cheese and add to the sweet potato mixture. Add the soy sauce, spices and seasonings. Spread the mixture in the pie shell and bake at 375F for 45 minutes to 1 hour, or until a knife inserted in the center comes out clean. Serve hot. *Serves 6 to 8*

Each serving contains: Cal-280, Prot-10g, Carb-40g, Fib-4g, Tot. Fat-9g, Sat. Fat-4g, Chol-125mg, Sdm-403mg

TOMATILLOS

Tomatillos, or *Mexican husk tomatoes*, may be purple or yellow when ripe, but nine times out of ten they are used when green. Tomatillos are usually cooked because this process enhances their lemony flavor and softens their usually tough hides. Raw, they have a sweet plum taste or a harsh, acidic flavor.

Tomatillos are available off and on all year. Look for fruit that is hard and firm with clean tight husks and no bruises or signs of shriveling. Store them unwashed in a paper-lined basket for up to a month.

Tomatillos make a superb and unique garnish if you simply pull back the husk without removing it. Before cooking, however, the husk must be peeled off and the fruit inside washed. Cooked, they make a lovely full-flavored, mellow sauce. Tomatillos are traditionally used in salsa and if you are a salsa lover, chances are you'll not be able to get enough of this little fruit.

Salsa

Salsa can be made with tomatoes, or for a little treat, with tomatillos. Try this garden-fresh combination with crunchy corn chips or as a sauce on many dishes.

3 red peppers, finely chopped
1 green pepper, finely chopped
1 small Spanish onion, diced
10 tomatillos, finely chopped
3 Tbsp fresh lime juice
1 Tbsp olive oil
Salt to taste

<u>1/2-cup serving contains</u>: Cal-87, Prot-2g, Carb-12g, Fib-3g, Tot. Fat-4g, Sat. Fat-0g, Chol-0mg, Sdm-70mg

Combine all the ingredients in a medium-size bowl and let stand for 30 minutes. *Makes about 2 cups*

Tomatillo Salad

This is the easiest recipe for tomatillos that I have ever come across. It is a good introduction to the fruit.

1 pound tomatillos, peeled, washed and thinly sliced
1/4 cup olive oil
2 Tbsp lime juice
1 cup Parmesan cheese, grated
2 tsp basil, chopped
Pepper
Cilantro (coriander)

<u>Each serving contains</u>: Cal-271, Prot-12g, Carb-8g, Fib-2g, Tot. Fat-22g, Sat. Fat-7g, Chol-20mg, Sdm-468mg

Arrange the sliced tomatillos on a platter. Blend the oil and lime juice and drizzle over the fruit. Sprinkle with grated cheese and basil. Grind on some pepper. Garnish with cilantro (coriander). *Serves 4*

TOMATOES

Pete says never, never, never store tomatoes in the refrigerator unless they are absolutely ripe, and then only for a short time. To bring out their flavor, keep them at room temperature.

There is nothing in the world like a vine-ripened tomato. Although there is little that is not available almost "farm-fresh" at Pete's all winter long, not even the most expensive, most luxurious-looking hothouse tomatoes can match the taste of a tomato picked fresh from the garden. My grandfather has some very happy memories of summer afternoons spent in the tomato field with nothing but a salt shaker.

It is important to choose tomatoes that are smooth, firm, nicely shaped and heavy for their size, preferably with good color. Tomatoes with stems attached lose moisture more slowly and will keep fresh longer. Usually the tomatoes found in the markets during the winter months are not yet ripe. The best way to ripen them is to place them stem down in a paper bag in a cool place away from direct sunlight, until they become slightly soft. D*o not* store tomatoes in the refrigerator. Once they are ripe, tomatoes should be used as soon as possible.

Tomatoes are high in vitamin C and one medium tomato has about 25 calories.

To peel tomatoes, immerse them in boiling water for 15 to 20 seconds; then plunge them into ice water immediately. Let them cool and peel them with a sharp knife.

To seed tomatoes, cut them in half horizontally and squeeze them until the seeds fall out.

Cherry tomatoes are a nice idea for a salad because all you need to do is give them a rinse and toss them in whole. They look neater, are less work and taste as good as larger tomatoes. And as Pete notes, sliced tomatoes add a lot of moisture to a salad.

Cherry Tomatoes Vinaigrette

2 pints cherry tomatoes

VINAIGRETTE
1/4 tsp sugar
1/4 cup fresh lemon juice
3/4 cup peanut oil
2 cloves garlic, minced
1 tsp fresh thyme, finely chopped
1 tsp fresh basil, finely chopped
1 Tbsp parsley, chopped
2 or 3 green onions, thinly sliced

Mix the vinaigrette and add the washed and stemmed tomatoes. Chill several hours or overnight. *Serves 6*

Each serving contains: Cal-277, Prot-1g, Carb-9g, Fib-2g, Tot. Fat-28g, Sat. Fat-5g, Chol-0mg, Sdm-15mg

Stuffed Tomatoes

1-1/2 cups cottage cheese

1/2 cup yogurt

1/2 to 1 cup Parmesan cheese

1 green onion, finely chopped

1/4 cup celery, chopped

4 large tomatoes

1/4 cup cilantro (coriander) or parsley, chopped

Mix the cottage cheese, yogurt, Parmesan, onion and celery. Cover and refrigerate.

Cut each tomato in 4 or 6 pieces down to within 1 inch of the base. Separate the sections and place the cheese mixture in the middle. Garnish with cilantro or parsley. *Serves 4*

Each serving contains: Cal-255, Prot-23g, Carb-13g, Fib-2g, Tot. Fat-13g, Sat. Fat-8g, Chol-35mg, Sdm-822mg

Broiled Herbed Tomatoes

1/3 cup Cheddar cheese, grated

4 Tbsp parsley, chopped

4 Tbsp fresh dill or basil, chopped

2 cloves garlic, finely chopped

3 large tomatoes, cut in half

2 Tbsp butter or olive oil

Mix the cheese, parsley, dill or basil and garlic together, and sprinkle the mixture on the tops of the halved tomatoes. Dot with butter or drizzle with the olive oil. Broil the tomatoes for 10 minutes, until they are heated through. Garnish with a little extra parsley. *Serves 6*

Each serving contains: Cal-78, Prot-2g, Carb-4g, Fib-1g, Tot. Fat-6g, Sat. Fat-4g, Chol-17mg, Sdm-86mg

Pete's Stuffed Baked Tomatoes

8 large ripe, firm tomatoes

1/2 cup olive oil

1/3 cup minced parsley

2 cloves garlic, minced

1 cup uncooked long-grain rice

1 tsp saffron

2 cups hot vegetable stock

Salt and pepper

1/2 tsp cinnamon

Dill or basil

Slice off the top of each tomato and carefully scoop out the pulp, leaving the shell whole. Strain the pulp and set pulp and juice aside. Arrange the tomatoes in a shallow baking dish, sprinkling each one with a few drops of the oil.

Heat the remaining oil in a skillet. Sauté the parsley and garlic for 2 minutes. Add the rice and simmer for another 3 minutes, stirring constantly. Stir the saffron into the stock and pour the hot stock onto the rice and parsley.

Simmer the rice mixture, covered, over low heat for 10 minutes, stirring frequently until rice is almost done. Remove from the heat and season with salt, pepper and cinnamon.

Fill the tomato shells with the rice mixture. Spoon the reserved tomato pulp on top of the tomatoes. Pour the reserved tomato juice around the tomatoes, adding water to a depth of 1 inch.

Bake the tomatoes at 350F for 30 minutes or until the rice is tender and the liquid has been absorbed. Watch to make sure the tomatoes don't scorch. Add water if necessary. Baste occasionally with the pan juices. Serve hot or at room temperature. Garnish with dill or basil just before serving. *Serves 6*

Each serving contains: Cal-322, Prot-5g, Carb-36g, Fib-4g, Tot. Fat-19g, Sat. Fat-3g, Chol-0mg, Sdm-68mg

TURNIPS AND RUTABAGAS

Another vegetable neglected by North Americans! Turnips and turnip greens are widely used in Asian countries, northern Europe, France, Austria, Switzerland, Germany and Great Britain. On this side of the ocean, however, they are regarded as a lowly root and too often relegated to stews. Although Pete sells quite a few turnips, I have a sneaking suspicion that this vegetable is not being used to its best advantage.

I displayed my ignorance by looking confused when Pete started explaining the difference between turnip and rutabaga. I had always assumed that rutabaga was an American name for turnip. Not so. Rutabagas look different from turnips; they are longer and rounder, and while turnips tend to have purple-tinged skin surrounding clean, white flesh, rutabagas have a red-brown and beige skin with cream-colored flesh.

Rutabagas also taste different; they are sweeter, more flavorful and possess a drier flesh than turnips. But if you are one of those who share my ignorance and worry that you may have been committing a grave error by mistaking rutabaga for turnip, fear not. The two are interchangeable in any recipe and the taste and texture are so close that only the most discerning could tell them apart.

Turnips and rutabagas are available all year round, with their peak season between early November and late March. Choose medium to small turnips (2 to 3 inches in diameter) and small

Turnip and rutabaga are not the same thing. Rutabagas are longer and rounder than turnips, which have a purple-tinged skin and white flesh. Rutabagas taste sweeter and have cream-colored flesh.

rutabagas (3 to 4 inches in diameter) that are firm, heavy for their size and have smooth unblemished skins. Large turnips and light rutabagas tend to be fibrous.

Turnips and rutabagas should be stored in cool, well-ventilated, dry surroundings, or in a plastic bag in the refrigerator. A rutabaga can be stored for a couple of months in the former, a week in the latter. If you bought turnips with the greens attached, cut the greens off, wash them, shake them dry, wrap them in plastic and put them in the refrigerator. A turnip stored in plastic in the refrigerator will keep for 3 weeks, the greens for 2 to 4 days.

Turnips are an excellent source of vitamins A and C, especially the greens; they also provide potassium and calcium. Rutabagas have even more vitamin C and are a good source of potassium. Four ounces of raw turnip have 33 calories; the same amount of raw rutabaga has 55 calories.

Turnip greens are particularly sharp in flavor so the most popular cooking technique is to boil them, thereby dulling their kick a little. When preparing the greens for cooking, simply put the damp leaves in a pot with a tightly fitting lid with an inch or two of water and boil them, covered, for 5 to 10 minutes, until tender but not mushy. Serve the greens with butter, salt, pepper and a sprinkle of Parmesan cheese.

Pete, of course, likes turnip and rutabaga as he likes almost every vegetable—boiled, steamed or baked with lots of butter and pepper. For variety, he adds basil, dill or bacon bits. He is particularly fond of mashed turnip and apples. When the turnip has boiled for about 15 minutes, he just adds half as much peeled, cored and quartered apple as turnip. He then boils the two together until tender and mashes them as usual, adding a little nutmeg with the seasonings. According to Pete, the apple adds a delicious sweetness to the turnip.

To bake turnip or rutabaga, peel and slice the root into 1/4-inch slices, arranging them in a shallow baking dish. Dot with butter, sprinkle with salt, water and a little freshly ground pepper. Cover and bake at 350F for 30 to 40 minutes until tender.

To boil turnip or rutabaga, simply place the whole, peeled vegetable in enough water to cover it and boil for 30 minutes until tender. If you want to speed things up, cut the turnip into chunks.

Turnips or rutabagas are also good in a **stir-fry.** Simply peel the roots, slice them into 1/4-inch slices or julienne strips and give the strips about 5 minutes in the wok.

Both vegetables are also delicious raw on a vegetable tray or in salads.

The following recipes refer to turnips but feel free to use rutabagas instead. The cooking time for a rutabaga may be a little longer.

Turnip au Gratin

6 small or 4 medium turnips (2 to 3 lbs), peeled and sliced
Salt and pepper
1 medium-size onion, sliced
2 Tbsp oil
2 cups cooked rice
1 tsp fresh thyme, chopped
1 tsp fresh basil, chopped
4 Tbsp butter
1 cup Mozzarella cheese, grated
2 Tbsp parsley, chopped

Cook the turnips in boiling salted water until tender. Drain. Add salt and pepper to taste. Sauté the onion in the oil until transparent. Mix the rice and onion together.

In a baking dish, arrange the turnip in alternating layers with the rice mixture, sprinkling on the herbs as you go. Dot with butter. Bake at 350F for 15 minutes.

Remove from the oven and sprinkle with cheese and parsley, returning the dish to the oven until the cheese has melted. *Serves 4 to 6*

Each serving contains: Cal-476, Prot-12g, Carb-53g, Fib-9g, Tot. Fat-25g, Sat. Fat-12g, Chol-53mg, Sdm-519mg

Curried Turnips

1 medium onion, minced
3 Tbsp butter
1 Tbsp curry powder
1 cup hot vegetable stock, more or less
2 pounds turnips, peeled and cut into 1-inch cubes
2 medium apples, peeled and sliced
Salt and pepper
1/2 cup yogurt
2 Tbsp fresh basil, coarsely chopped

Sauté the onion in the butter until transparent. Add the curry powder and cook for 2 or 3 minutes, stirring constantly. Add 1/2 cup of the stock.

Add the turnips. Simmer, covered, over very low heat. After 10 minutes, add the apples. Simmer for another 10 minutes or until the turnip is tender. Add more stock, a little bit at a time, if necessary to prevent scorching. Season with salt and pepper. Remove the turnip mixture from the heat and stir in the yogurt. Sprinkle with basil and serve immediately. *Serves 4 to 6*

Each serving contains: Cal-220, Prot-4g, Carb-31g, Fib-8g, Tot. Fat-10g, Sat. Fat-6g, Chol-27mg, Sdm-326mg

WINTER SQUASH

There was some discussion between Pete and me about what types of winter squash to present here. It was a difficult decision because there are so many types of squash that are similar. We decided on butternut, buttercup and acorn, because these are the three most popular winter squash and Pete's particular favorites.

Squash was a staple food for North Americans before the advent of Europeans to this continent. The Indians relied on it along with beans and corn. To this day, it is still far more popular with North Americans than Europeans.

Squash keeps for such a long time that you can buy it and store it until you decide how you want to serve it. I always have squash around because I am the ultimate disorganized cook, and I can buy it without deciding ahead how it will be served. A versatile vegetable, squash can be used in soup, in a main course or in a dessert.

Acorn squash, also known as *pepper squash*, is acorn-shaped with wide ribs. It is usually 5 to 8 inches long and about 5 inches in diameter. The shell is smooth, hard and thin, and it varies in color from a solid, deep green to a green with bright orange areas. The flesh is pale orange, tender, moist and fibrous with a large seed cavity.

Buttercup squash is sometimes called a *turban squash* because of the funny turban-like cap at the blossom end. Its shape resembles that of a pumpkin, being 4 to 5 inches long and 6 to 8 inches across. The shell is quite hard and thin and its color is between dark ivy and dull blackish green with grayish spots and faint dull gray stripes. The flesh is orange, fine-textured, dry and sweet.

Butternut squash is cylindrical, usually about 12 inches long, with a bulb at the bottom, and 3 to 5 inches wide. The shell is hard and smooth, and anywhere from light beige to dark yellow in color. The flesh is yellow and fine-grained. Butternut squash is a particularly good value, because this variety tends to have a lot of flesh.

In all instances, look for squash that is hard, blemish-free and heavy for its size. Avoid squash with soft or decaying spots or cracks. Store it in a dry, well-ventilated place for up to a month.

On average, winter squash is an excellent source of vitamin A and a good source of vitamin C, although acorn squash contains less vitamin A. Four ounces of baked squash contain 50 calories.

When Pete does his taste tests for "Mid-day," this is how he cooks his squash, and with a little butter and black pepper, he and the CBC crew are all set. When the filming is done they all enjoy the leftovers.

Each serving contains: Cal-113, Prot-2g, Carb-20g, Fib-6g, Tot. Fat-4g, Sat. Fat-2g, Chol-8mg, Sdm-623mg

Each serving contains: Cal-229, Prot-3g, Carb-33g, Fib-10g, Tot. Fat-12g, Sat. Fat-7g, Chol-31mg, Sdm-193mg

Each serving contains: Cal-320, Prot-2g, Carb-30g, Fib-6g, Tot. Fat-23g, Sat. Fat-14g, Chol-62mg, Sdm-313mg

Simplicity Squash Recipe

1 winter squash, split in half
Butter
Salt and pepper

Poke holes in the squash with a fork and either wrap in plastic wrap and microwave on HIGH (100%) about 6 to 7 minutes or wrap in foil and bake in the oven at 350F for 15 to 20 minutes, depending on the size of the squash. The foil will keep the squash from drying out and will speed up the cooking time.

Unwrap, dot with butter and sprinkle with salt and pepper. Serve piping hot. *Serves* 4

Pete's Sautéed Buttercup Squash

1 medium-size buttercup squash, peeled, seeded and cut lengthwise in slivers
4 Tbsp butter
Salt and pepper
Nutmeg or minced fresh tarragon

Simply sauté the squash slivers in the butter until golden-brown and slightly soft. Drizzle the squash with some extra melted butter, and season with salt, pepper and either nutmeg or fresh tarragon. Pete's personal favorite is tarragon, but he insists that it must be fresh! *Serves* 4

Baked Butternut Squash

1 large butternut squash, peeled, seeded and cut into 1-inch cubes
Salt and pepper
2 tsp anise seed, crushed
1/8 tsp ground cardamom
2 or 3 Tbsp brown sugar
2 Tbsp lemon juice
1/2 cup melted butter

Place the squash into a buttered 2-quart casserole. Sprinkle with the salt, pepper, anise seed, cardamom and sugar. Drizzle with the lemon juice and butter. Bake, uncovered, at 350F for 30 minutes or until tender. *Serves* 4

Golden Soufflé

1-1/2 cups puréed cooked winter squash

Salt, pepper and nutmeg

6 Tbsp butter

5 egg yolks

7 egg whites

Blend the squash with the seasonings and butter and beat lightly. Mix in the egg yolks one at a time, beating each in well.

Beat the egg whites until stiff but not dry. Fold one-quarter of the whites into the purée, mixing carefully. Gently fold the remaining whites into the purée. Pour the mixture into a well-oiled 1-1/2-quart soufflé dish. Bake at 375F for 25 to 30 minutes. *Serves 6*

Each serving contains: Cal-194, Prot-7g, Carb-6g, Fib-2g, Tot. Fat-16g, Sat. Fat-9g, Chol-208mg, Sdm-232mg

Harvest Soup

This is the soup recipe that got me through college. You can use any winter squash you like, including pumpkin. For a little luxury, add a spoonful of yogurt to each serving.

1/3 cup diced onions

4 Tbsp butter

1 large potato, peeled, chopped

1 cup vegetable stock

2 cups cooked winter squash

Salt and pepper

3/4 tsp curry powder

3/4 cup milk

Paprika

Sauté the onions in butter until soft. Add the potato, stock, squash, salt, pepper and curry powder. Simmer for 10 minutes, or until potato is tender. Blend in the milk. Sprinkle with paprika. *Serves 4*

Each serving contains: Cal-219, Prot-4g, Carb-22g, Fib-5g, Tot. Fat-14g, Sat. Fat-8g, Chol-37mg, Sdm-491mg

Baked Acorn Squash

2 large acorn squash, washed and cut in half lengthwise, with the seeds removed

Salt and pepper

1 small onion, grated

4 Tbsp brown sugar

4 Tbsp butter

Place the squash, cut side down, on a shallow baking dish and add 1/4 inch of hot water. Bake at 350F for 20 to 30 minutes or until the squash is tender to the touch.

Drain any water left in the tray and turn over the squash. Sprinkle each half with salt, pepper, onion, sugar and butter. Return it to the oven and bake another 10 to 15 minutes. *Serves 4*

Honey-glazed Acorn Squash: substitute honey or maple syrup and nutmeg for the onion and brown sugar.

Each serving contains: Cal-269, Prot-3g, Carb-43g, Fib-10g, Tot. Fat-12g, Sat. Fat-7g, Chol-31mg, Sdm-197mg

BITTER MELON

I am pushing things a little by including *Balsam pear*, or bitter melon, in this section, but it is a squash, so look for it in the squash section of your produce supplier. It looks like a wrinkled cucumber, 5 to 8 inches long, green in color when immature and orange when completely ripe. For eating, you'll want one that is greenish-yellow. Inside the melon is a pink or white spongy pulp and seeds. The skin is edible, but do remove the seeds and the core.

The vegetable is well-named because it is in fact bitter. To remove the bitterness, simply soak the vegetable in salty water, give it a good rinse and pat it dry. Bitter melon is at its best when sliced and added to a stir-fry. It is also good stuffed or curried. If you want to get into bitter melon with any sincerity, consult an Asian cookbook, for bitter melon is an Asian specialty.

Bitter melon is available without much regularity, all year round. Look for melons that are well-shaped and firm, with good skin color and without any dark spots or soft areas. Although the skin of the bitter melon is wrinkled, avoid vegetables with withered skin. Store bitter melon in a plastic bag in a cool place for 3 days at the most.

Joe's Bitter Melon Stir-Fry

Joe ran the Nipa Hut, a little lunch counter in the corner of the Saint John City Market. This is his favorite way of preparing bitter melon and a nice introduction to the vegetable.

2 Tbsp peanut oil

1 clove garlic, minced

1 medium onion, sliced

1 tomato, diced

1/2 cup sliced mushrooms

1 Tbsp grated fresh ginger

Salt or soy sauce

3 bitter melons, cut lengthwise, seeded, with core pulp removed, and cut in 1/4-inch slices, soaked in salt water as described above, if desired

Heat the oil in a wok or frying pan. Brown the garlic, add the onion, tomato, mushrooms and ginger and sauté the mixture until the onion is transparent. Add some salt or soy sauce and simmer for 3 minutes. Add the bitter melon and simmer until the bitter melon is soft and the flavors well-blended. Serve hot with rice. *Serves 4*

Each serving contains: Cal-110, Prot-3g, Carb-11g, Fib-3g, Tot. Fat-7g, Sat. Fat-1g, Chol-0mg, Sdm-143mg

YUCCA ROOT

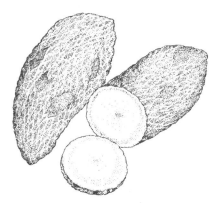

Don't look to yucca root if you'd like something unusual for your next tray of crudités. It should *never* be eaten raw—you could become very ill. Cooked, it is an extraordinarily versatile vegetable and can be added to a stew, a stir-fry or any number of side dishes.

If you like tapioca, you'll like yucca root . . . because the flesh of the yucca plant, known as *manioc* or *cassava* in South America, is used as a base for the pudding that most of us have eaten as children and secretly crave as adults.

In South America, a flour is made from dried, grated yucca root and sprinkled on starchy dishes or used to make a hard flat cake called *cassava bread*.

Yucca root looks more like a branch than a root. Shaped like a sweet potato and covered with a rough pinky-brown bark, yucca root usually weighs between half a pound and three pounds. The flesh is pure white, dense and heavy. A good source of iron, yucca root contains about 40 calories in 1/2 cup of the cooked vegetable.

When buying yucca, look for roots with firm skin, avoiding those with hairline cracks (a sign of dryness) or any sign of mold. A good sniff will often lead you to a good root, because yucca roots tend to smell acrid or sour when they begin to age. You might even want to ask your grocer to cut a root for you to ensure that the flesh is clean and free from rot.

Yucca root should be used soon after it is purchased, because it does not store well. If necessary, you may keep the root in a cool, dark, well-ventilated place, but for no more than 2 days. Or you can freeze it raw. Just peel and rinse the chunks, wrap them tightly and place them in the freezer.

To use yucca root, simply peel it and remove the fibrous central core. Because the root is very hard, it may be necessary to cut the root into chunks before making an incision in the bark. A knife can then be used to peel away the bark and its underpadding.

A versatile vegetable, yucca may be fried, boiled, sautéed or added to a stew. When cooked, it absorbs the flavor of other vegetables and becomes almost translucent with a sticky, densely buttery chewiness of which Pete is particularly fond. Yucca root is also a natural thickening agent, so be sure to include it in your stews and soups.

The very first time I had yucca root, I just put it in boiling water, added some garlic and simmered the root for 20 minutes. Although this is still my favorite way of eating yucca root, it is also delicious served with a spicy tomato sauce, chopped green onions and cilantro (coriander).

Pete's Yucca Yummies

These little hors d'oeuvres are one of Pete's chewy, cheesy specialties.

> **1 pound yucca root, rinsed, peeled and cut into chunks**
> **1/3 cup Cheddar cheese, grated**
> **1 tsp Dijon-style mustard**
> **1 Tbsp melted butter**
> **3 eggs**
> **1 tsp salt**
> **1 Serrano or Jalapeño pepper, minced**
> **1/2 tsp sugar**
> **Oil**

Grate the yucca root and blend it with the cheese, mustard, melted butter, eggs, salt, pepper and sugar. When well blended, form the mixture into small balls, 1 inch in diameter. Deep-fry the balls until golden, about 5 minutes. Drain the yucca balls on a paper towel and serve hot. *Serves 5*

<u>Each serving contains</u>: Cal-233, Prot-9g Carb-26g, Fib-0g, Tot. Fat-11g, Sat. Fat-4g, Chol-142mg, Sdm-779mg

ZUCCHINI AND SUMMER SQUASH

Zucchini is a summer squash, but because it is the most popular and most common, Pete and I decided to include summer squash with zucchini rather than vice versa. Probably most of us don't even think of zucchini as a summer squash anymore. It is wonderfully versatile, and delicious both raw and cooked. Zucchini are a great favorite at summer fairs because, if encouraged, they will grow to be absolutely enormous. Until about 20 years ago, zucchini was all but unknown, except to people of Mediterranean descent and to the French, but today it is very popular and easy to find.

This section refers most often to zucchini but, unless otherwise indicated, the same descriptions apply to the other varieties of summer squash as well. Every recipe for zucchini can be used with summer squash and vice versa. After zucchini, the most common varieties of summer squash are the yellow crookneck, the yellow straightneck and the golden zucchini.

Zucchini is available all year round, its peak season being from June to August, while summer squash is, as the name implies, only available during the summer. Look for firm, smooth, glossy, well-shaped zucchini, about 6 to 10 inches long and 1 to 2 inches in diameter. Avoid zucchini with soft spots or torn skin.

Store zucchini in a plastic bag in the refrigerator. Although it will keep for 5 days, it is a good idea to use as soon as possible.

Zucchini is a good source of vitamin C. Raw, it has only 20 calories in 4 ounces.

Sautéed Zucchini and Variations

6 Tbsp olive oil or butter
1-1/2 pounds zucchini, thinly sliced
Salt and pepper

Heat the olive oil or butter, or some of each, in a skillet. Add the zucchini and sauté for 4 or 5 minutes over medium to high heat, tossing well. Season with salt and pepper. Serve hot. *Serves 4 to 6*

With garlic and herbs: add 3 large cloves of finely chopped garlic to the oil and sauté with the zucchini. Sprinkle with 3 tablespoons chopped parsley and 1 tablespoon chopped fresh basil and serve.

Zucchini is a wonderfully versatile squash. Like carrots, zucchini is delicious both raw and cooked and lends itself to sweet and savory dishes.

With shallots: before adding the zucchini, sauté 1/2 cup of finely chopped shallots in the oil or butter until they are transparent.

With walnuts: simply add 1/2 cup of coarsely chopped walnuts to the zucchini. Cook with the vegetable. Sprinkle with 2 tablespoons of chopped parsley and a few more nuts just before serving.

With cheese: once the zucchini is cooked, sprinkle generously with freshly grated Parmesan cheese and broil for 2 minutes or until the cheese is melted and golden brown.

With tomatoes and peppers: sauté the zucchini with a generous handful of halved cherry tomatoes and 1 small green pepper cut into strips. When the zucchini is tender, sprinkle the mélange with 2 tablespoons of fresh chopped basil and a generous amount of grated Parmesan cheese.

Chilled Zucchini Soup

2 pounds zucchini, washed and grated
1 cup green onions, chopped
4 Tbsp butter
2-1/2 cups vegetable stock
2-1/2 cups buttermilk
Salt and pepper
6 Tbsp dill, chopped

Cook the zucchini and onions gently in butter until soft, about 8 minutes. Stir in the stock and purée the mixture. Add the buttermilk, salt, pepper and 4 tablespoons of the dill. Chill for at least 4 hours. Garnish with the remaining dill just before serving. *Serves 6*

Variation: add 1 tablespoon each of curry and cumin to the zucchini and onions before adding the stock. Omit the dill.

Pete's Zucchini Muffins

This recipe does not belong to Pete Luckett but to my brother Pete. He makes the most amazing muffins and my mom grows vast quantities of zucchini, so when the two of them get together, we all feast on these delicacies.

2 cups zucchini, grated

2 eggs, well beaten

1 cup buttermilk

1/2 cup brown sugar

3 Tbsp honey

1/2 cup raisins

1 tsp vanilla

1 cup oil

1-1/2 cups whole-wheat flour

1-1/2 cups bran

2 tsp baking powder

1 tsp baking soda

1 tsp cinnamon

1 tsp salt

1/4 tsp nutmeg

Mix together the zucchini, eggs, buttermilk, brown sugar, honey, raisins, vanilla and oil.

In a separate bowl, mix the flour, bran, baking powder, baking soda, cinnamon, salt and nutmeg. Blend the dry ingredients with the zucchini mixture, just until moist. Spoon into greased muffin tins and bake for 25 minutes at 375F. *Makes 12 large muffins*

<u>Each muffin contains</u>: Cal-310, Prot-5g, Carb-33g, Fib-5g, Tot. Fat-20g, Sat. Fat-2g, Chol-36mg, Sdm-245mg

Zucchini-Ginger Jam

My mother makes this jam every summer and it is really wonderful stuff. If you grow your own zucchini this is a great way to use up the squash, which often grow too big.

4 pounds zucchini, peeled and cut into small cubes

6 cups sugar

3 lemons, juiced and rinds grated

1-1/2-inch piece ginger root, peeled

1/4 pound candied or preserved ginger, slivered

Place the zucchini in a large bowl, cover with sugar and let stand overnight. Drain off the liquid and bring it to a boil with the lemon juice and grated rind. Add the ginger root tied in a cheesecloth bag. (My mom just grates the ginger and leaves it in, making the jam extra gingery.) Simmer for 1 hour. Add the candied or preserved ginger and the zucchini. Simmer 1 hour longer or until zucchini becomes transparent. Remove the cheesecloth bag, and spoon the jam into hot sterilized jars. Seal. *Makes 4 pints*

<u>1 tablespoon contains</u>: Cal-42, Prot-0g, Carb-11g, Fib-0g, Tot. Fat-0g, Sat. Fat-0g, Chol-0mg, Sdm-1mg

Zucchini-and-Tomato Casserole

1 small onion, minced

1/2 pound mushrooms, sliced

1 small red pepper, sliced

2 cloves garlic, minced

4 Tbsp olive oil

2 to 3 pounds zucchini, trimmed and cut into 1/4-inch slices

2 Tbsp fresh basil or dill, minced

1/2 cup Cheddar cheese, grated

4 large tomatoes, peeled and sliced

Salt and pepper

2 Tbsp melted butter

1/2 cup soft breadcrumbs

Sauté the onion, mushrooms, pepper and garlic in the olive oil, stirring frequently, for 4 minutes or until the onion is soft. Add the zucchini. Sauté over medium heat, stirring constantly, for 5 minutes or until the zucchini is golden, but still firm.

In a buttered 1-1/2-quart casserole, spread a layer of the zucchini mixture. Sprinkle with basil or dill and some of the Cheddar cheese, cover with a layer of tomatoes and sprinkle with salt and pepper. Repeat the layers.

Combine the melted butter and the breadcrumbs and sprinkle them on top of the zucchini mixture. Bake, uncovered, at 350F for 20 minutes or until golden-brown. *Serves 6*

Each serving contains: Cal-261, Prot-8g, Carb-22g, Fib-5g, Tot. Fat-17g, Sat. Fat-6g, Chol-20mg, Sdm-234mg

Zucchini Frittata

2 Tbsp olive oil

1 small red onion, sliced paper-thin

2 pounds zucchini, trimmed and thinly sliced

1 large tomato, sliced

6 eggs

1/4 cup parsley, minced

2 Tbsp fresh basil or dill, minced

Salt and pepper

Heat the olive oil in a frying pan and sauté the onion for 2 minutes at high heat; add the zucchini and continue cooking for 2 or 3 minutes. Lower the temperature and lay the tomatoes on top of the zucchini and onion.

Beat the eggs and herbs together. Season with salt and pepper and pour the mixture over the zucchini. Fry over low heat for about 5 minutes or until the bottom is set and browned. Turn the omelet over and cook for another 2 or 3 minutes. Cut into wedges and serve. *Serves 3*

Each serving contains: Cal-299, Prot-17g, Carb-16g, Fib-5g, Tot. Fat-20g, Sat. Fat-4g, Chol-425mg, Sdm-233mg

FRUITS

APPLES

North Americans consume vast amounts of apples. And no wonder: apples can be eaten raw or prepared a hundred ways. They are good with cheese and with other fruits and vegetables. In a pie, a salad or as a snack, apples are a staple in the North American diet.

Most of the apples we find in our markets are those that ship and store well; but in the autumn, less-popular varieties are readily available for apple lovers. Unfortunately, many types of apples are no longer grown in quantity, simply because they do not travel well. Their scarcity only makes them more of a treat. Pete particularly recommends anything that ends in "pippin"; his favorite is a Cox's Orange Pippin. If you can find one of these, buy it, eat it, and think of Pete and England, where they are bestsellers.

Four common types of apples are available virtually all year round: Red and Golden Delicious, Granny Smith and McIntosh. The Red and Golden Delicious apples outsell all other varieties of apples in North America. The **Red Delicious** is an eating apple (it loses its shape and some of its taste when cooked); the **Golden Delicious,** on the other hand, is excellent eaten out of hand or cooked. **Granny Smiths,** originally from Australia, are enjoying increasing popularity. Although they demand a particularly warm climate for growing, they travel well. "Grannies" are equally delicious eaten raw or cooked. The Delicious varieties and Granny Smith apples are available all year round and are always in good supply. **McIntosh** apples are also very popular, but they have one peculiarity—they dissolve when baked. Nevertheless, they are a favorite for out-of-hand eating or for pies. They are especially abundant in the autumn, and the stored apples are usually in good supply until late summer.

In recent years a new arrival, picked and shipped fresh, has been imported from New Zealand. These apples have a crunchy freshness that is unique to apples that have not been in storage. So if you are fond of fresh apples, keep an eye out for New Zealand's exports in late spring and early summer, in particular, **Gala, Royal Gala** and **Braeburn** varieties.

The popularity of the apple is such that there are recipe books exclusively about apples . . . there is little that has not been done with apples. I *could* tell you how to make a swan out of a Granny Smith apple. But that wouldn't be of much use, would it? Instead I will pass on one all-purpose apple recipe, which can be added to your collection of apple pie, apple pudding, apple cookies, applesauce, apple bread, apple muffins, apple-everything recipes. This culinary gem is something different—something you will be amazed that you ever did without.

Crêperie Apples

When I worked at a crêperie in France, one of our most popular dessert crêpes was "Pommes, crème fraîche, Calvados." This consisted of a crêpe with an apple mixture and a dollop of crème fraîche inside, all rolled up and flambéed with Calvados, an apple liqueur. What a fabulous dessert! I still dream about it. Every couple of days I would make the apple filling, and although it was intended for the crêpes, when the crêperie doors were closed, we found a thousand other uses for it. We spooned it over ice cream, over cake, mixed it with yogurt, poured cream over it, put it on toast. Its uses are infinite!

You may wish to adapt this recipe to your particular taste. I use Granny Smith apples because of their tartness.

> 1/4 cup all-purpose flour
> 3 pounds apples, peeled and cut in thick slices
> 3 Tbsp butter
> 1/2 cup brown sugar
> 2 tsp cinnamon
> 1 tsp nutmeg
> Pinch of salt
> 1/2 cup cider or apple juice

Put the flour in a paper bag and toss the apple pieces in the flour until they are well coated.

Melt the butter in a frying pan. Add the apples and sauté for about 5 minutes. In the meantime, blend the sugar and spices. When the apples begin to turn golden, add the sugar-spice mixture and the salt, and cook for a few more minutes. Add the cider, turn the heat to low and simmer, covered, for 15 minutes, until the apples are tender. Depending on your taste, you can add more or less juice to this mixture. You can also include some brandy or Calvados, an excellent addition if you intend to serve crêperie apples with ice cream. *Serves 8, depending on how you use it of course*

Each serving contains: Cal-197, Prot-1g, Carb-41g, Fib-4g, Tot. Fat-5g, Sat. Fat-3g, Chol-12mg, Sdm-81mg

APRICOTS

Apricots have been cultivated in the United States for about 300 years, making them one of the first cultivated fruits in North America. These sweet little beauties are among the earliest fruits to reach the markets each summer, and they dry so well that we can enjoy them all winter too. But ripe apricots do not stand up to shipping. And although new, tougher varieties have been developed, we often exchange sweetness for firmness.

If you want to eat apricots immediately, choose softer ones; if you won't be using them for a day or two, choose apricots that are less ripe. They will ripen nicely if you just leave them on the counter, out of direct sunlight. To hurry the ripening process, wrap them loosely in a paper bag.

My grandmother, who lives 1,000 miles away, has several apricot trees, which some years give the most magnificent crop. Other years they produce nothing! Unfortunately, these wonderful little fruits do not travel well, and every time I eat an apricot that is not from one of her trees, I long to taste one of those soft, richly flavored little jewels. I am a fan of the old-fashioned apricot which, I guess, means that I am not a proponent of the "bright" flavors of the new hybrids!

Apricots are available from New Zealand and Chile from January to March. Domestic apricots are available from late May to early August. Look for firm, golden-colored apricots. Once they are ripe, you may keep them in the refrigerator in a plastic bag for up to 2 days.

Apricots are a good source of vitamin A and C. One medium-size apricot has about 17 calories.

Apricots are delicious rinsed and eaten out of hand. You can cut them in half, remove the pit and fill the hollow with Brie or any soft cheese, making a nice appetizer. For breakfast, add slices of apricot to your cereal or pancakes. Toss them into a fruit salad or add them to ice cream and top with toasted almonds.

Apricots and Sour Cream

12 apricots, halved
1/2 cup brown sugar
1 cup sour cream
Pinch of nutmeg

Place apricot halves in a baking dish. Sprinkle with brown sugar and spread the sour cream over them. Grate on a little nutmeg. Bake at 325F for 15 minutes or until apricots are soft. *Serves 6*

Each serving contains: Cal-161, Prot-2g, Carb-21g, Fib-1g, Tot. Fat-8g, Sat. Fat-5g, Chol-17mg, Sdm-26mg

ASIAN PEARS

This is the fruit for me! If you love crisp texture with the richness of a soft fruit taste, then Asian pears are also the fruit for you. The Asian pear tastes like a soft ripe pear, but is crisp and juicy like a firm apple. Its granular texture is offset by mild flavor and aroma. The most common of all Asian pears is sold at Pete's under the name *Japanese pear*. Its Japanese name is *Nijisseiki*, or translated into English, "Twentieth Century." It has the shape, size and color of a large Golden Delicious apple and although its flesh is not as juicy as that of some varieties, it is slightly sweeter.

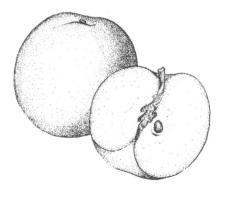

Asian pears are available almost all year, their peak month being September. They are sold ripe, and their storage life is incredible. You may leave them on the counter for up to 2 weeks. Left unwashed in a plastic or paper bag in the refrigerator, they will keep for up to 3 months!

Asian pears are a good source of vitamin C and a great source of fiber, as are most fruits.

The very best way to eat Asian pears is raw. Because of their juiciness and the texture of their flesh, the pears also cook well, remaining dense and retaining their shape. Try them sautéed with toasted sliced almonds or slivers of preserved ginger, or make them into a pie, adding some thickener to make up for their juiciness.

An Asian pear is a perfect end to a meal. Serve it slightly chilled with a wedge of lime on the side or sliced horizontally to expose its flower-shaped seed center. An Asian pear is a great dessert for a child's lunchbox or for a snack; it is a refreshing, juicy change of pace and nothing beats its crisp, minty freshness.

More than 25 varieties of Asian pears are available in North America—of every color and size. They are always extremely crisp, almost unbelievably juicy and well-suited to being sliced transparently thin.

BANANAS

Bananas are one of those rare fruits that ripen better off the tree. They are picked and shipped green, then stored and ripened in special rooms. Owing to the increased demand for exotic fruits, we can look for a few delicious surprises on the banana shelf of our local markets. The apple, or finger banana, sold at Pete's as a *baby banana*, is a small, fat banana that is rich, super sweet and firm when ripe. Its seeds are slightly crunchy, giving the fruit a unique texture. *Red bananas* are also available in limited quantities. These bananas really are red until they ripen, when they become almost black or a very dark purple. They have very creamy flesh and are surprisingly sweet.

Bananas are available all year round from Central and South America. The red and baby bananas are available sporadically. Choose fruit that is slightly green at the ends if you like bananas firmer and slightly less sweet, clear yellow with an occasional black spot if you like them softer and sweeter. You can store fully ripe bananas in the refrigerator. The cold will retard the ripening process but will keep the texture of the flesh, despite blackening the skins. Bananas will ripen nicely at room temperature, out of direct sunlight.

Bananas are an excellent source of potassium. One medium-size banana has about 100 calories.

Cut bananas should be coated with citrus juice to prevent them from blackening. They are delicious eaten out of hand or sliced on cereal, pancakes or waffles. Add them to a fruit salad or a fruit tray. The next time you make a cheesecake that doesn't need baking, try lining the inside of the cake with sliced bananas; simply cover the bottom crust with sliced bananas before you pour in the filling.

Baked Bananas

Baked bananas are an easy, delectable dessert. Slit the bananas down one side and bake in a 325F oven for about 15 minutes or until they are soft but not mushy. Drizzle the bananas with some melted butter and sprinkle with brown sugar. Bake them for another 5 or 10 minutes until the sugar has dissolved. Serve them with yogurt or sour cream.

Each serving contains: Cal-271, Prot-1g, Carb-44g, Fib-2g, Tot. Fat-12g, Sat. Fat-7g, Chol-31mg, Sdm-119mg

Sautéed Bananas

Peel and slice the bananas on a diagonal. Heat some butter in a frying pan and gently add the fruit. Turn once to coat each slice with butter and cook slowly until soft. Sprinkle with some brown sugar and continue cooking until the fruit is glazed. Serve the bananas very hot.

For a special treat, flambé the fruit in Grand Marnier or brandy, and serve with ice cream or yogurt. Delicious!

Each serving contains: Cal-241, Prot-1g, Carb 36g, Fib-2g, Tot. Fat-12g, Sat. Fat-7g, Chol-31mg, Sdm-122mg

BLACKBERRIES

There are several types of blackberries, including the red loganberries, *all of which grow on upright or trailing bushes.*

One of my happiest memories from childhood is picking black-berries, or *brambleberries* as they are sometimes called, at my grand-mother's farm. I would wander down the lane behind the fields and fill a bowl with wild berries. Adding as much cream as my grand-mother could spare, I would indulge in these little treasures until I couldn't eat any more. Now I can't eat blackberries without remembering those days.

Blackberries are available off and on all summer, from May until mid-September. It is a good idea to plan on using black-berries within 2 days of purchasing them. As with all berries, Pete's advice is, "Don't keep 'em, eat 'em." To keep them in perfect condi-tion, refrigerate them, unwashed, on a cookie sheet lined with paper towels; cover them with another layer of paper towels and wrap them in plastic. Rinse the berries quickly before serving them.

Blackberries are delicious in a fruit salad or on breakfast cereal. Try tossing a handful into pancake or waffle batter. Serve them *au naturel* with cream or ice cream and a little sugar. For visual appeal, sprinkle a few onto a slice of cantaloupe, or serve a mixture of sliced strawberries and blackberries with a little sour cream or yogurt. Try them on meringue, ice cream or fresh pound cake.

Blackberries are a good source of vitamin C. One cup has only 75 calories.

Blackberry Concentrate

The idea of mixing fruit and vinegar surprises some people but this concoction produces the most delicious syrup. You can mix it with water, about 4 tablespoons with 10 ounces of water, and make a delicious thirst quencher. Or, you can pour this syrup over ice cream or yogurt for a summer dessert.

1 cup white vinegar, mixed with
1 cup water
1 quart blackberries
2 to 3 cups sugar

Pour the vinegar and water over the berries and let them stand for at least 24 hours.

Press the whole mixture through a strainer, squeezing as many of the berries through as possible. Add the sugar and boil for 30 minutes, stirring occasionally. Cool the syrup and keep it in the refrigerator until you are ready to use it. This syrup also freezes well. *Makes 1 quart*

1/4-cup serving contains: Cal-166, Prot-0g, Carb-43g, Fib-2g, Tot. Fat-0g, Sat. Fat-0g, Chol-0mg, Sdm-1mg

BLUEBERRIES

Three hundred and fifty years ago the blueberry was already an established North American native. Indians were gathering, drying, and using blueberries as an integral part of their daily diet.

Blueberries grow in other countries but nowhere are they as enthusiastically greeted as in the United States and Canada. They grow with wild abandon over much of North America, and although there are several types of blueberries, high-bush and low-bush are the most common varieties. The larger berries tend to come from the cultivated high bushes while the smaller, wild blueberries come from the low bushes.

Blueberries ship well and are transported around the country, so no matter what your local season, the fresh fruit is available from early summer to early fall. Look for plump, firm little berries with a slight grayish hue. To store the berries, either refrigerate them in the box or, if you want to keep them in perfect condition, place them between layers of paper towels and wrap them in plastic. Blueberries can be stored in this manner for 4 days, but like all berries, they are perishable and you are wise to use them as soon as you purchase them.

To freeze blueberries, simply lay them, unwashed, on a cookie sheet in a single layer, place them in the freezer and, when they are firm, put them in bags. It isn't necessary to thaw them before cooking, but be sure to give them a quick rinse before using.

In some ways blueberries are the ultimate fruit, with nothing to hull, nothing to peel, nothing you can't use, nothing to throw away. Whether you love wild or cultivated berries, all of them are juicy, slightly crunchy little morsels of tart-sweet flavor.

Blueberries are an excellent source of vitamin C. One serving, about four ounces, contains only 23 calories!

Blueberries can be found in a wealth of recipes, from muffins and pies to cakes and pancakes. They are delicious simply rinsed and served with ice cream, sour cream or yogurt and some sugar and cinnamon. They are super with crème de cassis or Cointreau.

Blueberry Cake

4 eggs

1 cup sugar

1 cup oil

2-1/2 cups all-purpose flour

3 tsp baking powder

1/2 cup orange juice

1/4 tsp salt

Rind of 1 orange, grated

3 cups blueberries

In a large bowl, beat the eggs. Add the sugar, beating until almost white, and beat in the oil. Sift the dry ingredients, reserving 1/2 cup flour for flouring the berries. Alternately add the dry ingredients and the orange juice, mixed with the salt and orange rind, to the mixture. Fold in the floured berries and pour the batter into an oiled Bundt pan.

Bake at 325F for 45 to 60 minutes. *Serves 12*

Each serving contains: Cal-371, Prot-5g, Carb-43g, Fib-2g, Tot. Fat-20g, Sat. Fat-2g, Chol-71mg, Sdm-190mg

BREADFRUIT

Breadfruit is eaten as a vegetable. The green fruit, which is about the size of a large cantaloupe, is covered with bumps, almost like scales. Inside, it is rather like a potato, both in texture and taste. When slightly ripe, breadfuit resembles partially baked bread. When completely ripe, the fruit develops a muskiness present in many tropical fruits; its texture becomes soft and slightly runny. Breadfruit does not keep once it becomes ripe and must be used immediately, although in some tropical countries, it is eaten after it has fermented.

Breadfruit is available all year round and is easier to find in an area with a Caribbean population. A good breadfruit will weigh close to 5 pounds. Look for fruit with large, well-developed "scales." It should be completely green if you want to keep it for some time. Avoid fruit with hard spots, dents and dark areas.

In the South Sea islands, breadfruit is called "the staff of life." It is usually stored in water and sold whole.

145

Breadfruit is jammed with calories, with around 120 in 4 ounces. It is also loaded with vitamin C and potassium.

Most popularly used like potatoes, breadfruit makes a gorgeous side dish, baked for 1 hour at 425F. It is also good boiled, steamed, mashed, creamed, puréed, fried or roasted. You might like to try roasting it, eating it sliced or deep-frying the slices and reheating them in a spicy or cheese-flavored sauce.

If you live in an area where breadfruit is common, buy some and try it. Some will warn you that it is an acquired taste. They are right. It is. But, I'm told that once you've acquired it, you will never let it go.

CACTUS PEARS

Cactus pears are among the most attractive garnishes in the market. Drop a slice of cactus pear into a cocktail or serve it with roasted or grilled vegetables. Lime juice accents the flavor.

Tuna is the fruit of a cactus native to Mexico. Surprised? Thought it was a kind of fish, right? *Tuna, Indian fig* and *prickly pear* are all names for the cactus pear: a spiky, egg-shaped fruit, usually disarmed by the time it has reached the shelves of our markets. Mexico produces more cactus pears than the world produces apricots—which gives you some idea of just how popular the fruit is.

Most of the cactus pears sold in our markets are grown in the desert areas of the United States, with occasional imports from Central and South America. There are two main varieties. One type has a dull, gray-maroon exterior and scarlet flesh. The other has a grayish, green-yellow skin and yellow flesh. Both varieties of fruit taste the same, contain the same edible seeds, are the same shape and the same size. A combination of the sliced flesh from both varieties provides an exquisite contrast of color.

Although the fruit is usually harmless by the time you buy it, some authorities recommend wearing rubber gloves or using tongs to handle the fruit, to avoid being pierced! Pete considers this procedure totally unnecessary. To remove the skin, simply hold the fruit and slice off both ends; make a lengthwise slit in the skin and peel it away from the flesh. Cactus-pear skin comes off surprisingly easily, revealing a barrel-shaped fruit.

Cactus pears are available from August to December. Look for ripe fruit that is a deep color all over and gives a little to gentle pressure. Choose fresh-looking fruit; avoid those with mold. You may store the ripe fruit in a plastic bag in the refrigerator for 5 days. Cactus pears will ripen at home, on the counter, out of the sun; when tender, retire them to the refrigerator.

Cactus pears are a good source of vitamin C and rich in potassium and fiber. One cactus pear has 45 calories.

Pete prefers that cactus pears be served chilled. If you serve them raw, have a little fun with their color: try mixing them with kiwi, oranges and bananas in a salad or on a fruit plate.

Cactus-Pear Smoothie

2 cactus pears, peeled and sliced
1 very large banana, peeled and sliced
4 ice cubes
2 Tbsp honey
Squirt of lime juice
1/2 cup milk
1/2 cup yogurt

In a blender, purée the pears and the banana for one minute. Add the remaining ingredients and whirl until smooth. *Serves 2*

Each serving contains: Cal-234, Prot-6g, Carb-46g, Fib-5g, Tot. Fat-5g, Sat. Fat-3g Chol-16mg, Sdm-65mg

Cactus-Pear Sauce

This sauce is delicious served hot with ice cream, sour cream or yogurt. It also complements fresh fruit. It can be served hot, warm or cold.

3 cactus pears, peeled, sliced and puréed
1 Tbsp cornstarch
1/4 cup sugar
2 Tbsp lime juice
1 Tbsp butter
1 tsp vanilla extract

Blend the purée, cornstarch and sugar. Cook over medium heat until the mixture boils and thickens. Remove from the heat and add the lime juice, butter and vanilla. *Makes 1 cup*

1/4-cup serving contains: Cal-117, Prot-1g, Carb-22g, Fib-3g, Tot. Fat-3g, Sat. Fat-2g, Chol-8mg, Sdm-35mg

CARAMBOLA

The carambola, or *star fruit*, is a beautiful garnishing fruit. It is ellipsoidal, with four to six ridges running its entire length. When sliced, it makes exquisite star shapes. I make a fruit plate composed of peeled, sliced kiwi fruit, sliced strawberries and sliced carambolas; the combination of colors and shapes couldn't be more beautiful.

Carambola come in yellow or white, although the white variety is rare. You can buy green carambola, but these are simply the yellow fruit before it is ripe. Carambola is a versatile and decorative fruit. It can be added to vegetable or fruit salads and is particularly attractive in drinks. The carambola, originally a native of India and Sri Lanka, is now produced in Thailand, tropical Africa, Brazil, India and, happily for North Americans, in Florida.

The taste of the star fruit is rather difficult to describe. The one problem is knowing whether you are getting a wonderfully sweet plum-and-roses tasting fruit or a lemon-lime tart fruit. Although there is no certain way to be sure which is which, Pete can usually tell. But that is due to years of experience. As a general rule, the sweeter carambolas tend to have thick ribs, while the more sour ones have narrow ribs. A white carambola, a different variety from the yellow, will definitely be sweet.

Carambola are available from January to May and from July to October. If you can buy the fruit unripe, do so; it will ripen at room temperature. What's more, because the fruit is delicate and doesn't stand up very well to the poking and pinching that customers occasionally inflict on it, it will probably be safer on your kitchen counter than on a grocer's shelves.

When fully developed, a ripe carambola will give off the most wonderful aroma, a fruity, flowery perfume, and according to Pete, the ridges of the fruit will probably be brown. If you are using the fruit chiefly for its appearance, try to avoid those with brown marks—the marks don't affect the taste but they mar the appearance a little.

Store the fruit at room temperature; even ripe, it will keep for 3 days. If you won't be using them for a week, keep carambolas where they will not be damaged, in the warmest part of the refrigerator. Carambola are a good source of vitamin C. A medium-size fruit has only 40 calories.

Sliced carambola can be sautéed in butter for a few moments and served as a garnish. Slice up star fruit and add it to your next fruit salad or as a garnish on your next vegetable salad, but don't use too much—half of one fruit is plenty in a salad for four.

Carambola and Avocado

These fruits were made to go together.

2 ripe avocados, halved lengthwise and thinly sliced
Orange juice
4 small carambolas, thinly sliced
Salt and pepper

Dip the avocado slices in the orange juice. Arrange slices of carambola and avocado on a serving plate. Squeeze on a little orange juice and sprinkle with salt and pepper. *Serves 4*

Each serving contains: Cal-207, Prot-3g, Carb-18g, Fib-8g, Tot. Fat-16g, Sat. Fat-2g, Chol-0mg, Sdm-79mg

CHERIMOYAS

Pete's favorite tropical fruit is cherimoya, also known as *soursop* or *sherbet fruit*. He describes it as being every tropical fruit blended together and poured into a skin. But what a skin! In all honesty, cherimoyas are not attractive from the outside. They look interesting, but not appealing. They have greenish-gray skin and what appears to be an attempt at scales on the outside. Despite their rather rough-and-ready appearance, cherimoyas are extremely delicate; even a leaf brushing on the skin during the growing period will leave a mark on this leathery covering. But the exterior belies the beauty of the fruit inside, which is both appealing to the taste buds and attractive to the eye.

The skin is filled with a creamy white flesh that is studded with beautiful, inedible, large black seeds. Apparently, steps have been taken to develop a seedless cherimoya but, like watermelon, half the fun of eating this fruit is spitting the seeds out, unless you are at a fancy dinner party—but when was the last time you were served cherimoya at a dinner party?

Cherimoyas are expensive. They require complicated and time-consuming pollinating techniques and because they are so tender, they must be harvested by hand and shipped with extreme care; considerable effort is put into their packing so that they arrive, after having been shipped by air, looking as unblemished as possible.

The taste of a cherimoya is a taste of heaven and it is greatly enhanced by the smooth, creamy texture of the fruit. You hardly need to use your teeth on a cherimoya; just mush it around in your mouth until it dissolves. Sweet, almost fermented and slightly musky, cherimoya tastes like paradise or what I imagine paradise to taste like. One mouthful and you can sense the warmth of a tropical breeze on your cheeks, feel the sun filtering through the leaves of a palm tree and hear the waves lapping at the white sand.

The flavor of cherimoya has been described as a combination of tropical fruits: mango, pineapple, banana and papaya. But the best description of the fruit's flavor is Pete's: every tropical fruit you ever tasted blended together into a thick cream.

Cherimoyas are in season when we most need to dream of tropical climes—from November until the end of April. They are picked hard and left to ripen en route to your table, or mouth. Buy them green and hard, and let them ripen at home, out of direct sunlight, turning them frequently so that they ripen evenly.

A ripe cherimoya can be anywhere from pale green to a darkish green with brown speckles; it may even turn slightly gray when ripe. Watch out for darkened fruit, which may not ripen properly, the dark spot indicating that it may have been subjected to cold. Markings on the skin, called *surface scars*, will not affect the quality of the fruit. Buy either large or small cherimoyas because their size has no effect on the taste; if they are sold individually rather than by the pound, buy a big one and get more for your money. A large one will probably last you all day.

Cherimoyas are high in calories: a 4-ounce serving has about 100 calories. They are a good source of vitamin C and contain niacin and thiamin, two of the B vitamins.

The best way to eat cherimoya is all by yourself. That way you get more. They are exquisite slightly chilled, cut up and eaten like watermelon. A quick 30 minutes in the freezer and you will have sherbet fruit, just like an exotic sherbet. Because the fruit will darken once exposed to the air, squeeze some lemon or lime juice on the cut surface to protect the creamy white color.

Serve cherimoyas cut in halves or quarters to be eaten with a spoon. Remember to cut out the small central core. Cherimoyas may also be puréed, by pushing pieces of the fruit through a sieve, and mixed with a little lime or lemon juice to give the fruit an edge. Try the purée mixed with a little cream and a sprinkle of nutmeg, or blended with other delicate fruits like raspberries, grapes or melon.

Cherimoya Soufflé

1 ripe cherimoya

3 Tbsp orange juice or 1-1/2 Tbsp lime juice

3/4 cup whipping cream, whipped

A sprinkling of nutmeg

Purée the flesh of the cherimoya with the fruit juice. Gently fold in the whipped cream. Sprinkle with nutmeg and chill well. *Serves* 4

Cherimoya Sauce

1 ripe cherimoya

1 tsp lemon or lime juice

1/2 cup half-and-half

Purée the flesh of the cherimoya with the fruit juice. Stir in the half-and-half. Chill. Serve with delicate fruit or ice cream. *Makes* 1 *cup*

This isn't really a soufflé but it is similar in texture. It was concocted by Pete for a friend who complained that he found the cherimoya a little over-whelming.

Each serving contains: Cal-288, Prot-3g, Carb-35g, Fib-3g, Tot. Fat-17g, Sat. Fat-10g, Chol-61mg, Sdm-17mg

1/4-cup serving contains: Cal-168, Prot-3g, Carb-34g, Fib-3g, Tot. Fat-4g, Sat. Fat-2g, Chol-11mg, Sdm-12mg

ATEMOYAS

The atemoya is a cousin of the cherimoya. It looks like a wax artichoke that was stored on the mantelpiece and melted a bit. It also looks like a cherimoya with rounded scales. In color, it is a grayish green. In taste, it is uncannily like cherimoya, but milkier, as opposed to creamier. Its texture is similar to the cherimoya, although it has fewer seeds. Serve it chilled as you would cherimoya. And why not be totally decadent? Pour a little cream over the fruit.

Atemoyas are available from late August to November. Take them home unripe and ripen them on the counter. If they split, as they often do en route to perfect ripeness, don't worry, just cover them with a clean towel. Do not refrigerate the fruit until it is ripe or you will ruin it. Once ripe, it will yield to gentle pressure, and you can keep it for a day or two in the refrigerator. The cold will darken the skin of the fruit but that will not affect the taste.

Atemoya is high in calories, with 93 in 1/3 cup, and is a good source of protein and potassium.

I'm going to let you in on a secret. For a dinner party, Pete covered atemoya halves with sour cream and a generous sprinkling of brown sugar. Then he chilled them for about 15 minutes. There is no more magnificent dessert in the world. I promise!

CHERRIES

"Don't keep 'em, eat 'em!" Pete's words are as true for cherries as for any berries. Because they are very perishable, cherries should be eaten as soon as possible after purchase.

One day at Pete's we received a case of cherries, and it was immediately obvious that every single cherry had been packed by hand! Each tiny berry was neatly placed in line with those below, above and beside it. All the stems pointed in the same direction; not one of the cherries was squashed, damaged or even out of line. I gazed at this in astonishment when Pete's right-hand man, Geoff, came up to me. "Amazin' in't it? You gotta treat 'em li'l beau'ies wif' such care." Wow, he wasn't kidding! I wasn't surprised when I saw the price per pound. They were expensive, but they were magnificent!

In the summer months cherries can be found relatively easily and at a reasonable price. Cherry lovers in North America are particularly lucky because more cherries grow here than any other place in the world; they are also the sweetest and best.

There are, of course, two different types of cherries: tart and sweet. Certain types of tart cherries can be eaten out of hand, but generally they are used in cooking. Ninety percent of the crop is processed, and when you buy commercial cherry-pie filling or cherry jam, more often than not it is made with the tart cherries.

151

In the sweet-cherry category, there are the light-skinned, or yellow, cherries which, unfortunately, do not ship very well. However, the dark, almost-black cherries ship beautifully, the most popular and most common variety being the sweet, dark-purple Bing. These are the ones we buy to eat by the handful.

Cherries are available from late May until early August. You may be lucky enough to find some New Zealand imports around Christmas; however, only a small quantity is imported, so if you are frantic for them, be prepared to search a little. The ripest cherries are also the biggest, the sweetest and the most richly colored. In sweet and tart cherries, look for fruit that is plump, firm and brightly colored.

Cherries are very perishable. They should be eaten as soon after purchase as possible. However, if you must, cherries may be stored in the refrigerator for up to 3 days, if you arrange them between paper towels on a cookie sheet and wrap them in plastic.

Sweet cherries are a good source of vitamin C; tart cherries are a good source of vitamin A. Four ounces of raw sweet cherries have 80 calories; 4 ounces of sour cherries have 65 calories.

In my opinion, the best way to eat sweet cherries is to give them a quick rinse and eat them raw. If you want something a little more adventurous, you can cut them in half, remove the pits and add them to a fruit salad. Stewed cherries are good with ice cream or yogurt. Tart cherries, or a mixture of tart and sweet cherries, make a wonderful deep-dish, fresh-fruit pie. Garnish a plain cake or a lonely meringue with a mixture of fresh and stewed cherries. For real, true-blue adventure, combine pitted, halved cherries with a little brandy, let them marinate for about 15 minutes and blend in some sour cream, or sour cream and yogurt. Garnish with some minced tarragon and toasted slivered almonds. You can also use Grand Marnier and add a little grated orange rind to the sour cream. Go ahead, create something!

Triple-Cherry Sauce

1-1/2 cups cherry juice

1/2 cup sugar

1 Tbsp cornstarch

1 cup pitted fresh sweet cherries

1 Tbsp kirsch (cherry liqueur)

In a saucepan combine the juice, sugar and cornstarch. Cook, stirring, until thickened. Add the cherries. When heated, stir in the kirsch. *Makes 2 cups*

1/4-cup serving contains: Cal-94, Prot-0g, Carb-23g, Fib-0g, Tot. Fat-0g, Sat. Fat-0g, Chol-0mg, Sdm-1mg

COCONUT

Use fresh coconut in place of dried, packaged coconut without having to adjust the recipe. Try grating it coarsely and adding it to a fruit salad or serving it with curry.

This hairy, hard-shelled fruit is a delight for kids. It is amazing how many children will try to convince their mothers to buy a coconut when they see them at Pete's. I still remember the excitement among my brothers and sister and me when we managed to squeeze a coconut onto the shopping list. In many tropical and subtropical regions, coconuts are an important source of food, as common as apples for us.

Coconuts are available all year, being most plentiful in October, November and December. A good coconut will be clean on the outside, without any damp spots or mold. It should be heavy for its size, and when you shake it, you should be able to hear the liquid inside.

If you want to keep a coconut for a while, store it in the refrigerator; but the fruit will also be fine on the counter for a week or two if you can guard it from the kids. The grated flesh will keep in the refrigerator for 2 weeks.

Getting into a coconut can be difficult if you don't know the formula. Here is the easiest way to get the most out of this fruit. One end of a coconut is usually more pointed than the other, and on the rounder end, there are three little depressions called the *eyes*. Drill two holes in the eyes and drain out the liquid. One way of extracting the liquid is to stick a straw in and drink it; the other is to let the fruit sit upside down on a bowl or mug and let the liquid drip out. This juice is superb added to fruit salad or mixed with rum. Incidentally, this is *not* coconut milk.

For the next stage you have two choices. The first is to pound away at the coconut until you manage to break it. The second is to put it in the oven at 350F for 15 minutes, until the shell begins to crack; let the nut cool briefly and then whack it with a hammer along the crack. The shell should split open. You can then pry out the flesh out with a knife or a clean screwdriver.

Three-quarters of a cup of coconut meat contains about 150 calories. It is a good source of potassium and fiber; it also contains saturated fat—a rarity for a fruit or vegetable.

Coconut Milk

Use coconut milk and some grated coconut to make an interesting sauce for curry. Try a little coconut milk in a cocktail, or with your favorite dessert.

1 cup fresh coconut cut into 1/2-inch chunks
1 cup hot water

Whirl the coconut and the hot water in a blender or food processor for 20 to 30 seconds until the chunks have all but disappeared, or until the mixture is thick and pulpy.

Let the liquid steep for 30 minutes. Strain through a double thickness of cheesecloth, wringing it well to remove the liquid. Discard the coconut.

The milk, covered and refrigerated, will keep for up to 3 days. *Makes 1 cup*

Polka Dot Coconut Macaroons

3 egg whites
1 cup sugar
1/2 teaspoon almond extract
1-1/4 cups shredded coconut
1/2 cup chocolate bits

Preheat the oven to 325F; line cookie sheets with foil. Beat the egg whites until foamy. Gradually beat in the sugar until stiff. Fold in extract, coconut and chocolate bits. Drop by teaspoonfuls onto the cookie sheets. Bake 15 to 18 minutes. *Makes about 45 macaroons*

CRANBERRIES

North America is the only producer of cranberries. I know, because cranberry juice is one of my favorites and I have searched a large part of continental Europe for the ruby liquid, to no avail.

There are three types of cranberries: bog, bush and rock. The ones most of us buy in plastic bags for Thanksgiving and Christmas are bog cranberries. This wild fruit is cultivated all along the eastern seaboard as well as in Wisconsin and British Columbia. Occasionally, you'll find bush and rock cranberries for sale locally from late summer to mid-autumn.

Cranberries are abundant from September to the end of November, and they freeze like a dream. Simply drop the bag in the freezer; you don't even need to thaw the berries before cooking. Look for plump, firm berries and avoid withered or shriveled ones. Cranberries keep for up to 8 weeks—much longer than most berries.

Cranberries are a great source of vitamin A. One cup has only 55 calories; that's without sugar, of course!

Although the lowly cranberry was relegated to jelly and sauce for a long time, it is finally coming into its own and recipes abound for cranberry cookies, cranberry bread, cranberry coffee cake, cranberry muffins and cranberry pudding. It is about time, for this tart little berry has been overlooked for too long.

Cranberry-Wine Sorbet

2 cups fresh or frozen cranberries
1/2 cup sugar
1/2 cup red wine
1-1/2 cups orange juice
2 tsp grated orange rind

Combine all the ingredients in a saucepan and simmer over medium heat until the cranberries are cooked and split open. Cool. Purée the mixture in a blender or food processor.

Pour the purée into an ice-cream maker and freeze according to the manufacturer's instructions, or pour the purée into a loaf pan and cover with foil or plastic wrap. Freeze for 4 hours or until firm. Chop the mixture with a knife or fork until it looks like crushed ice. You can also break up the frozen sorbet and whirl it in a food processor just before serving, chilling the bowl first. *Makes 3 cups*

1/2-cup serving contains: Cal-123, Prot-1g, Carb-28g, Fib-1g, Tot. Fat-0g, Sat. Fat-0g, Chol-0mg, Sdm-2mg

Cranberry-Blueberry Pie

Pete told me about this pie. It is deliciously different and hopelessly easy.

2 cups cranberries
2 cups blueberries
3/4 cup sugar
2 Tbsp cornstarch
1/4 tsp nutmeg
2 Tbsp grated orange rind
Pastry for a 9-inch pie shell
Sour cream
Cointreau

Mix the filling ingredients in a medium-sized bowl and pour the mixture into the pie shell. Bake at 425F for 15 minutes; reduce the oven temperature to 375F and bake for another 35 minutes.

Just before serving, add a dollop of sour cream flavored with a small amount of Cointreau. *Serves 6*

Each serving contains: Cal-206, Prot-1g, Carb-41g, Fib-3g, Tot. Fat-5g, Sat. Fat-3g, Chol-9mg, Sdm-27mg

DATES

I am not sure why Pete keeps selling dates at his stall. He maintains, with great vehemence, that the staff eats more than they sell. On behalf of the staff, I would like to say that probably, all put together, we eat far fewer dates than he does. Who can blame him, or us, for that matter?

There are three types of dates: soft, semi-dry and dry. The soft dates are invert or liquid-sugar dates and the dry, cane-sugar dates. Although there are more than a hundred different varieties of dates, North Americans are familiar with fewer than ten.

The most common date is the **Deglet Noor,** which translated means "Date of the Light." It is a semi-dry date, probably what most of us expect a date to be: superb, plump, smooth-skinned with a beautiful golden-brown color. Chances are good that when you buy packaged dates, you are getting Deglet Noor.

Pete's favorite date is the **Medjool,** which is often sold loose as fresh fruit. Big, soft and immensely sweet, the Medjool is wrapped in a dark, rather wrinkled skin.

The **Barhi** is the softest and tenderest date. It has a thin, slightly crunchy skin and flesh that dissolves in your mouth. The **Zahidi, Halawy** and **Khadrawy** dates are all invert-sugar dates. The **Halawy,** usually imported from Iraq, is semi-dry and often steamed to fatten it up. The **Thoory,** a light, golden-colored date, is the driest variety, sometimes called a *bread date,* and a favorite snack for athletes.

If stored properly, dates will keep indefinitely. You can put them in plastic bags in the freezer and forget them for as long as 5 years! Although you can keep them in the refrigerator for up to a year, it is important to keep dates away from foods with a strong odor, such as onions, because dates have a tendency to absorb smells, which does little to enhance their taste.

Dates contain some of the B vitamins and, despite their sugary sweetness, only 25 calories in a single fruit.

Great eaten out of hand for a quick energy renewer, dates are also a delicious addition to a wide variety of dishes. Try sprinkling a handful on your breakfast cereal, pancakes, waffles or French toast. Include a few coarsely chopped dates the next time you make bran muffins. For something really different, add some cut-up dates to a fruit salad.

An exquisite treat for an appetizer or a light dessert can be made quickly and easily by filling a few date halves with cream cheese, topping each half with a walnut, or by sliding pieces of Brie into date halves and warming them a little. You can use chopped dates in place of raisins in any recipe. If you like playing with your food, toss a few into a bowl of ice cream, yogurt or sour cream. Now that you have a few ideas . . . experiment a little and see what you can come up with!

For a sweet energy booster, dates are hard to beat. Contrary to popular opinion, dates are not dried fruit. They are fresh, but because they are so dry and sugar-packed, they are often mistaken for dried fruit.

Chocolate-Date Confection

1 teaspoon orange extract
1/2 cup (3 oz.) chocolate chips, melted
10-ounce package pitted dates
3/4 cup finely chopped nuts

Stir the orange extract into the melted chocolate. Using a fork, dip the dates into the chocolate, drain briefly over the chocolate, then roll in the nuts. Place on wax paper to cool. *Makes 32 to 36*

<u>1 confection contains:</u> Cal-56, Prot-1g, Carb-8g, Fib-1g, Tot. Fat-3g, Sat. Fat-1g, Chol-1mg, Sdm-2mg

FEIJOAS

A feijoa is not a pineapple guava. If you ever hear anyone refer to a feijoa as a pineapple guava, you have Pete's permission to correct him. No, even better, you have a request from Pete to correct him. A feijoa tastes vaguely like pineapple, among other things, and like guava, it is a member of the myrtle family; but it is not a guava.

A delicious, if rather innocuous-looking fruit, a feijoa is about 2-1/2 to 3 inches in length and shaped like a football with flattened ends. The thin skin can be anywhere from mild lime green to a dark olive in color. Inside is a dense, somewhat gritty, tan-colored flesh similar in texture to that of a very ripe guava with tiny, edible seeds.

Feijoas are on the market in the autumn and winter from California and in the spring and summer from New Zealand. If the fruit is not completely ripe when you buy it, it will ripen uncovered, out of direct sunlight. To speed things up, put a feijoa in a paper bag with a ripe apple until the feijoa feels like a soft ripe pear and smells wonderfully fragrant. But don't wait for much of a change in color; the skin may become only a little darker. Once ripe, feijoas may be refrigerated, uncovered, on a tray lined with paper towels, for up to 2 days.

Feijoas are a good source of vitamin C; four ounces of the fruit have 40 calories.

Feijoa will darken quickly once cut, so if you want to serve them sliced, in a fruit salad or on pancakes or waffles, a squeeze of lemon will help.

For a delicious dessert, serve halved, poached feijoas with un-whipped heavy cream. If you have a large budget, are lucky enough to be able to buy feijoas inexpensively or are simply extravagant, scoop out the flesh of several feijoas, purée it in a food processor or blender, and serve it over sliced bananas, strawberries and oranges. Sprinkle with minced crystallized ginger and you have the dessert of a lifetime!

A delicious treat for breakfast is half a feijoa with a little lime or lemon juice, or if the fruit is a little tart, with a sprinkle of sugar. If you feel like really indulging, scoop a little of the flesh out of the center of a halved fruit, drop in a dollop of vanilla ice cream or a citrus-flavored sherbet and pour a little Cointreau over the top.

Feijoas in Orange Syrup

1/2 cup water

1/4 cup sugar

1/4 cup frozen orange-juice concentrate

Half an orange rind, grated

3 large ripe feijoas, peeled, halved and sliced

In a saucepan, bring the water, sugar, orange juice and orange rind to a boil. Add the sliced feijoas. Lower the heat, cover and gently poach the feijoas for 5 minutes or until the fruit has become slightly soft. Chill for at least 4 hours.

This concoction is great with vanilla ice cream, or with lemon or lime sherbet. But beware of using too much. It is highly concentrated! *Makes 1-1/2 cups*

1/4-cup serving contains: Cal-64, Prot-1g, Carb-16g, Fib-1g, Tot. Fat-0g, Sat. Fat-0g, Chol-0mg, Sdm-2mg

FIGS

Most of us are probably more familiar with dried figs than we are with the fresh fruit. Dried figs are 50% sugar while the fresh contain only 12%. Fresh figs are delicate and must be handled with extreme care. They can be white, green, purple or black, depending on their variety. The flesh can be anywhere from a deep pinkish-red to a yellowish-white, and can be either a mass of tiny edible seeds or seedless.

The very best figs are tree-ripened, but because they are so perishable, they are usually picked and shipped before they are ripe. This means that we rarely get good figs in Canada, but at Pete's we often get beautiful figs. And in some ethnic markets in larger cities, you may occasionally stumble across an excellent fig or two.

Fig season lasts for most of June and from August to late September. Perfectly ripe figs, which should be used immediately, are soft to the touch. When buying figs, avoid those with brown or grayish spots on the skin which indicate that the fruit has turned sour and should not be eaten; they can sour and ferment easily. If you must store them, lay them on a paper towel, cover them with plastic wrap and keep them in the refrigerator, but for no more than 3 days.

Fresh figs are a good source of calcium, phosphorus and iron. Two large figs have about 100 calories.

A ripe fresh fig is delicious simply eaten out of hand; you can eat the skin if you wish, or you can eat the flesh out of the skin. Try some fresh fruit with crusty French bread and cheese or sprinkle fresh figs with kirsch or lime juice and a dollop of fresh cream. A delicious and easy dessert can be made by cutting an "X" in the

For a refreshing starter, cut fresh figs in quarters and drizzle with raspberry liqueur. Serve with slices of goat cheese sprinkled with chopped nuts.

bottom of a fresh fig, stuffing it with some cream cheese and a little mixed spice, wrapping it in foil and baking it in a hot oven for 15 minutes. For an extra-special treat, serve this dessert with fresh gingersnaps.

Figs and Cream

**16 fresh Black Mission figs, peeled, or unpeeled and
    cut into quarters**
Raspberry liqueur
1/4 cup fresh raspberries
1 cup whipping cream

Divide the figs among four separate bowls. Sprinkle with liqueur. Mash the raspberries and blend them into the cream, which can be whipped or not, depending on your preference. Divide the raspberry mash among the four bowls and chill for 2 hours. *Serves* 4

Each serving contains: Cal-365, Prot-3g, Carb-41g, Fib-7g, Tot. Fat-23g, Sat. Fat-14g, Chol-82mg, Sdm-24mg

Figs, Cognac and Cream

A decadent version of Figs and Cream.

8 to 10 fresh figs
3 Tbsp sugar
2 Tbsp cognac
3/4 cup whipping or sour cream
1/4 cup curaçao

Cut the figs in half from top to bottom. Lay them cut side down on a large plate or tray. Sprinkle with sugar and drizzle the cognac over them. Cover and refrigerate for an hour or more.

Mix the cream and curaçao and refrigerate.

To serve, put the figs in a bowl and pour the cream over them. *Serves* 4

Each serving contains: Cal-331, Prot-2g, Carb-35g, Fib-4g, Tot. Fat-17g, Sat. Fat-10g, Chol-61mg, Sdm-18mg

GRAPEFRUIT

Have you ever wondered where the grapefruit got its name? It certainly wasn't because it tastes like grapes. I would tell you if I knew, but no one seems to know for sure where the name came from. It's probably because the fruit grows in clusters like grapes . . . as many as 25 in a cluster!

Grapefruit are certainly a popular fruit and Pete sells them by the truckload. We think the best quality citrus fruit is the Indian River fruit, grown in Indian River, Florida, which has the perfect soil and climate conditions for growing good citrus fruit. But Arizona, California and Texas also produce excellent fruit. The pink and white grapefruit are different in color, but not in flavor or juiciness.

Grapefruit are available all year round, and although they are most abundant from January to June, they are most flavorful and juicy in March and April. Look for fruit with smooth, thin skins that are either well-rounded or slightly flat at both ends. Fruit that is heavy for its size promises juiciness and because the grapefruit is almost three-quarters liquid, juiciness means flavor. Avoid coarse, rough or puffy fruit, or those with a pointed end—an indication that the flesh will be dry and nearly flavorless.

Grapefruit like temperatures around 50F, so unless you are keeping them for more than a week, leave them on the counter. If they are going to be around for more than a week, store them in the refrigerator.

One 8-ounce glass of fresh grapefruit juice has more than enough vitamin C to give you your daily requirement. Half a grapefruit has only 50 calories. For a change, try eating one peeled, like an orange, in segments. They are delicious and nutritious like this.

We all know what a great beginning to the day grapefruit is: its tang is what we need to get us going. If they could come up with a grapefruit that was good with coffee, or a coffee that was good with grapefruit, we'd be all set.

Grapefruit Mousse

3 large eggs, separated
1/2 cup sugar
2 large grapefruit, puréed
Rind of 2 oranges, finely grated
1 Tbsp unflavored gelatin, softened in
1/4 cup cold water
1 cup whipping cream, whipped
Fresh strawberries

Mix the egg yolks and all but 2 tablespoons of the sugar. Beat well. Stir in the puréed grapefruit. Simmer the mixture in the top of a double boiler for 5 minutes or until thick, stirring frequently.

Remove from the heat and stir in the orange rind and gelatin. Transfer the mixture to a large bowl and place it in the freezer, stirring occasionally, until the mixture is thick enough to mound slightly.

Beat the egg whites with the remaining sugar until they are stiff but not dry.

Remove the grapefruit mixture from the freezer and fold it into the whipped cream a little at a time. Then fold one-quarter of the grapefruit-whipped-cream mixture into the egg whites. Fold the egg whites into the rest of the grapefruit-whipped-cream mix. This must be done with great care so that you do not lose the lightness you have beaten into the egg whites.

Put the mousse into individual dessert dishes or a large glass bowl. Chill for at least 5 hours. Serve garnished with a few sliced strawberries. *Serves 6*

Each serving contains: Cal-269, Prot-5g, Carb-25g, Fib-1g, Tot. Fat-17g, Sat. Fat-10g, Chol-161mg, Sdm-49mg

Broiled Grapefruit

2 grapefruit, halved

1 Tbsp melted butter

4 Tbsp honey

Nutmeg

4 Tbsp crème de cassis

Place the grapefruit in a pan close enough together so that they stand upright. Drizzle the melted butter and honey on each half and dust with a little nutmeg.

Pour some water into the bottom of the pan and broil the fruit for 8 minutes, or until they are very hot. For a little excitement, drizzle some crème de cassis on each grapefruit half. *Serves 4*

Each serving contains: Cal-159, Prot-1g, Carb-27g, Fib-2g, Tot. Fat-3g, Sat. Fat-2g, Chol-8mg, Sdm-30mg

GRAPES

There is a bewildering array of grapes of various sizes, colors and tastes: Thompson seedless, Flame seedless, Ruby seedless, Tokay, Emperor, Almeria, Calmeria, Cardinal, Ribier and Muscatels. There are grapes with seeds and those without. Some grapes are small, others are large. They may be red, green or black.

Grapes are available all year. The first six months of the year see our shelves filled with imported grapes, mainly from Chile; the last six months load us down with the fruit from California. When buying grapes, look for plump, firm fruit. White grapes (or *green grapes*, as they are more commonly called) have a tinge of amber at their sweetest. Darker grapes, red and purple ones, should have no signs of green. Although seedless grapes are more popular, grapes with seeds usually have a richer, fuller flavor.

Grapes don't ripen once they leave the vine, so they are ready to eat the moment you buy them. Refrigerate them in a plastic or paper bag for up to 4 days, depending on the variety, but because they are extremely perishable, they should be eaten as soon as possible after purchase.

Grapes contain small amounts of several nutrients. The number of calories they contain, ranging from 70 to 140 calories per cup, depends on the type of grape.

Grapes are most commonly eaten out of hand after a quick wash. They are the perfect complement to ripe soft cheeses, before or after a meal. Try adding a handful to your next vegetable salad for the occasional sweet bite. For an attractive centerpiece, dip grapes, still on the stem, first into beaten egg whites and then granulated sugar, refrigerating them until firm. For an attractive fruit plate, arrange a small bunch of Ribier (or another black grape) with strawberries and sliced kiwi. The color combination is beautiful. For a delicious, nutritious snack for the kids, pop some Flame grapes into the freezer. They'll love them!

Grapes don't ripen once they leave the vine, so they are ready to eat the moment you buy them.

Grapes, Honey and Cognac

1/4 cup mild, fragrant honey

3 Tbsp cognac

1 tsp lime juice

1 pound green seedless grapes, rinsed, drained and dried

Yogurt or sour cream

Mix the honey, cognac and lime juice together. Add the grapes and toss carefully. Chill overnight. Serve with a dollop of yogurt or sour cream. *Serves 4*

Each serving contains: Cal-188, Prot-2g, Carb 39g, Fib-1g, Tot. Fat-2g, Sat. Fat-1g, Chol-4mg, Sdm-17mg

GUAVAS

This luscious tropical fruit may be a little difficult to put your finger on because it occurs in 140 species! But don't rush to your nearest market to see how many types of guavas they sell because most varieties are not easy to find outside their habitat—Australia, India, South Africa, South America and the Caribbean. Guavas can be rounded or pear-shaped; the flesh may range from a hot pink to a gentle salmon color, or it may be white or yellow. The fruit may be loaded with seeds or virtually seedless and sweet or sour. They may taste like pineapples, lemons, strawberries or bananas. The skin is usually a yellowish-green or a dull yellow.

The one constant is the strong fragrance of guavas. Pete has described the smell as varying from that of a pair of sweaty old sneakers to the Garden of Eden. A ripe guava has a rich, heady floral aroma; the less-ripe fruit smells much less appealing.

The peak season for guavas is summer, starting a little early and ending a little late, when they can be purchased either at the peak of their ripeness, or taken home unripe and left on the counter to ripen, filling your kitchen with their sweet aroma. When ripe, guavas will be yellow in color and yield to gentle pressure. Use guavas promptly once ripened, or store them in the refrigerator in a plastic or paper bag for up to 5 days. But remember, handle the ripe fruit with care. Guavas bruise easily.

Guavas are full of vitamin C and a good source of potassium. Four ounces of the raw fruit have about 70 calories.

The pink-fleshed guava is especially satisfying because its color is so unusual. It is a must in a fruit salad, especially in combination with the emerald kiwi, the clear-yellow carambola or the velvet-orange mango. Pink-guava purée is glorious added to whipped cream, snow pudding or rice pudding or spooned over sponge cake. A brief tour with a spoon leaves slashes of pink and streaks of flavor through an otherwise ordinary dessert. But if you are not lucky enough to find a pink guava, you only lose out on visual appeal; no matter what its color, the taste is just as miraculously delicious!

A guava is also delicious eaten out of hand. You can either peel it or eat it from the inside out. If you are a curry lover and have not been savoring the delectable fruit after a curry, do so without delay. A slightly chilled guava is perfect after a spicy meal, cleansing and refreshing. A few slices of peeled guava added to an apple pie before baking will make an exquisite dessert you'll not soon forget. And guava purée over gingerbread is an unusually welcome treat. Guava can be a delicious addition in the most unlikely situations. Come on, be daring. Explore!

Guava-and-Avocado Dessert

A delicious and interesting dessert demonstrating the versatility of the avocado while displaying the wonderful taste of the guava.

1 large avocado, peeled and diced
4 fresh guavas, peeled and diced
Juice of 1 orange
Juice of 1 lime
Sugar to taste
1/2 cup yogurt
1 Tbsp sugar
1 tsp vanilla
Cream
Orange slices or sliced strawberries

Mix the diced avocado and guava with orange juice. Add the lime juice and sugar to taste. Chill the mixture.

Sweeten the yogurt with 1 tablespoon sugar. Add vanilla and enough cream to thin it out just a bit.

Place alternating layers of yogurt and the guava mixture in a glass bowl or individual parfait glasses. Decorate with orange slices or sliced strawberries. *Serves 4*

Each serving contains: Cal-227, Prot-3g, Carb-30g, Fib-8g, Tot. Fat-12g, Sat. Fat-4g, Chol-14mg, Sdm-25mg

KIWANOS

This truly exotic-looking fruit is a cherished favorite of the African hippopotamus. At least, that's what Pete says. If they are a favorite of the hippos, that is because they do not have to pay for them. It is just about as expensive as any exotic fruit on the market and you certainly aren't paying for taste.

A kiwano looks like a very large Easter Egg and is indeed beautiful in appearance. Its color can range from deep yellow to golden-orange. In shape, it is spherical and covered with little round-ended spikes. Inside is a soft, textured flesh looking rather like kiwi fruit, but packed with white edible seeds.

If you had seen Pete feature this fruit on CBC's "Midday," you would have seen him do his taste test. No doubt three-quarters of the viewers were watching the spoonful of gorgeous, emerald-colored, seed-laden fruit as it moved towards Pete's mouth. We all waited for his ecstatic "Delicious!" Instead we got "Yuck!"

Kiwanos are cucumber jelly in one of the most beautiful coverings Mother Nature ever designed. Although they may be superbly refreshing if you live in one of the hottest climates on earth, and especially if you're a hippo, in North America these fruit should probably be purchased exclusively for their appearance or not at all.

Kiwanos were discovered by a New Zealander on holiday—a clever New Zealander on holiday. He took the fruit home with him and grew acres and acres of it and started shipping it around the world, marketing it as a brand-new fruit.

Kiwi

Although this fruit is native to China, it did so well when introduced to New Zealand that it was renamed after that country's national symbol—the kiwi bird. Kiwi is grown in Israel, California, Italy, Spain, France and Chile, to name a few of the countries, but most of the fruit found in North American markets comes from New Zealand or California. This exotic fruit exploded onto the North American marketplace and has become so popular that it is now almost as easy to find as apples. There is no doubt that this little brown fruit is here to stay. (It is rather interesting to note that several years ago the kiwi, then known as the *Chinese gooseberry*, made an attempt to "explode" onto the fruit market. Its lack of success then is now largely attributed to its unappealing former name.)

Thanks to the New Zealand-California balance, kiwis are in good supply all year round, with California fruit in our markets from October to May and New Zealand fruit from May to October.

When purchasing kiwi, choose fruit that is firm. You can allow them to ripen as much or as little as you like. Just keep them uncovered and out of direct sunlight for a few days. If you want them to ripen more quickly, put them in a paper bag with a ripe apple, banana or pear. If you are buying kiwis to eat immediately, choose those that are uniformly soft or firm without squishy areas. They should yield to gentle pressure. Fruit that is too soft will be mealy and lack flavor. Once ripe, kiwis will retain their texture and flavor, if stored in a paper or plastic bag and refrigerated, for up to a week.

One small kiwi contains enough vitamin C for your daily requirement; 4 ounces of the flesh—one fairly large kiwi—contain 40 calories.

A real treat when working on the kiwi display at Pete's is to find a split kiwi. We break the fruit in half and eat it right out of the skin. The skin is edible but not too many people enjoy it. My brother, who is a kiwi fanatic, worked hard at eating the skin, but he gave up after about a month, claiming that it was not worth the effort.

The fruit is not easy to peel; use a sharp knife or a vegetable peeler. Inside is beautiful emerald flesh surrounding an edible, white center, around which are swirls of tiny black seeds. Peeled and sliced, kiwis are beautiful in fruit salads or served with fresh or poached fruit. In combination with strawberries, they make a splendid garnish on sponge or angel-food cake.

Kiwi contains an enzyme that prevents gelatin from setting, so use kiwi only as a garnish for gelatin molds. Some glazes, if used on kiwi, will become watery if they are allowed to stand, so don't glaze kiwi unless you plan to serve it right away. Another enzyme in kiwi will separate milk, but don't worry about mixing kiwis with ice cream or other milk products; if the two are mixed, just serve them immediately.

Kiwis are one of the hardiest fruits for shipping and handling. They are picked green and they have their own built-in protection in the form of a fuzzy skin, which, although thin, is tough. If they are refrigerated the moment they are picked, they will not ripen until moved to warmer temperatures.

Cooking with kiwi is generally not recommended; the fruit loses some of its tang and turns a rather unpleasant shade of olive green. And because the fruit is so beautiful and so wonderfully refreshing, there is no reason to eat it any way but raw.

Kiwi Sorbet

This is a wonderful end to a meal. The last time I made it, I served it in individual cups, surrounded by sliced strawberries and topped with whipped cream. It looked magnificent and tasted even better.

2/3 cup sugar
1-1/2 cups water
1/4 cup fresh lime juice
1/4 cup fresh lemon juice
2 cups kiwi, puréed
3/4 cup orange juice

Stir the sugar into the water and bring to a boil. Simmer for 5 minutes and then cool the mixture, refrigerating it for 1 hour.

Add the lime and lemon juices to the kiwi purée and chill. Blend the syrup, the purée and the orange juice. Pour the mixture into an ice-cream maker and proceed according to the manufacturer's instructions.

Like most sherbets, kiwi sorbet profits from a rest in the freezer for a day or two. *Makes 1 quart*

1/2-cup serving contains: Cal-114, Prot-1g, Carb-29g, Fib-1g, Tot. Fat-0g, Sat. Fat-0g, Chol-0mg, Sdm-3mg

KUMQUATS

Occasionally when I am making fruit baskets at Pete's, I happen to be lucky enough to find a box of kumquats with which to decorate the baskets. This is bliss, for not only do the tiny oblong, orange-colored kumquats make a fruit basket look heavenly, they are the best things to pop in your mouth and munch on every once in a while. The combination of the silky-sweet peel and the lip-curling, sour pulp makes them wonderfully out-of-the-ordinary, strangely delicious and refreshing. And, from an aesthetic point of view, these cheerful, bright-orange creations are hard to beat.

Kumquats are a winter fruit, appearing in November and, if we're lucky, lasting until late April or early May. Look for firm, not squishy-soft, fruit. Don't be afraid to give a kumquat a gentle squeeze. If you buy kumquats planning to use them within a few days, leave them out; otherwise you can store them in the refrigerator for up to 2 weeks. They tend to spoil more rapidly than oranges because they are so thin-skinned.

Kumquats are the ideal garnish. All you do is wash them and use them— no peeling, no trimming. Put kumquat slices on your next carrot cake after it has been iced.

Kumquats are an excellent source of vitamin C. Four of these tiny fruits contain 75 calories.

There is no need to waste anything with kumquats. All you do is wash them and use them. No peeling, nothing to cut off, nothing to throw away. Because they make beautiful garnishes, they may be blanched in boiling water for 15 seconds, chilled in ice water, dried, sliced thinly and tossed by the handful onto a fruit or vegetable salad.

If you want to add a little color and pizzazz to your fruit bowl, toss them where they will look splendid nestling among black grapes. If you can manage to get your hands on some strawberries too, you will be astonished at how beautiful a combination the three can be. But of course the easiest way of all to eat these little wonders is to give them a quick roll between your finger and thumb, blending the flavor of skin and flesh, and pop them in your mouth. What a treat!

Kumquat-and-Broccoli Salad

Pete never lets kumquat season pass without making this salad at least once. He doesn't remember where he got the recipe but he has never forgotten it. It is not only great-tasting, but great-looking too.

1 bunch broccoli

10 kumquats

4 Tbsp extra-virgin olive oil

1 clove garlic, minced

2 Tbsp lime juice

1/2 tsp sugar

Salt and pepper

Pinch of savory

10 black olives

Peel broccoli stems and cut them into smallish pieces; cut the head into florets. Steam for 3 minutes, or until the broccoli is bright green but still firm.

Boil the kumquats in the broccoli water for 15 seconds. Chill the fruit in ice water. Cut half the kumquats into quarters; slice the rest thinly.

Heat the oil and garlic very slowly, until the garlic becomes a very light beige, about 5 minutes. Add the lime juice, sugar, salt, pepper, savory and quartered kumquats, and purée the mixture in a blender or food processor.

Add the purée to the broccoli and sliced kumquats and toss well. Chill. Add the olives just before serving; sprinkle with salt and grind on some pepper. *Serves 2*

Each serving contains: Cal-397, Prot-8g, Carb-31g, Fib 14g, Tot. Fat-30g, Sat. Fat-4g, Chol-0mg, Sdm-399mg

LEMONS

Where would we be without lemons? On salads, in mayonnaise, in sauces, in butter for vegetables, in desserts, cakes, soufflés, pies and sherbet—so much is enhanced by a little lemon juice. Sliced lemons provide a colorful and tasty garnish; lemon rind is a zesty addition to just about anything. It may seem an odd parallel, but the lemon is perhaps the onion of the fruit world. Just as there are few vegetable recipes that aren't enhanced by the addition of onion, so there are few fruits as indispensable as the lemon.

The Gold Rush of 1849 first drew attention to the lemon. High in vitamin C, this yellow citrus fruit was used as a cure and as a preventive for scurvy; miners were willing to pay exorbitant sums for a single lemon. This instant demand caused lemon trees to be planted in such numbers that we are still reaping the benefits more than 100 years later.

Lemons are available all year. The lemons you'll see in the U. S. markets come from Arizona, California, Florida, South America and Spain. When buying lemons, look for fine-textured skins and for fruit that is heavy for its size. Coarse-skinned lemons, or those that are light in weight, don't have as much juice. Pale-yellow lemons or fruit with green overtones are likely to be acidic. Deep-yellow lemons are more mature and generally not as sour. Lemons may be kept for several weeks in the refrigerator or on the counter.

If you or any of your acquaintances should happen to contract a dose of scurvy, lemons are the answer. Lemons are an excellent source of vitamin C, a good source of calcium, phosphorus and potassium. Four ounces of the peeled fruit contain about 25 calories.

Lemons are indispensable—as a garnish, a flavor and a source of vitamins, in desserts, cakes, sauces and a hundred other ways.

Lemon Poppy-Seed Bread

If you are a lemon lover, you will become devoted to this bread.

4 eggs

1-1/2 cups oil

1-1/2 cups half-and-half

2 Tbsp lemon juice

1/2 cup poppy seeds

Rind of 2 lemons

1-1/2 cups sugar

3 cups flour

1-1/2 tsp baking soda

2 tsp baking powder

1 tsp salt

GLAZE
Juice of 2 lemons
1/4 cup sugar

Beat together the eggs, oil, half-and-half, 2 tablespoons lemon juice and poppy seeds.

In a separate bowl, combine the lemon rind, sugar, flour, baking soda, baking powder and salt. Stir the dry ingredients into the egg mixture and blend until smooth and uniform.

Pour the batter into 2 greased loaf pans. Bake at 325F for 1 hour.

Combine ingredients for the glaze and pour it over the loaves while they are hot and still in the pans. *Makes 2 loaves*

LIMES

Do you know why Englishmen are called *limeys*? Pete told me that during the California Gold Rush, lemons were almost as dear as the gold itself. Why? Because they could provide enough vitamin C to prevent scurvy. In an effort to combat this complaint without paying the ludicrous prices demanded for lemons, English soldiers were rationed one lime a day. A more-common explanation is that a century earlier lime juice was given to British sailors for the same reason. Brits have been known as *limeys* ever since.

Limes are a funny little fruit, largely overlooked by many cooks. This is unfortunate, because limes add a little zap, which brightens up many foods. There are many different types of limes, the Persian being the most common.

Nothing is more refreshing on a really hot day than lime sherbet. Add some slices of lime in your iced tea or, like Pete, insist on lime in your gin and tonic. Try squeezing a lime over your salad.

Limes are available all year round, because they are now grown in a number of tropical countries, as well as in California and Arizona. Look for limes that are firm and bright; heavy fruit will be juicy. Because the skin on a lime is thinner than that of a lemon, be careful when handling them. Limes will keep well in the refrigerator for 3 weeks.

Limes are an excellent source of vitamin C. A 4-ounce lime has less than 30 calories.

1/8 of a loaf contains: Cal-425, Prot-5g, Carb-43, Fib-1g, Tot. Fat-27g, Sat. Fat-4g, Chol-61mg, Sdm-339mg

Lemons and limes are more than vaguely alike. They have the same distinctive shape and the taste is similar, but limes are less acidic and much more fragrant.

Spiced Limeade

On the hottest, driest day of the year, try this thirst quencher.

1/2 cup sugar, or to taste
2 sticks of cinnamon
5 whole cloves
1 cup water
Juice of 6 large limes
Ginger ale
1 lime, sliced
Sprigs of mint

Simmer the sugar, cinnamon and cloves in the water for 10 minutes. Cool and add the lime juice.

Fill glasses with crushed ice or ice cubes, and fill each half full with the lime-juice mixture. Top up the glasses with ginger ale, and garnish with a slice of lime and a sprig of mint. *Serves 4*

1 serving contains: Cal-162, Prot-0g, Carb-44g, Fib-1g, Tot. Fat-0g, Sat. Fat-0g, Chol-0mg, Sdm-10mg

Lime Butter

This easy butter is delicious on hot vegetables.

1 cup soft butter
8 tsp lime juice
2 tsp finely grated lime peel

Beat the butter until light and fluffy. Blend in the lime juice and lime peel. Mix well. *Makes 1 cup*

1 tablespoon contains: Cal-102, Prot-0g, Carb-0g, Fib-0g, Tot. Fat-12g, Sat. Fat-7g, Chol-31mg, Sdm-117mg

LOQUATS

Loquats are delicious with kiwi and strawberries or raspberries. The fruit in syrup is great any time, as a snack or with a meal. Try them in meringue shells or with pound cake.

One morning when we were setting up the stall, Pete handed me a rather odd-looking little fruit and said, "Try this, I think they're absolu'ely beau'iful!" I looked dubiously at the little thing in my hand, steeled my nerves and ate it. (Pete has been known to invite new employees to eat a hot pepper. An unpleasant surprise!) To my delight, it was delicious!

Loquats have one big problem. In a market that places so much importance on appearance, ripe loquats look rather insignificant; they are small and they bruise easily. Throughout the Mediterranean and in countries where loquats are popular, such as Portugal, China and India, loquats are eaten and enjoyed without regard to their less-than-perfect appearance.

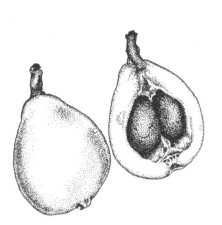

A loquat looks something like an apricot, is 1 to 2 inches in length and usually egg-shaped. It has a downy skin that is a dark golden-yellow and firm flesh ranging from cream to orange with one or more large seeds. In taste, it walks the tightrope between tart and sweet and can vary from mild to densely rich.

In North America, loquats are available only fleetingly, from March to June. When buying them, choose large fruit that is soft and sweetly aromatic, preferably without stems. Loquats should be refrigerated only if they are moments away from spoiling. Otherwise, you'd be smarter to cook them in a syrup to preserve all of their wonderful taste and aroma.

Loquats are a first-rate source of vitamin A and a good source of potassium. They are also low in calories, with only 50 in four ounces of the flesh.

Most loquats don't need peeling. Quarter and seed them, or, if you like, cut the fruit in half, like Pete, without worrying too much about the seeds. Just be sure to remove the stems.

Loquat Heaven

1 cup loquat chunks

3 bananas, sliced

1 orange, peeled and sliced

1 cup pineapple chunks

1/2 cup grated coconut

Toss together the loquat, bananas, orange and pineapple. Sprinkle with the coconut just before serving. *Serves 4*

Each serving contains: Cal-125, Prot-2g, Carb-32g, Fib-4g, Tot. Fat-4g, Sat. Fat-3g, Chol-0mg, Sdm-3mg

Loquats in Syrup

1 cup water

1/2 cup sugar

Juice and peel from 1 small lemon

1 pound ripe loquats, rinsed and stemmed, with the blossom ends cut off

Simmer the water, sugar, lemon juice and lemon peel, covered, for 3 minutes. Let the syrup stand for about 10 minutes to let the flavor develop. Add the fruit to the syrup and simmer gently, covered, for five minutes or until the fruit is tender. Cool, uncovered, in the syrup and chill.

Loquats in syrup keep for months in a plastic container in the freezer. *Serves 4*

Each serving contains: Cal-154, Prot-1g, Carb-40g, Fib-2g, Tot. Fat-0g, Sat. Fat-0g, Chol-0mg, Sdm-3mg

LYCHEES

These perfectly wonderful little fruits are almost indescribable. Known as *lychees*, *litchis* and *lichees*, they are usually expensive; but they are worth the price, no matter what it is.

When we have them at Pete's, it is rare that Pete will pass the lychee display without picking up a few to savor. And they are a fruit to be savored. They are small, about 1 to 2 inches in diameter, and have a warty, thin, tough skin that ranges in color from a warm rose to a dull brown. Inside this rather inconspicuous outside lies a true tropical delight. The flesh of this fruit is tight, translucent and a shiny white in color. The consistency is similar to that of a peeled grape and the taste is rather musky and grapey, with a hint of violets—a juicy paradise for your taste buds. In the midst of this delectable flesh is a smooth, mahogany-colored pit, beautiful but inedible.

Lychees are available from December to May and in July and August. Grown in Israel, China, Taiwan, South Africa and Thailand, they are also grown in Florida, but in extremely limited numbers because they are very susceptible to the cold.

Look for full, heavy lychees that still have some of the stem attached. Fruit with a hint of red color tends to be fresher. Don't worry if the shell is mottled with brown; this occurs very soon after the fruit has been picked. But avoid shriveled or cracked fruit or those that seem too soft. Although they will lose some of their heavenly perfume, lychees will keep for 2 weeks in the refrigerator or 1 week at room temperature.

Lychees are packed with vitamin C and are a good source of potassium. Surprisingly, for all that sweetness, they contain only about 80 calories in 4 ounces.

Pete maintains, rightly, that the only way to eat these little fruits is fresh. They are excellent stuffed with cream cheese (thinned with a bit of milk or mayonnaise) and topped with a walnut or two. They are also superb in a fruit salad: peel them and remove the pits by cutting the fruit in half, gently loosening the pit and lifting it out. But best of all, simply put a bowl of lychees in the middle of the table, give everyone a plate for skins and pits and watch them enjoy!

One day a customer approached my cash register with a large bag of lychees. I told her the price, which was almost $20, and asked if she wanted to put some back. She smiled serenely and said, "No, it's all right. They are worth every penny." I have to agree.

In some areas only canned lychees are available. Drain before using, then split and fill them with sweetened cream cheese for a quick dessert. Perfect following a Chinese meal.

Lychees Stuffed with Ginger Cream

3 ounces cream cheese

2 tablespoons chopped crystallized ginger

2 tablespoons orange or pineapple juice

1 11-ounce can lychees, drained

In a small bowl combine cream cheese, ginger and orange or pineapple juice. Spoon into lychee cavities. *Makes 16 to 18*

1 confection contains: Cal-43, Prot-1g, Carb-6g, Fib-0g, Tot. Fat-2g, Sat. Fat-1g, Chol-6mg, Sdm-16mg

MANGOES

Mangoes are relatively easy to find in season, which is fortunate for those of us who love them.

The fruit is common in the tropics and no longer the rarity it once was in North America. A ripe, fresh mango is almost unbeatable in terms of its flavor and, if properly cut, the texture is blissful. Mangoes tend to be very fibrous and, without a knife, they are difficult to eat out of hand. It takes about half an hour to consume a mango and at least an hour to get the fibrous bits of the flesh out from between your teeth. But let me assure you that it is more than worth it. In flavor, a mango is a cross between apricots and peaches, although even sweeter and with a hint of something tropical. The texture is smooth and dense.

The best way to deal with a mango is to cut it down each side, from top to bottom. Do *not* try to twist the fruit away from the seed; the two are firmly connected! Insert your knife into the middle of the fruit and cut the flesh away from the seed. Then lay the fruit halves skin side down on a cutting board. Slice the flesh, but not the skin, lengthwise and then crosswise. (This technique deals with the stringiness of the fruit and makes it much easier to eat.) Then all you have to do is push the skin so that the flesh pops up and voilà, mango cubes beautifully displayed on their own serving dish! If you are adding the fruit to a salad or a dessert, simply slice the cubes of flesh from the skin.

Mangoes are available from January to August, with their peak season in early summer. Coming in 101 different shapes and colors, they can be round, heart-shaped, kidney-shaped or oval; they might be green, yellow, orange, red or any combination of these colors. Look for mangoes with nice tight skins, and avoid those with loose, wrinkled-looking skin or soft spots.

A ripe mango should yield to gentle pressure like a ripe peach. The stem end will smell sweetly fragrant, the aroma faint but noticeable. Avoid those that smell acidic.

An unripe mango will ripen on your counter, uncovered, out of direct sunlight. Mangoes do not like the cold, although the fruit is especially good if chilled briefly before serving. Gentle thumb pressure is the best way to tell if a mango is ripe because, despite the variety of colors mangoes come in, few of them go through any noticeable color change as they ripen. If you must store the fruit, keep it in a plastic or paper bag in the refrigerator for no more than a day or two.

Mangoes are an excellent source of vitamins A and C and a good source of potassium. Four ounces of the flesh have 75 calories.

For a truly exotic sauce, purée mango flesh in a food processor or blender and spoon it over fresh fruit, or sauté sliced mangoes in butter, sugar and your favorite liqueur and serve it over ice cream, yogurt, or a simple light cake. Mangoes are, of course, delicious simply eaten out of hand, without any embellishment.

Mangoes are delicious raw or cooked. Try mango cubes on your waffles or pancakes, or as a delicious addition to fruit salad.

Pete's Mango Heaven

This is the next best thing to paradise. Try it with yogurt, ice cream or sour cream.

- **2 Tbsp butter**
- **1 Tbsp lime juice**
- **1 Tbsp brown sugar**
- **1 ripe mango, about 1 pound, peeled and cut into about 10 slices**
- **1 large firm, ripe banana, sliced**
- **3 Tbsp Grand Marnier**
- **3 Tbsp brandy**
- **Freshly grated coconut**

Melt the butter in a frying pan and add the lime juice and sugar, stirring until the sugar is dissolved. Add the sliced fruit and cook for 2 minutes on each side until heated through and slightly soft.

Add the alcohol and flambé. Garnish with the grated coconut. Serve immediately. *Serves 4*

Each serving contains: Cal-153, Prot 1g, Carb-18g, Fib-2g, Tot. Fat-7g, Sat. Fat-4g, Chol-16mg, Sdm-62mg

MANGOSTEENS

Yet another delight from southern climes! Mangosteens are miraculous little things, one of the most fragrant tropical fruits you will find anywhere. They are not particularly remarkable on the outside; a short, thick, dark-green stem is attached to the fruit where four symmetrical sepals meet the reddish-purple shell. Inside the tough, hard skin are two comparatively large, inedible seeds and a spherical collection of pure white syrupy sections, one of the most tender-fleshed fruits you will ever experience.

Mangosteens are bought ripe because they are sold ripe, because they are picked ripe and do not ripen once harvested. So you can savor one of these delights without having to exercise your patience! This fruit, which is often sold by weight, is expensive, especially so because it is heavy and most of the weight is in the inedible skin and seeds. The actual fruit is usually no more than 2 inches in diameter.

The shells, which are full of tannin and used in the Far East for tanning leather or making ink, make getting at the fruit a bit of an adventure. The best way to release the fruit is to cut through the shell with a knife, being careful not to slice the flesh, and gently pry out the sections of the fruit.

The best way to eat mangosteens is raw. You can serve them with half their shells off or without the shell, all by themselves, in a fruit salad or folded into whipped cream.

Mangosteens are available off and on all year. They are grown in Indonesia, Thailand and central Brazil. Because of their thick shell, they keep well in the refrigerator for up to a week or on the counter for 3 days.

Mangosteens are a good source of vitamin C. Four ounces of the flesh have 75 calories.

Mangosteen-Champagne Sorbet

6 mangosteens, peeled and pushed through a sieve

2/3 cup champagne or sparkling white wine

1 egg white

1 Tbsp sugar

1/2 cup raspberries, puréed or pushed through a sieve

1 kiwi, thinly sliced

Mix the mangosteen pulp with the champagne. In a separate bowl, beat the egg white until stiff, gradually adding the sugar. Fold the mangosteen into the egg white and freeze, stirring occasionally, so that the sorbet remains light.

Serve with the raspberry purée and decorate with slices of kiwi.
Serves 3 to 4

Each serving contains: Cal-146, Prot-2g, Carb-28g, Fib-1g, Tot. Fat-1g, Sat. Fat-0g, Chol-0mg, Sdm-17mg

Pete's Tropical Paradise

One evening Pete asked me to get something together for him for dessert: a coconut, some bananas and about 6 mangosteens.

I asked him the next day, "How was the dessert?" He got a dreamy look in his eye and said, "Beau'iful, absolu'ly beau'iful." I asked him what he had done and he explained that he had poached the bananas in the coconut liquid for about 5 to 7 minutes. He then added some coarsely grated coconut flesh and the mangosteens, which he poached for 2 minutes, just until warmed through. Pete then flambéed the whole thing in Cointreau and served it over ice cream. And if that doesn't sound heavenly, I don't know what does. If you are feeling particularly adventurous and in the mood for a truly exquisite dessert . . . you now know what to try!

MELONS

When we have cantaloupes cut in half and ready to eat on the sale shelf at Pete's, I take one home and eat half for supper and the other half for breakfast. True indulgence, but 100% enjoyable!

One of the saddest stories I know involves my mother, my grandmother and a field of Crenshaw melons. (At least we think they were Crenshaws. They were grown from special seeds, imported by a friend from Arizona.) About 25 years ago my grandmother, who has a farm in the fruit belt in Ontario, had a field of melons that were painfully close to being ripe. She and my mother went out to have a look at the fruit and decided that it would be ready to be picked and eaten the next day. The whole family went to bed with dreams of the luscious treats. They got up the next morning, raced out to harvest the fruit and found that every last melon was gone! The horses had beaten them to it; they had gone into the field and eaten every Crenshaw. I don't think my grandmother has ever grown melons again. Even now, when she tells that story, a tear comes to her eye. Mine too!

Summer and melons go together, and even in midwinter a slice of melon is a slice of sunshine.

Cantaloupe, honeydew and watermelon, the more common melons, are available all year round; other melons have definite seasons. At Pete's, we have them from New Zealand, Chile, Mexico, Arizona, California and Israel, to name just a few places. Most melons are sold underripe and can do with a day or two at room temperature. Look for melons that are evenly ripe, without soft or damp spots. Ripe melons should be stored in the refrigerator, tightly wrapped in plastic, because a ripe melon will give off ethylene gas and cause other produce to spoil.

Melons are a good source of vitamin C; cantaloupe and honeydew are rich in potassium and most melons with red or deep-orange flesh provide some vitamin A. Four ounces of melon flesh have between 30 and 40 calories.

Cantaloupes are available year round; they are especially abundant in the summer months during the California and Arizona harvest. To make sure that they're perfectly ripe, give cantaloupes a day or two at room temperature before serving them; the flesh will be softer and juicier. Look for melons that are slightly oval, at least 5 inches in diameter, with a golden background color. Both pronounced netting and a very small crack or two at the stem end are signs of sweetness. The fruit should also give a little when pressed.

Honeydews are usually available from May to November. The ripe fruit should have an aroma and be a little soft at the stem end. An unripe melon will ripen at room temperature if kept out of direct sunlight. *Green honeydews* are yellowish-white, tinged with green with a satiny blush. Choose melons that weigh at least five pounds and are smooth and firm. *Orange-flesh honeydews* are a cross between a cantaloupe and a honeydew. The outside looks like a honeydew but

A good melon is one of the chief delights of the fruit world. A slice of ripe, juicy melon is a wonderful way to start or end a day. Look for Ogen or Galia melons from Israel. They are wonderfully sweet and heavily scented.

inside, the flesh looks and tastes like a cantaloupe. When ripe, the skin should be a light pink.

Casabas are golden-yellow in color with a hint of green at the stem end. They will keep, uncut, in a cool place for a month.

The **Santa Claus** looks like a small watermelon with the flesh of not-quite-so-sweet honeydew. As with green honeydews, look for melons that weigh at least 5 pounds and have bright-yellow stripes.

The **Canary** melon is Pete's favorite. A ripe canary will be sweet, juicy and fragrant and will have a firm, crisp texture. Look for a melon weighing from 4 to 5 pounds, and canary yellow in color.

The **Myan** melon was developed by horticulturists in Texas to be grown specifically in the Guatemalan highlands where, in fact, most of them are now grown. The Myan is a cross between a honey-dew and a casaba melon. The taste is slightly richer than a honey-dew, the color rich and creamy, the flesh a very light green. Myan melons are ready to eat by the time they reach your market.

Watermelon: the only way to be sure that you are getting a good watermelon is to buy it cut. If you are buying a whole water-melon and want a crisp, sweet-fleshed melon, look for one with dull skin and a velvety bloom of symmetrical shape. The back-ground color of the skin should be turning from white or pale green to a creamy, light-yellowish color.

Specialty melons: keep an eye out for *Ogen* or *Galia* melons from Israel. Both are wonderfully sweet and heavily scented. The Galia tastes like an ultra-sweet, juicy cross between a honeydew and a cantaloupe. It has thick, light-colored flesh and a barky, golden skin when ripe. Galia melons are available from October to January.

Melons are a very versatile fruit, mainly because the fruit is sweet and delicately flavored. Serve slices of melon topped with ice cream or fruit sorbet; put melon balls in your next fruit salad. Halve a cantaloupe and fill it with cubes or balls of different types of melon, drizzle the whole thing with some fruit-flavored liqueur and serve it with yogurt or vanilla ice cream.

Cantaloupe Ice Cream

A super way to eat cantaloupe. Cold, refreshing, delicious and beautiful.

> 1 medium cantaloupe, flesh removed from rind
> 2 Tbsp lemon juice
> 1/4 cup honey
> 1/4 cup sugar
> 3 cups whipping cream
> 1 tsp vanilla extract

Cut fruit into small pieces and purée it with lemon juice in a blender or food processor.

2/3-cup serving contains: Cal-260, Prot-2g, Carb-16g, Fib-0g, Tot. Fat-22g, Sat. Fat-14g, Chol-82mg, Sdm-27mg

In a separate bowl, blend the honey, sugar and cream. Add the melon purée and the vanilla. Stir until the sugar is dissolved.

Pour the mixture into an ice-cream maker and freeze according to the manufacturer's instructions, or pour it into a large square pan, cover with foil and put it in the freezer for 4 hours or until firm, stirring 2 or 3 times. *Makes 2 quarts*

Honeydew Sorbet

A superbly refreshing ice.

1-1/2 cups sugar

1-1/2 cups water

1 medium honeydew, flesh removed from rind and cut up

2 tsp lime juice

Put the sugar and water in a medium-size saucepan, stirring over medium heat until the sugar is dissolved. Cook until the syrup reaches 220F on a candy thermometer, or until the syrup makes a thread when poured from a spoon into cold water.

Cool the syrup at room temperature for 10 minutes.

Purée melon and lime juice in a blender or food processor. Pour the purée into the syrup, and blend.

Pour the mixture into an ice-cream maker and freeze according to the manufacturer's instructions, or pour the mixture into a large square pan, cover with foil and put it in the freezer for 4 hours or until firm, stirring 2 or 3 times. *Makes 2 quarts*

2/3-cup serving contains: Cal-136, Prot-1g, Carb-35g, Fib-1g, Tot. Fat-0g, Sat. Fat-0g, Chol-0mg, Sdm-12mg

NECTARINES

There are many, many varieties of nectarines, but only two types—the freestone and the clingstone. Most nectarines that are now available are red, rather than peach-colored, and have firm, sweet flesh. Nectarines are a versatile fruit, standing up well to cooking and combining well with other fruits, berries or dairy products. They can be substituted for peaches in any recipe, but be prepared to make an allowance for the fact that they are not quite as juicy.

Happily for nectarine eaters, the harvesting of the California fruit (the main source for most of North America) extends from early June until the middle of September, so we can enjoy them throughout the summer. Nectarines are also available from New Zealand and Chile from Christmas until mid-March. Look for fruit that has an orange-yellow background with red areas. The fruit should be plump and bright, and firm to moderately hard.

Nectarines are not a cross between plums and peaches, as people often think. A nectarine is a nectarine is a nectarine, and has been for many centuries.

If you are buying a nectarine for lunch or to eat on your way back to the office, choose one that yields to gentle palm pressure. The fruit should almost be as soft as a ripe peach. Avoid fruit that is shriveled, dull or hard, indicating that it was probably immature when picked. Nectarines, like peaches, don't get more sugary once they have been harvested. You can, however, ripen nearly ripe fruit at room temperature, out of direct sunlight. You can also store the ripe fruit in a paper or plastic bag in the refrigerator for up to a week.

Nectarines are a good source of vitamins A and C. One medium-size fruit has 70 calories. As an added bonus, nectarines are a "detergent fruit," excellent for your teeth.

Nectarines are delicious simply washed and eaten out of hand. Try them sliced on cereal or pancakes; add slices of nectarine to fruit or mixed-green salads. Sautéed, grilled or baked, nectarines are a delicious addition to any meal. Try serving nectarines with ice cream or plain yogurt, or poaching them in water, sugar and white wine to serve over pound cake or fresh sponge cake.

Nectarine Sort-of Pie

A delicious and original end to a meal.

> **3 eggs, well beaten**
> **1/2 cup milk**
> **1/2 cup cake flour**
> **Pinch of salt**
>
> **FILLING**
> **2 cups nectarines, sliced**
> **3 Tbsp honey**
> **1 Tbsp lemon juice**
> **Sour cream**
> **Cinnamon**

Beat the eggs, milk, cake flour and salt together and pour the mixture into a buttered 9-inch pie pan. Bake at 450F for 15 minutes, pricking as needed to release some of the air. Bake at 350F for another 10 minutes or until golden. Let the crust cool for a few minutes.

In a medium-size bowl, blend the nectarines with the honey and let them stand for at least 5 minutes.

Sprinkle lemon juice on the cooked crust and cover with the nectarines and honey. Spread with sour cream and sprinkle with cinnamon. *Serves 6*

Each serving contains: Cal-224, Prot-7g, Carb-25g, Fib-1g, Tot. Fat-12g, Sat. Fat-6g, Chol-126mg, Sdm-107mg

ORANGES

Under this rather broad heading you can expect to find any orange-colored fruit larger than a kumquat. It is not really fair to lump mandarins, clementines, satsumas, Minneolas, tangelos and tangerines together under "oranges," because they are not oranges. However, it does seem the simplest way to deal with this diverse group of citrus fruits.

All members of the orange family are excellent sources of vitamin C, with approximately 62 calories in a single fruit.

The best of the orange season extends from November until April, because this is when the Florida and California seasons are in full swing. The oranges from these two states are some of the sweetest and juiciest in the world.

The season starts with several different types of seeded **Valencia** juice oranges, the most common types being the Pineapple and the Hamlin. Both tend to be fibrous, although flavorful. Valencias are good for eating but are renowned for their juice. They are more fibrous than the navels. California Valencias are on the market from late May until early mid-November.

From Christmas, until mid-May, California provides the North American market with its most popular eating orange, the seedless **navel.** It is the only orange that is consistently seedless, but it does not have the juiciness of the Valencias. The navel usually peels easily and separates in tender segments without any tough pith. Pete does, however, issue a warning: although navels have a reputation for being sweet, and indeed, as the season progresses, some of the sweetest oranges are navels, be careful with the early fruit as it can be a little sharp.

California grows more navels than Florida, and because North Americans are now beginning to see significant imports of navel oranges from countries in the southern hemisphere, such as Argentina, Pete thinks that in a few years we will have a good supply of fresh navels year-round.

It is worth noting that there are "specialty" oranges available in small quantities at higher prices and for short periods of time. For about one month each year, we sell **Seville** oranges at Pete's. They are set well away from the rest of the oranges and adorned with a large sign that advises the unwary of their incredibly tart nature. I was warning one customer about eating them and she looked at me and said, "Oh, I buy them to eat them." I asked her if she had ever eaten them before. "Sure have! I like them." My mouth fell open and I looked at her as if she were a lunatic. Then she grinned and added, "I like eating lemons too." Most of the Seville orange crop is used in orange marmalade. The Seville orange rind is coveted for this purpose but the flesh is unpleasantly tart for most palates.

Question: Are Florida or California oranges better? Pete explains: California oranges tend to look better—cleaner and brighter—but they are thicker skinned and less juicy than their Florida counterparts. A California fan can tell you that their oranges are infinitely better than Florida's, and vice versa. Most of California's oranges are grown to be eaten; Florida's are grown for processing.

The other specialty orange worth mention is the **blood** orange. Usually available longer than the Seville orange and later in the year, its supply is also limited. These oranges are very popular in Mediterranean countries. They are inclined to be tart-sweet with a faint berry-like flavor. From the outside they look like any other orange, although they have a red blush. Inside they have the most incredible flesh, ranging in color from pink to burgundy, sometimes with beautiful slashes of brilliant red. Most blood oranges are imported from southern Italy.

Mandarin is a very broad term that encompasses all the different tangerines, satsumas and clementines. The original Japanese mandarin is now called a *satsuma* and is grown in Japan, North America and Spain. More often than not, it is sold simply as a tangerine. It is a smallish, basically seedless fruit that is sweet and juicy. The **clementine,** another variety of mandarin sometimes called the *clemie,* is Pete's favorite in the mandarin family. It is seedless, with an easy-to-peel skin and a rich flavor. Grown chiefly in Morocco and southern Spain, it is available from December until February.

The last member of the mandarin family, the **tangerine,** is so called because it was developed in the North African country of Tangiers. There are numerous tangerine varieties; they are all generally small and fairly soft, having a deep-orange, thin, pebbly skin and soft, sweet flesh. Most tangerines are available in profusion from December through February and in declining quantities through March and April.

Last but not least, we find the hybrid family of **tangelos,** of which there are several types. Be careful of the fruit that arrives on the market in November because, as with other early oranges, it is inclined to be bitter. The most popular and very best tangelo, according to Pete, is the *Minneola,* which is available from Florida in February and March. The Minneola tangelo, as distinct from the Minneola tangerine, is exquisitely juicy and flavorful, so tender "it'll mel' in your mouf, darlin'" and virtually seedless. It is not a particularly sweet fruit. Sometimes called a *Honeybelle,* it is hard to miss, being rather large and having a knobbly bump at one end. Tangelos are available from December to April.

The last "orange" that should be brought to light is the **temple** orange, also known as the *royal mandarin* by California growers, although it is neither an orange nor a mandarin, but a cross between a tangerine and an orange: a tangor. Resembling a large tangerine, the temple is very seedy, but wonderfully juicy and superbly sweet. Look for temples from January until May.

Pete's Seville Thrill

12 Seville oranges
6 quarts cold water
1/4 cup lemon juice
8 cups white sugar
6 red maraschino cherries, chopped

Peel the oranges and place the peel and the cold water in a kettle. Bring to a simmer and cook until tender. Save 4 cups of the liquid and set aside.

Scrape the white pith from the peel and shred the peel to desired thickness and length. Add the reserved liquid, lemon juice, and the pulp and juice from the oranges. Bring to a boil, add the sugar and simmer for 2 to 3 hours. Add chopped maraschino cherries before pouring the mixture into hot, sterilized jars. *Makes 12 8-ounce jars*

PAPAYAS

Although we'll probably never see them, the rarely imported Mexican variety of papayas can grow as large as soccer balls and weigh from 10 to 15 pounds! The flesh of this variety is often a glorious salmon pink, although it varies from region to region. Ninety percent of the papayas that we find in our markets are the Solo variety, shipped from California and Hawaii. This tropical fruit can be eaten ripe, as a fruit, or unripe, cooked like a zucchini.

The first time I tasted one was at Pete's. We had cut some of the ripe ones in half, garnished them with a few thin slices of lime and were selling them on the sale shelf. I bought one and tasted it without the lime, and it immediately became clear to me why we were selling them with a slice of lime: the flesh is subtly sweet and demands the tart freshness of a lime.

Papayas are beautiful when cut in half. The flesh is a deep orange with a central cavity filled with tiny black seeds; when ripe, it has a soft, juicy texture and a vaguely musky aroma.

Unfortunately, papayas are picked when still green to survive the rigors of shipping, so most of us in North America will never taste the extraordinary flavor of a tree-ripened papaya. Nevertheless, the ones I have tasted at Pete's are pretty wonderful, and if that's as close as I get, then I'm happy.

Papayas are available more or less all year because the plant has no specific fruiting or flowering time. Never buy green fruit as it may not ripen properly at home. Look for partially yellow fruit, and do not be put off by a spotted appearance, because the yellow coloring under all the marking is the important thing. If the fruit is

1 tablespoon contains: Cal-37, Prot-0g, Carb-9g, Fib-0g, Tot. Fat-0g, Sat. Fat-0g, Chol-0mg, Sdm-1mg

Papaya, delicious raw, can also be enjoyed cooked.

unripe, put it in a dark place at room temperature or, to speed things up, put it in a paper bag with a ripe banana. The fruit, when ripe, should give under gentle thumb pressure like a ripe avocado. Do not put papayas in the refrigerator unless they are completely ripe; even then, do not keep them there for more than 2 days. And do not serve papaya chilled; cool temperatures deaden the taste.

Papaya is an excellent source of vitamins A and C and a good source of potassium and fiber. Despite its sweetness, it has only 55 calories in 1 cup of the flesh.

Papaya, like so many tropical fruits, is not cheap and it seems unfortunate to cook it when it is so delicious raw. But just in case you happen to run into a bumper crop of cheap papayas, I'll mention some things you can do with cooked papaya and some ways to cook it. Unripe papaya does cook well, retaining its shape and remaining firm. It is great cut in cubes and included in a kebab. Unpeeled halves are natural containers for salads.

Sautéed papaya is delicious with ice cream, on thin pancakes with a squeeze of lemon or lime, or on thin slices of pound cake. Uncooked papaya is wonderful alone, or in a fruit salad with slightly acidic fruits like pineapple, coconut or oranges. Above all, don't forget the lime. The fruit is lovely arranged with kiwi slices and strawberries or with a scoop of ice cream dropped into the pit cavity.

Papaya-Ginger Ice Cream

There is a place in Toronto that makes truly magnificent ice cream, including the most heavenly papaya-ginger ice cream. This recipe produces something that is very close to the original.

> **1 completely ripe papaya, seeded, peeled and sliced**
>
> **2 Tbsp candied ginger, finely minced**
>
> **3 Tbsp white rum, or to taste**
>
> **1/4 cup sugar**
>
> **2 tsp maple syrup or corn syrup**
>
> **2 cups milk, chilled**

Toss the papaya, ginger and rum together in a bowl. Sprinkle with the sugar and let the flavors blend for about an hour at room temperature, occasionally giving the fruit a gentle stir. Purée the papaya and its "marinade" in a food processor and, with processor still running, gradually pour in the syrup and milk. Add more rum and sugar if you like. Pour the mixture into an ice-cream maker and proceed according to the manufacturer's instructions.

This ice cream improves if stored in the freezer for a day or two. *Makes 1-1/2 quarts*

3/4-cup serving contains: Cal-104, Prot-2g, Carb-17g, Fib-1g, Tot. Fat-2g, Sat. Fat-1g, Chol-8mg, Sdm-31mg

PASSION FRUIT

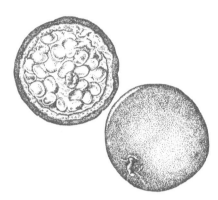

For years I thought this fruit was named for the reaction that it elicited from its eaters. Not so. It was named by Christian missionaries who saw the symbols of Christ's Passion in the flowers of the passion-fruit tree. Nevertheless, I am sure that I am not alone in my passionate feelings toward this little treat. I was familiar with the flavor of passion fruit before I actually ate one. One summer in France, I worked at a crêperie where we had a great deal of trouble finding passion-fruit juice, a vital ingredient in some cocktails. When we finally found it, I decided to taste it to find out what all the fuss was about. It was wonderful.

I was delighted when, six months and 4,000 miles later, I encountered passion fruit once again, this time at Pete's. I bought one, tasted it and, surprisingly, it tasted exactly like the juice. Even if the fruit did not evoke such powerful and pleasant memories, I think that I would still find some passion for the little wrinkled purple thing.

There are several types of passion fruit, but only two that North Americans really need to know about: the small brownish-purple ones (1 to 2 inches in diameter), which sometimes sport purple labels saying "Wrinkled is ripe," and the larger (2 to 3 inches) yellow or orange, hard-shelled fruit. The small round fruit is sold at Pete's as *passion fruit*, the larger spherical fruit as *granadilla*. They taste very similar: tart but sweet, rather like a mixture of jasmine, banana and lime, and are so rich and powerful that it is almost as difficult to forget as it is to describe.

It's helpful to know what the flesh of the fruit looks like. I bought a granadilla at Pete's a few months ago, broke the shell open and did a tour among my coworkers, offering them all a taste. They all, without exception, declined, and I must admit I was not especially surprised. It doesn't look like much just sitting there. A granadilla has a hard, smooth shell that protects the flesh from drying out. Inside are a lot of black seeds sitting in what looks rather like cloudy grapefruit flesh. The seeds are edible and provide a little crunch in what looks and feels like semi-set gelatin.

The purple passion fruit is much the same except that this gelatinous fruit is yellow and surrounded by a thin, tough skin, which is wrinkled when the fruit is ripe. As for the taste? The granadilla is slightly more subtle in flavor than the passion fruit and a little more perfumed without the edge. Both are heavenly!

Granadillas, Florida's passion fruit, are available from late summer until about Christmas time. Passion fruit from New Zealand are available from early spring until early summer. At Pete's we have also had passion fruit from Colombia and Ecuador. So, with occasional breaks when the supply of passion fruit is a little low, these tropical delights are available all year.

Like many tropical fruits, passion fruit blends particularly well with other fruit. Try passion fruit with bananas, kiwi and grapes because these four seem to get along especially well. But be careful not to overwhelm the fruit; mix it with delicately flavored ingredients or eat it, as Pete prefers it, with absolutely nothing else.

It is hard to get a passion fruit that is past its prime, because its prime lasts for quite a while. If the skin is wrinkled and shriveled, buy it! The fruit is ready to eat. If the skin is smooth and firm and the fruit still rounded, keep it at room temperature until the skin is dimpled and the fruit sounds loose and damp when shaken. Granadillas are a gorgeous orange-yellow when ripe and because of this shell, completely unwrinkled. Passion fruit should be stored in the refrigerator when completely ripe, preferably in a protected spot so that it won't be knocked or squashed by anything else.

There are several ways to eat passion fruit or granadillas. The way Pete prefers is simply to cut away the skin or shell and scoop out the flesh—an especially delicious treat if the fruit is slightly chilled. Some people like to add a drop or two of lemon or lime juice, others like passion fruit with a little sugar. The flesh is superb with vanilla or fruit ice cream, or you can mix it in with whipped cream or sour cream and serve it with fruit salad.

Passion fruit has some vitamin C and, unless strained, is a good source of fiber. One passion fruit has about 15 calories.

Passion Fruit and Mango à la Pete

This is true decadence and absolute bliss.

> **4 passion fruit**
> **1 ripe mango**
> **1 Tbsp butter**
> **2 tsp sugar**
> **2 Tbsp brandy**
> **2 Tbsp Cointreau**

Scoop the flesh and seeds out of the passion fruit and cut the flesh from the skin. Take the seed out of the mango. Mix the fruit with the butter and sugar. Add the brandy and Cointreau and flambé the mixture.

If you really want to go overboard on decadence, serve it with ice cream. *Serves 4*

Each serving contains: Cal-117, Prot-1g, Carb-15g, Fib-3g, Tot. Fat-3g, Sat. Fat-2g, Chol-8mg, Sdm-36mg

PEACHES

Serve peach slices on your cereal in the morning, or add them to pancakes, waffles or French toast. The fruit is also a delicious addition to a mixed-green salad.

The easiest way to peel a peach is the same way you peel a tomato. Give the fruit 15 to 30 seconds in boiling water, lift it out, immerse it in ice water and when cool, peel it with a knife.

Often referred to as "The queen of fruit," the peach is among the four most popular fruits in North America. Little will delight a family more than a shopper returning home with a basket of ripe peaches.

Look for local peaches at your market and at farmers' markets, because there are many varieties of flavorful peaches that are not widely available simply because they do not travel particularly well. The newer varieties of the fruit are firmer, bigger but not as sweet, yet because they stand up better to the rigors of packing and shipping, they are more commonly available.

Basically there are two types of peaches: freestone and clingstone. In a ripe freestone peach, the stone (pit) will almost fall out into your hand when you cut the fruit in half. In a cling, the fruit is firmly attached to the stone and needs to be pried out, no matter how ripe the fruit is. Most of the fruit available early in the season is cling or semi-freestone; many of the later varieties are freestone. Clings tend to have firmer flesh; freestones have a little more flavor.

The peak season for domestic peaches is from mid-May to early October. During the winter months, from late December to March, fruit is imported from Chile and New Zealand. You cannot tell whether a peach is fresh by looking at the red blush. What is important is the background color. In a good fruit, it will be cream colored, or better yet, yellow. Avoid fruit whose background color is green. It means that the fruit was probably harvested when immature and will not ripen properly. Unripe peaches will ripen at home on the counter out of direct sunlight or more quickly in a loosely closed paper bag.

For eating out of hand you will want soft, ripe peaches. For cooking and using later on, choose firm, ripe fruit. Ripening peaches at home will not make the fruit sweeter but will soften it and make it juicier. Keep the ripe fruit in the refrigerator in a plastic or paper bag for up to 5 days.

Peaches are a good source of vitamins A and C and potassium. A medium-size fruit has about 45 calories.

A fresh peach is delicious simply eaten out of hand. Give it a good rinse and if you are not partial to fuzz, peel it. By rubbing your thumb over the fruit, you can remove most of the fuzz and still get the added fiber of the skin.

You can also make a wonderful all-purpose concoction of peaches and honey by slicing some peaches into a bowl and drizzling a little honey over them. How much depends on how sweet your peaches and how sweet your tooth. Cover this mixture and let it sit. The whole thing blends together wonderfully, with the peach juice and the honey making a delicious light sauce that really enhances the fruit. Serve the fruit alone or with sour cream, yogurt or ice cream. Add a little raspberry sauce for a Peach Melba. With fresh pound cake, some whipped cream and a little cognac or brandy, you have a gourmet delight.

Peach and Blueberry Bliss

2 pounds peaches peeled, pitted and sliced

1 pint blueberries, washed

1/2 cup sugar

1 cup all-purpose flour

1 tsp baking powder

1/4 tsp salt

1 tsp cinnamon

1 tsp vanilla extract

1 egg

5 Tbsp butter, melted

Put the peaches in a well-oiled 2-quart casserole. Cover with the berries and sprinkle with a little of the sugar.

Mix remaining sugar, flour, baking powder, salt and cinnamon in a medium-size bowl. Add the vanilla and the egg and mix until coarsely blended and the dry ingredients dampened. Sprinkle the sugar mixture over the fruit and drizzle with melted butter.

Bake, uncovered, on the highest shelf in the oven for 15 minutes at 375F, then bake for another 10 to 15 minutes at 400F or until the topping is golden.

Serve the casserole hot, warm, cool, cold, any way at all. Try it with ice cream or yogurt. *Serves 6*

Each serving contains: Cal-332, Prot-5g, Carb-56g, Fib-5g, Tot. Fat-11g, Sat. Fat-6g, Chol-61mg, Sdm-282mg

Peach-Orange Frozen Yogurt

Even more refreshing than ice cream on a hot day is frozen yogurt, and this one is really special.

1/4 cup sugar

1 Tbsp unflavored gelatin

1/2 cup corn syrup

1 cup orange juice

5 large ripe peaches, peeled, halved and pitted

1 Tbsp lemon juice

3 cups plain yogurt

1 tsp vanilla extract

Grated rind of 1/2 orange

Mix the sugar and gelatin and blend in the corn syrup and orange juice. Simmer over low heat until the sugar and gelatin dissolve. Cool for 15 minutes.

Purée the peaches and lemon juice in a blender or food processor. Blend the fruit with the gelatin mixture.

Whisk the yogurt in a large bowl and gradually blend in the gelatin-peach mixture. Stir in the vanilla and orange rind.

Pour the mixture into a loaf pan and cover with plastic or foil. Freeze until firm, stirring a few times while freezing. *Makes 2 quarts*

2/3-cup serving contains: Cal-123, Prot-3g, Carb-25g, Fib-1g, Tot. Fat-2g, Sat. Fat-1g, Chol-8mg, Sdm-47mg

PEARS

I grew up without any particular fondness for pears. They seemed to me a rather dull version of an apple, but working for Pete over the last few years has given me a new appreciation for these heavenly creatures. I think now I would choose a pear over an apple any day.

The key to pears is eating them at their peak—not too early and not too late. I tended to be impatient and eat the fruit too soon, sacrificing flavor for texture. Never again. The flavor of a fresh, ripe pear is only enhanced by its buttery softness. Boscs, d'Anjous, Bartletts and Packhams are all sweet, juicy delights in their own right. They are an excellent source of fiber and each one contains about 99 calories.

Pears are available all year, with different types at different times. For cooking, choose Boscs, d'Anjous and Bartletts at the firm-ripe stage. For eating, pears should be soft-ripe, yielding to gentle pressure. Have you ever wondered why there are so many unripe pears in your market? Maybe it's different where you shop, but at Pete's most of the pears sell before they are ripe. It is because they have a finer flavor and are smoother textured when they are ripened off the tree, so they are picked, shipped and sold mature, but green.

Occasionally at Pete's we come across a crate of pears that have ripened, but for the most part, we put them out and sell them before they are perfectly ripe. If you buy your pears unripe, remember that they can take up to 7 days to ripen completely. Be patient; they are worth it! Bartletts and Packhams become a beautiful rich yellow when they are ripe; d'Anjous may remain green or turn slightly yellow and Boscs become a warm cinnamon. To ripen pears, keep them in a warm spot in a loosely closed paper bag. If you wish, you can keep the pears in the refrigerator for a week or two to slow the ripening process.

Bartletts, probably the most popular domestic variety of pear, are the first to appear on the North American market, being available from July to November. They are bell-shaped, with a thin, clear, yellow skin when ripe. There is also a red Bartlett, which is a surprisingly bright crimson, but like the regular Bartlett in taste and shape. They tend to be a little smaller than their yellow cousins. A fresh, ripe Bartlett is extremely juicy with a rich flavor and smooth white flesh.

D'Anjous are available from October to May. Anjous are largish pears with short necks. The flesh is a yellowish-white, with a juicy, spicy flavor. The texture is buttery and can be a bit granular near the center. The fruit may be yellow, greenish-yellow or even green when ripe. The stem end should yield to gentle thumb pressure. The importance of letting Anjou pears ripen cannot be overstated. I ate them for years while they were still hard and granular and, unfortunately, almost flavorless. When you let them ripen completely they become a delicious, mellow fruit.

Boscs are often called the "aristocrat of pears," and it is easy to see and taste why. This winter variety has a completely different type of appeal than the others, tending to be smaller with a slender, tapering neck and beautiful dark-yellow skin overlaid with a brownish color. The flesh is yellowish white, juicy, crunchy and buttery with a tendency to be slightly granular in the middle. A superb pear for eating fresh or for cooking.

Packhams, a later winter variety, are medium to large, with a bumpy surface. This leading spring import variety looks rather like a Bartlett—although perhaps not quite as symmetrical—and like a Bartlett, it turns from green to yellow as it ripens. The skin is thicker on a Packham than a Bartlett, but the flesh is more buttery and the flavor noticeably richer.

One cannot continue without mentioning the **Passe Crassane** and **Comice** pears. Both of these varieties are hard to find, but if you are lucky enough to trip over some in a market during the autumn or winter months, *do not pass by.* They are the most glorious of all pears, and their taste is exquisite. The Passe Crassane, imported from France, is an apple-shaped pear with skin like that of a ripe Bosc. The richly flavored flesh is juicy, sweet and granular, with a dry aftertaste. Pete describes it as having a flavor that will "blow your taste buds away!" The Comice is also roundish with a thick, greenish-yellow skin that is occasionally russeted. Its juicy flesh will literally melt in your mouth.

While discussing pears, Pete could not help but express dismay at the fact that most people eat pears like apples. He explained that the way to eat a pear is to pull the stem out and eat down, from the top to the bottom. It was a relief to discover that I eat pears correctly!

Pears are delicious eaten out of hand, if properly ripe. Firm-ripe pears are also a tasty addition to a fruit or mixed-green salad. Serve pears for dessert with blue cheese or Brie. Sliced, drizzled with orange liqueur, dusted with cinnamon and served with sour cream or yogurt, they are bliss! Try sautéed pears with chopped preserved ginger and a scoop of vanilla ice cream. For a light dessert, poach pears in a thin syrup for 10 minutes.

Pear Tart

Pastry to line a 9-inch pie pan or a 10-inch flan pan

5 or 6 firm-ripe pears, cored, thinly sliced and peeled, if you wish

Sugar

1 Tbsp vanilla extract

3 Tbsp butter

Powdered sugar

Line a pie or flan pan with the pastry. Arrange the pears on the pastry, sprinkle them with a little sugar, drizzle them with vanilla and

For eating out of hand, pears should be soft-ripe, yielding to gentle pressure. They have a finer flavor when they are ripened off the tree, which is why you should usually buy them underripe.

Each serving contains: Cal-162, Prot-1g, Carb-30g, Fib-3g, Tot. Fat-5g, Sat. Fat-3g, Chol-12mg, Sdm-54mg

This recipe is a specialty of some friends of mine in Toronto and one of Pete's favorite desserts after a spicy meal.

Each serving contains: Cal-106, Prot-1g, Carb-40g, Fib-4g, Tot. Fat-1g, Sat. Fat-0g, Chol-0mg, Sdm-2mg

dot them with butter. Bake for 30 minutes at 425F or until golden. Remove from oven, sprinkle with powdered sugar and broil for a few minutes, until the sugar melts and glazes the pie. Don't let it burn. *Serves 8*

Gingery Poached Pears

6 medium-size firm pears, Bartletts or Boscs
1 cup water
1/4 cup sugar
Rind of 2 lemons, finely grated
Juice of one lemon
3 Tbsp preserved ginger, finely diced
2 Tbsp cognac or rum

Using a saucepan big enough to hold all the pears upright, mix the water, sugar, rind and lemon juice over moderate heat until the mixture comes to a boil. Stir in the ginger and remove from heat. Carefully peel the pears. If they won't stand up alone, trim the bottoms a little so they do. Stand the pears in the syrup in the saucepan. Cover and cook the pears, basting frequently, over medium heat for 15 to 20 minutes, or until the pears pierce easily with a toothpick. When the pears are tender, place in a large serving dish or in individual bowls.

Boil the syrup, uncovered, for another 5 to 10 minutes. Add the cognac or rum and pour the sauce over the pears, basting frequently until cool. Cover and chill. *Serves 6*

PEPINOS

Pepino means "cucumber" in Spanish, a name well-suited to this melon. Its flavor is refreshing like a cucumber and rather bland like a cucumber; even the texture is cucumber-like. The flavor varies from one specimen to another, but it is usually a very subtle blend of honeydew and cantaloupe, a nuance that may be too subtle for North American tastes. The texture is certainly that of a melon, smooth and juicy but not as sweet.

When I asked at Pete's what the fruit tasted like, someone described it to me as "a cross between bananas, pineapple and strawberries." I tasted it, and although Geoff, Pete's right-hand man, was enthusiastic, I was a little baffled. Its taste was almost unnoticeable. I had a sneaking suspicion that the first one we tasted was underripe. I tried another one and the flavor was more pronounced but still very subtle.

Pepinos are a very delicate fruit. Hold one to your nose and inhale deeply. The aroma is superb and distinctly sweet, although very faint.

Try one for yourself and see. Pete enjoys them, and he is very particular, so they must be good! He adds that the fruit has to be very ripe before it is eaten and most people simply don't wait long enough.

Although pepinos are worth trying, I doubt that there will be a line-up of customers waiting to stock up on them the next time they are in season. They have been around for about 60 years and are still not very popular, except in Japan, where subtlety in food is prized.

The tiny pepino is available from February to mid-May from New Zealand and Peru, and from August to December from California. It is exotic in appearance and does not at all resemble a melon. Usually between 2 and 4 inches long, it is shaped like a teardrop with satiny smooth skin and a pale-yellowish base covered with streaks or splotches of purple. It deepens to a gold color when the fruit is ripe.

Pepinos will ripen nicely at room temperature, out of direct sun. Once the skin under the purple markings is golden, the fruit is ready to eat. Although it will keep for a few days in a plastic or paper bag in the refrigerator, its delicate nature means that it is not at its best for very long. So eat it when it's at its best. When ripe, the fruit should feel like a ripe plum, firm but not squishy.

Pepinos are low in calories, like most melons, and high in vitamin C and potassium.

Like all members of the melon family, pepinos are best raw. Distributors say that the skin is edible, but it tends to be tough and does not enhance the flavor of the fruit. The Japanese and South Americans eat the fruit *au naturel*, with nothing, in nothing, all by itself. In New Zealand, where the fruit is just being discovered and where most of our pepinos come from, the melon is served in 101 different ways, from hors d'oeuvres, to garnishes, to desserts. For dessert, try one with a squeeze of lime or lemon. Pete's favorite pepino dessert consists of scooping the flesh out of halves of the fruit, mixing it with ice cream and heaping it back in the empty half skins. The pepino cries out for experimentation. Buy some and see what you can create!

PERSIMMONS

An unripe persimmon is perhaps one of the most cosmetically beautiful fruits, so perfect that it almost looks unreal. There are two major varieties of this Chinese native available in North America—the heart-shaped **Hachiya** and the **Fuyu,** which looks rather like a ripe tomato.

Persimmons are available from September until Christmas, being most abundant from mid-October until the end of November. In November and December, California persimmons are on the

Persimmons are deceptive little creatures and have surprised a lot of unwary consumers. They look perfectly ripe when they are nowhere near it. So now, when you are ready to try a persimmon, make sure, especially if you have a Hachiya in your hand, that it is ripe before you use it. It should look shriveled and a little ugly.

market and, to quote our friend Pete, "dirt cheap." Occasionally, you will find persimmons earlier in the year, from Chile, Brazil or Israel, but these fruits are very expensive because of the shipping costs.

If you buy persimmons before they are ripe, simply store them in a cool, dark place or in a loosely closed paper bag with an apple or banana until they are ripe. A hard Fuyu tastes like a cross between a date and an apple and can be eaten and enjoyed before it is ripe, but the Hachiya must feel like a sack full of water before it is ready to eat. It is very difficult to watch the fruit pass through what looks like perfect ripeness to overripeness, but trust the word of an expert. Pete says that to North American eyes the ripe fruit will appear overripe, but please be patient: once the fruit looks a little ugly and shriveled, it is perfect for eating.

If anyone tells you that you can ripen persimmons by freezing them, don't listen—the fruit will soften, but it retains a bitter taste and becomes mushy. If you want to keep the fruit once it is ripe, you can store it briefly in the refrigerator in a plastic bag.

The persimmon is an excellent source of vitamins A and C and has lots of fiber and potassium. A 4-ounce serving contains about 90 calories.

This gorgeous little fruit is amazingly versatile and can be used in breads, cookies, puddings, cakes or pies, although it seems rather a waste for a fruit that is virtually perfect solo. Try cutting a Hachiya in half and simply spooning the fruit into your mouth—you really can't eat it without a spoon. You might like to try scooping the flesh into a bowl and eating it with cream or milk. Or try pushing the flesh through a sieve and using it as a sauce for other fruit, a light cake or a pudding.

If you want to enhance the sweetness of the flesh, add some freshly squeezed lime juice. Cut the fruit in half, sprinkle it with brown sugar and dot it with a little butter. Place it under the broiler for no more than one minute, just 'til the sugar begins to bubble. Serve it with sour cream, whipping cream, yogurt or ice cream—butter-almond ice cream is especially good.

The Fuyu can be sliced while still firm and added to vegetable or fruit salads, or it can be enjoyed on its own. The peel is edible but may be removed if you prefer it that way.

Persimmon Pudding

1 cup sifted flour
1/2 tsp baking soda
1/2 cup sugar
1/2 tsp salt
1/4 tsp cinnamon
1/4 tsp nutmeg

1 cup persimmon pulp

2 eggs, well beaten

1 cup milk

1-1/2 Tbsp butter, melted

1/2 cup sliced almonds

1/2 cup chopped, dried apricots

1/2 cup dried currants

Mix the flour, soda, sugar, salt and spices. In a separate bowl, mix the persimmon pulp, eggs, milk, butter, almonds, apricots and currants. Blend the two mixtures into a soft batter, adding a little more milk if it is too dry. Pour the batter into a buttered casserole and bake at 350F for 30 to 45 minutes. Serve hot with whipped cream. *Serves 4*

Each serving contains: Cal-502, Prot-12g, Carb-84g, Fib-6g, Tot. Fat-15g, Sat. Fat-5g, Chol-126mg, Sdm-535mg

PINEAPPLES

Pineapples, named because of their resemblance to pine cones, should be picked at their peak of ripeness and flavor because they have no starch to convert to sugar; pineapples do not ripen once they have been harvested. Pineapples will soften somewhat and lose some of their acidity, but they do not get any riper.

Pineapples are available all year, with the peak season occurring from April to June. When choosing a pineapple, look for one that is as plump and as large as possible. Deep green, crisp-looking crown leaves are a good sign of freshness. Check out the core on the base of the pineapple for any blackness, which indicates that the pineapple has started to ferment. Don't bother trying to pull out the central leaves of the crown—this won't tell you anything except whether or not the leaves come out easily. A sweet ripe fruit may have a fragrant pleasant aroma—a good indication but not a guarantee, because some lovely fruit will not smell.

Pineapples do not store particularly well, so use the fruit as soon as possible. If you will not be using it promptly, you can leave it out on the counter, away from direct sunlight, for up to 2 days. A cut pineapple can be kept in plastic in the refrigerator for 4 days, but it too should be used as soon as possible. Four ounces of fresh pineapple have 60 calories.

Raw pineapple is an excellent source of vitamin C and contains an enzyme called *bromelin* that prevents gelatin from setting.

Although some markets offer fresh peeled, cored, sliced pineapple, this is not true for all of them. Cutting the fruit yourself is not particularly difficult. First, slice off the bottom of the pineapple so it will sit on the counter comfortably, then stand it on its end and cut off the skin with long vertical strokes of a sharp knife.

Remove the eyes individually with the tip of a knife, or cut long thin diagonal grooves around the fruit on either side of the eyes. (The latter is slightly more decorative.) Then slice the fruit in quarters lengthwise and cut out the core. You can give the core pieces to the kids for something to chew on. It is tasty but so fibrous that you simply chew it for a while and then spit out the pulp. It is also a favorite snack at Pete's, indulged in by the one chosen to put pineapples through the peeling and coring machine.

The sweet juicy taste of pineapples make them a natural addition to a fruit salad and delicious in combination with a mild solid or cream cheese. A hollowed-out pineapple half makes an attractive bowl for pineapple dishes. Try filling one with a combination of melon balls or cubes, sliced strawberries, sliced kiwi, grapes and orange sections, and grate some fresh coconut on top. Add some pineapple chunks to your next coleslaw for a juicy, delicious surprise. For a great low-calorie snack or dessert, top a slice of pineapple with a scoop of cottage cheese. Explore a bit—pineapple is a natural in almost any combination.

Pineapple-Orange Sorbet

1/2 cup light corn syrup

2 cups sour cream

1 to 1-1/2 cups pineapple, finely chopped, with juice

6 ounces orange-juice concentrate (1 can frozen orange juice)

Blend the corn syrup and sour cream until smooth. Add the pineapple and orange juice. Pour the mixture into an ice-cream maker and freeze according to the manufacturer's instructions, or pour the mixture into a baking pan, cover with foil or plastic and freeze for 4 hours, stirring 2 or 3 times. *Makes 1-1/2 quarts*

3/4-cup serving contains: Cal-229, Prot-2g, Carb-30g, Fib-1g, Tot. Fat-12g, Sat. Fat-7g, Chol-26mg, Sdm-56mg

Pineapple Tropical Cream

Add a little Cointreau or tropical liqueur for a touch of something special.

2 cups shredded pineapple

1/4 cup sugar

1 Tbsp lime juice

1 cup whipping cream, whipped

1/4 tsp ground nutmeg

Combine the pineapple, sugar and lime juice. Fold in the whipped cream and nutmeg. Chill. *Serves 4*

Each serving contains: Cal-189, Prot-1g, Carb-23g, Fib-1g, Tot. Fat-11g, Sat. Fat-7g, Chol-41mg, Sdm-12mg

PLUMS

The plum is a fruit that comes in almost every color, shape and flavor imaginable. But there are two clear distinctions—Japanese and European plums. During the peak seasons, most North Americans have easy access to both types of plums, although the Japanese varieties grown in California are more common. Medium to large and famous for their juiciness, they come in various shapes but are *never* purple or blue. European varieties, also grown in California, are *always* blue or purple and generally smaller and firmer, with a milder flavor. It is the European plums that are dried to make prunes.

Plums are available from early June to early October and during the winter months, from mid-January to mid-March. It can be tricky to tell ripe fruit if you are buying the dark-skinned plums, but look for fruit that is deeply colored. A ripe plum will give a little when lightly squeezed.

Store ripe plums, unwashed, in a plastic or paper bag for up to 4 days in the refrigerator. Fruit will ripen if left on the counter for a few days, out of direct sunlight. To hurry things up a little, put the fruit in a paper bag and leave it loosely closed—but keep an eye on it as the fruit ripens quickly.

Plums are rich in vitamins A and C. The European variety has a little less than half the calories of the Japanese; an average Japanese plum has 55 calories, a European, 20.

Plums are often cooked to bring out the best flavor of the fruit. Stewed plums are a delicious treat, particularly to kids! Well suited to poaching, plums will cook in 5 to 10 minutes in sugared water. Prick the skin before cooking so they don't explode. Serve them with cognac or port.

Plums are delicious eaten out of hand; give them a wash and they are ready. Pete's personal favorite for out-of-hand eating is the Laroda, a beautiful, juicy, red-skinned plum available early to mid-summer. The Japanese variety of plum is nice in fruit salads. Try plums sliced in cream, or fill the pit cavities of a European-type plum with a soft cheese such as Camembert.

Deep-Dish Plum Pie

It seems logical to make a pie with only a top or a bottom crust, especially when dealing with fresh fruit. It gives you more fruit to enjoy and fewer calories!

Don't be alarmed by how easy this recipe is. The only problem is getting it sweet enough, but not too sweet. I like it a little tart, something to keep in mind when you make this pie.

5 cups plums

1/4 cup sugar

2 Tbsp all-purpose flour

2 tsp cinnamon

Pastry for the top of one 9-inch pie

Sugar and cinnamon

Each serving contains: Cal-131, Prot-1g, Carb-30g, Fib-3g, Tot. Fat-2g, Sat. Fat-0g, Chol-0mg, Sdm-14mg

In many Eastern and Mediterranean cultures, pomegranate seeds are used as a garnish. Their wonderful sweet-sour flavor enhances almost everything. Try adding a handful to your next green salad!

Choose your favorite casserole or deep pie dish and assemble enough plums to fill it. Then cut the fruit in half and remove the pits. Combine the sugar, flour and cinnamon. Layer the fruit and the sugar mixture in the casserole. Place pastry on top and seal it to the sides of the dish. Cut slits in the top to allow the steam to escape. Bake at 400F until the pastry is golden and the fruit bubbling. Remove from the oven and sprinkle the crust with a little sugar and a touch of cinnamon. (I told you it was easy!) *Serves 6*

POMEGRANATES

Pomegranates originated in Persia, where they reputedly kept numerous travelers alive on treks through the desert and where they gave the brilliant red color to Persian rugs. The broken skin and juice of pomegranates make an excellent dye. The thick skin that made them invaluable in desert treks also made them one of the most common exotic fruits—available a long time before importing exotic fruit was as popular as it is now. The fruit will keep for a long time, well protected by its skin.

A pomegranate is a fruit that must be eaten at a leisurely pace. The name comes from the Latin *pomum granatum*, meaning "apple of many seeds." From the outside, the fruit does, indeed, resemble a pomum. It is the size of a large apple with a leathery skin that is a mottled, deep, reddish-purple. Inside, hundreds of little edible seeds are each surrounded by translucent, crimson flesh, held in place and shown to advantage by a coarse, ivory-colored, inedible membrane. A mouthful of the little ruby gems is a mouthful of tangy-sweet, juicy flavor.

Pomegranates are available from fall to early winter. Look for large fruit with deep color. A heavier fruit will have more juice. The skin should appear as if it is having trouble holding itself together around its rosy contents.

Pomegranates will keep in the refrigerator for 3 months. You can pack the seeds in an airtight container and pop them in the freezer where they'll keep for about 3 months. When you want to use them, just scrape out as much as you think you'll need and sprinkle them, still frozen, into the dish you are preparing.

Pomegranates are loaded with potassium and vitamin C. You can count on about 110 calories per fruit.

Removing the skin is a fine art, yet surprisingly simple when you know how. When I was growing up, I ate pomegranates by breaking them in half and digging out the seeds with my fingers— a dangerous method if you care about your clothes. Now I use a knife to split the skin, carefully, from the calyx—the little crown— to the stem end and peel back the skin. The seeds can then be gently removed, while taking care not to pierce the flesh.

This drink was traditionally made with pomegranates, but, as with many things, it is often made with substitutes these days. Making the real thing isn't difficult and not only is it better for you, but the taste is far superior to today's commercial grenadine.

1/4-cup serving contains: Cal-97, Prot-0g, Carb-25g, Fib-0g, Tot. Fat-0g, Sat. Fat-0g, Chol-0mg, Sdm-0mg

Once a common fruit, quince are now a specialty. This member of the apple family is most often used in preserves, jams or jellies.

Grenadine

2 cups pomegranate seeds, cut from 2 large pomegranates
2 cups sugar

Mix the seeds and sugar in a saucepan (not an aluminum one), and mash them until all of the little juice sacs have been broken. Let the liquid mixture stand overnight or up to 24 hours.

Bring the liquid to a boil, stirring constantly. Turn the heat to low and simmer for 2 minutes. Strain the juice through a cheese-cloth, wringing it to extract the liquid. Pour the liquid into a sterilized jar and cover it with a clean cloth towel until cool. Remove the towel, cap the jar and refrigerate. *Makes 3 cups*

QUINCE

I remember the first time I saw quince: it was at Pete's, not too long ago. They are a rather unusual looking fruit but I immediately felt drawn to them, first because they looked rather lonely—we only had about 20 at the stall—and second because my father's favorite jelly is quince jelly. I had been asking what a quince was for years and received vague explanations, and I couldn't help but feel a little excitement when I saw the real thing!

This member of the apple family, which was once very common, has become less so over the years, probably because it was most often used for jams and jellies. Unfortunately, it has now become a specialty item which, like Seville oranges, is available only in small quantities.

Quince can be the shape of a Delicious apple or a pear, and can vary in color from golden to yellow with red flecks; it can also be smooth-skinned or covered with a woolly fuzz. There is little that is constant about the quince except its aroma: strongly musky with a hint of pear or pineapple. In fact, you can put a quince in your closet for a few months to scent your clothes.

Quince are available in the fall, imported from California, from September until November. Look for large, smooth fruit because there is a lot of waste and work in preparing smaller or gnarled fruit. If you can't find unmarked fruit, don't forget that the fruit should most often be cooked—a process that covers a multitude of sins. Quince will keep for a couple of months individually wrapped in a double layer of plastic and stored in the refrigerator. But be sure to put them in a corner of the refrigerator where they won't get bumped, because the fruit bruises very easily.

Quince are rich in fiber, are a good source of vitamin C and provide some potassium. There are 65 calories in 4 ounces of the raw fruit.

Baked Quince

The fruit in this dish turns a wonderful pinky gold and the taste of baked quince and honey is gorgeous. Serve it warm with ice cream, sour cream or yogurt.

2 pounds quince, peeled, cored and sliced

5 Tbsp mild honey

2 Tbsp lime juice

6 Tbsp water

1/4 cup sliced almonds

Overlap the quince slices in a large rectangular baking dish and drizzle with honey to coat the slices. Sprinkle the fruit with lime juice and water. Cover tightly.

Bake at 300F for 45 minutes or until the quince are tender. Remove the cover and turn the heat up to 425F; sprinkle with the almonds and bake for 10 minutes, until the liquid is thickened and the slices golden. *Serves* 4

Each serving contains: Cal-246, Prot-2g, Carb-58g, Fib-5g, Tot. Fat-3g, Sat. Fat-0g, Chol-0mg, Sdm-13mg

Quince-and-Almond Tart

One of Pete's regular customers brought us each a sample of this tart one day. We all asked her for the recipe the next time she was in.

3 cups water

2 cups sugar

Juice of 1 lime

3 to 4 pounds quince, peeled, cored and sliced, with the seeds placed in a cheesecloth bag

1 stick cinnamon

2 whole cloves

Pastry for bottom and latticework top of a 9-inch pie

4 Tbsp almonds, lightly roasted

Boil the water, sugar and lime juice for one minute; add the quince, the cheesecloth bag containing the seeds and the spices. (The pectin in the seeds will help thicken the syrup.) Bring the mixture to a boil, turn down the heat and simmer for 1-1/2 hours or until the juice is thick, stirring occasionally. Remove the seeds, cloves and cinnamon. (If you want to stop here, you will have quince jam!)

Fill a pastry-lined pie or quiche dish with the quince mixture and cover with a latticework top. Bake at 375F for 20 to 30 minutes. Remove the tart from the oven and sprinkle with the almonds. Cool for at least 4 hours or overnight. Serve with whipped cream, sour cream, vanilla ice cream or yogurt. *Serves* 8

Each serving contains: Cal-362, Prot-2g, Carb-87g, Fib-5g, Tot. Fat-3g, Sat. Fat-0g, Chol-0mg, Sdm-28mg

RAMBUTANS

Rambutans are funny-looking little fruits, looking more like creatures than fruit. About 2 inches in diameter, reddish brown in color and covered with soft, flexible spikes, they look like an odd form of miniature hedgehog. They are also known as *hairy lychees*, a name that refers not only to their spikes but to their taste as well: the hairy for the spikes, the lychee for the taste. I may be alone in thinking that rambutan suffers in comparison to the lychee, because I am partial to lychees. Rambutans are not as sweet, not as juicy and not as richly flavored or scented as lychees.

When eaten on their own, without comparison, rambutans are a nice, delicately flavored, delicately scented tropical fruit, tasting and smelling vaguely like a mix of lychee and coconut. Covered with a thick, slightly flexible skin with a lengthwise seam running around the outside, the rambutan hides a tight, white, slightly opaque flesh, which has a texture similar to a lychee although drier and more granular. The flesh is thin around the brown, oblong, inedible seed, with a hard central section on the area that surrounds the seed.

Rambutans are available off and on from April to October. Look for fruit that feels firm but not hard. Fruit with a rosy hue tends to be fresher; a brown, shriveled skin is a sign of old age. Rambutans may be kept in a plastic bag in the refrigerator for up to a week.

Rambutans may be enjoyed the same way as lychees, eaten raw by simply cutting the skin open along its seam. Rambutans are wonderful in a light syrup flavored with lemon and crystallized ginger, or in any recipe that calls for lychees, although you must compensate for the fact that rambutans are not as sweet or as juicy as lychees.

Rambutans are eaten the same way as lychees and can be used as a substitute for lychees, but you will have to allow for the fact that the fruit is not as sweet or as juicy. The most wonderful way to serve rambutans is peeled and seeded, with coffee ice cream.

RASPBERRIES

Although most of us are familiar enough with the red raspberry, it is interesting to know that this fruit is also black, golden, purple, yellow and amber, although it is unlikely that you will run across anything but the red raspberry, which is still the popular favorite and the most common. Most of us have delicious memories of fabulous desserts made with this delicately flavored and textured berry. It is perhaps the most elusive of berries, its delicate sweetness making it the perfect complement to other fruit and its juicy richness making it a true delight when eaten alone.

If your supplier is a savvy importer, raspberries will be available from the end of May into December. The season for locally produced berries is much shorter and varies from region to region.

Pete calls raspberries one-day wonders because they are the most fragile of all the berries and must be handled with great care. Raspberries should be eaten, not stored.

Raspberries should be stored for as short a time as possible. Place them on a cookie sheet between paper towels, wrapped in plastic. When buying them, look for plump, well-shaped berries with no signs of dampness or mold. Raspberries that have been picked in damp conditions have a particularly short shelf life.

Raspberries are an excellent source of vitamin C and a good source of folate; they have 70 calories per cup.

Like most berries, raspberries are delicious alone or with cream, ice cream, sour cream or yogurt. Try them with your favorite breakfast; they are super on cereal, pancakes or waffles. Try mashing a few with a little sugar and spoon over ice cream, in a meringue, on a light cake or over strawberries. If you have never had raspberry shortcake, give it a try. It's a truly wonderful surprise!

Raspberry Supreme

1 to 2 pints raspberries, washed

3 Tbsp Grand Marnier or orange-flavored liqueur

1/2 cup whipping cream

1 Tbsp sugar

1/2 cup yogurt

1/4 cup toasted slivered almonds

Reserving 1/2 cup of the raspberries, divide the fruit among 4 dessert dishes. Pour the liqueur over the berries.

Whip the cream, add the sugar and fold the whipped cream into the yogurt. Mash the reserved berries and fold them into the cream mixture. Spoon the cream mixture onto the berries and liqueur, and sprinkle with toasted slivered almonds. *Serves* 4

Each serving contains: Cal-268, Prot-4g, Carb-21g, Fib-6g, Tot. Fat-17g, Sat. Fat-8g, Chol-45mg, Sdm-26mg

RHUBARB

Because we tend to eat rhubarb with sugar and in desserts, we consider it a fruit, but technically it is a vegetable. There are two types of rhubarb: hothouse-grown and field-grown. The field-grown rhubarb has large stalks that are streaked red and green. The younger stems, on which the leaves are not yet full-grown, are usually the most tender, having a more delicate flavor than the larger stalks. When buying rhubarb, look for firm, crisp, fresh stalks. If the leaves are attached, they should be stiff and vivid green in color. Avoid rhubarb with wilted leaves or flabby-looking stalks.

Hothouse rhubarb, the very name of which sends Pete into raptures, is available in early spring. Pete says there is nothing like sweet, tender hothouse rhubarb, which is mild pink and nearly stringless, but most people are unwilling to pay the price for it.

Rhubarb is wonderfully easy to grow and appears early in the spring, about the same time as fiddleheads.

Because rhubarb is sold ripe and ready for use, all you have to do is wash it before cooking. If you wish to keep it for a while, you may store it in the refrigerator, unwashed and in a plastic bag, for as long as a week.

Rhubarb is a good source of vitamin C and provides some calcium. Extremely low in calories, it has only 20 in 1 cup of the raw diced fruit. However, beware: a 4-ounce serving of cooked, sweetened rhubarb has about 160 calories depending, of course, on how sweet you like it.

Stewed Rhubarb

1 pound rhubarb, cut into 1-inch pieces

1/2 cup sugar

Add the rhubarb to a saucepan with a small amount of water and simmer for 5 minutes. Add the sugar and simmer for an additional 5 minutes or until the sugar is dissolved.

This is great with yogurt, on ice cream, on pancakes, with custard, all by itself or almost any way you care to serve it. *Serves* 4

Rhubarb Soup

A friend brought back this recipe from Sweden. I'll admit that I was a little dubious at first, but one mouthful won me over. This is great at either the beginning or the end of a meal. I have not tried it in the middle, but it would probably be good there too.

2 pounds ripe rhubarb, cut into 1-inch pieces and cooked in 8 cups of water

2 sticks cinnamon

1/2 lemon, sliced

1 cup sugar

2 Tbsp cornstarch

1 egg yolk, beaten

1/2 cup cream or half-and-half

When the rhubarb is tender, remove it from the cooking liquid and purée it in a blender or food processor. Heat the purée and the cooking liquid with the cinnamon and lemon for 5 minutes. Add the sugar. (Taste it, you may like it sweeter.)

Mix the cornstarch with 1/3 cup water and stir into the rhubarb juice. Simmer for another 5 minutes, and remove the lemon and cinnamon. Just before serving the soup, mix the egg yolk with the cream and stir into the soup.

I like to garnish the soup with thin slices of preserved ginger if I am serving it as a dessert. *Serves* 8

The easiest thing to do with rhubarb is to cut it into 1-inch pieces and cook it without a lid in a small amount of sugar and enough water to cover.

<u>Each serving contains:</u> Cal-121, Prot-1g, Carb-30g, Fib-2g, Tot. Fat-0g, Sat. Fat-0g, Chol-0mg, Sdm-5mg

<u>Each serving contains:</u> Cal-156, Prot-2g, Carb-33g, Fib-2g, Tot. Fat-3g, Sat. Fat-1g, Chol-32mg, Sdm-12mg

STRAWBERRIES

For most of us, the strawberry season starts with the influx of berries from California and Florida in early May and lasts until the end of July. Of course, strawberries are available just about all year long, but they are shipped halfway round the world to get to us, and are usually not as fresh when they arrive.

Strawberries will ripen only a little after they are picked so look for boxes of ripe berries that are not hulled. Don't hull them until you have washed them or they will absorb water. The size of the berry has little to do with its taste, so look for boxes of berries that are the size best suited to your needs.

Your best bet, because strawberries don't store especially well, is to use them within 3 days of buying them. To keep them in tip-top shape until you use them, lay the unwashed berries on trays lined with paper towels; then cover them with more paper towels and a layer of plastic. Fresh local berries don't need to be treated with such kid gloves—they are usually fine in their baskets.

You can freeze strawberries easily. Simply hull them and lay them in a single layer on a baking tray; when they are frozen hard, transfer them to plastic freezer bags. They will keep for up to 10 months.

Strawberries are a great source of vitamin C and have only 50 calories per cup.

Well, well, well—how to use strawberries. It would probably be easier to tell you how not to use these little creatures. They are gorgeous *au naturel*, with whipped cream, sour cream, or in yogurt with a sprinkling of sugar. For a real treat, dip a few fresh strawberries in melted dark or milk chocolate. Try them with a little Grand Marnier and a little whipped cream and you will be in the midst of decadence—a wonderful place to be with strawberries. They are superb in ice cream or with a fresh sponge cake and, of course, in strawberry shortcake. I don't know how you usually make strawberry shortcake, but be sure to try it with sweet biscuits and whipped cream.

Strawberries ripen only a little after picking. The size has little to do with taste.

Strawberry Pie

This is my mother's recipe and even Pete agrees that berries don't come much better than this.

1 quart fresh strawberries
1 9-inch baked pie shell
1/4 cup water
3/4 cup sugar
2 Tbsp cornstarch
Whipped cream

Mash enough berries to make 3/4 cup pulp and set aside. Fill the pie shell with the remaining berries, leaving them whole unless they are extra large, using as many berries as you need to make sure the shell is well filled.

Add the water, sugar and cornstarch to the mashed berries and boil over medium heat until thick, stirring frequently. Pour the mixture over the berries in the pie shell and chill for at least 30 minutes. Top with whipped cream. *Serves 6*

Each serving contains: Cal-198, Prot-1g, Carb-36g, Fib-2g, Tot. Fat-7g, Sat. Fat-4g, Chol-20mg, Sdm-21mg

Strawberries Extraordinaire

Ha, this is something I didn't mention when telling you how to eat strawberries. Actually I'd rather not tell you about it now either—some things should remain secrets—but this is so completely extraordinary Pete has forced me to share it with you.

1 quart fresh strawberries; use local ones for best flavor
3 ounces cream cheese, softened at room temperature
3 Tbsp Grand Marnier
3 Tbsp mild honey
1 cup whipping cream, whipped
3 Tbsp grated orange rind
Fresh mint leaves

Wash the berries quickly in a sieve under running water and drain on paper towels.

Beat the cream cheese, the Grand Marnier and the honey until very smooth. Fold in the whipped cream.

Divide the berries into 6 large wine glasses or crystal dessert dishes and add the cream-cheese mixture. Chill for 4 hours, sprinkle with grated orange rind, and garnish with mint leaves. Sounds wonderful, right? It is. *Serves 6*

Each serving contains: Cal-266, Prot-3g, Carb-18g, Fib-2g, Tot. Fat-20g, Sat. Fat-12g, Chol-70mg, Sdm-58mg

TAMARILLOS

The exquisite little tamarillo, or *tree tomato*, is memorably beautiful. Scarlet or a warm yellow, it is as smooth-skinned and perfectly formed as its cousin, the eggplant. Shaped rather like a pointed egg, the flesh is the texture of a plum, a beautiful orange-yellow color with two deep-red swirls of tiny edible seeds.

The unusual astringent flavor of this fruit is especially suited to cooking and benefits from the addition of a little sugar. Of the two varieties, the yellow tends to be sweeter and milder.

Tamarillos are available from March to October, with the fruit being most plentiful during the summer months. Because tamarillos hold up wonderfully well to shipping and storing, nine times out of ten you will find them in perfect condition in markets. A ripe tamarillo will yield to pressure like a firm, ripe plum. It will also develop a fragrance somewhere between that of an apricot and a tomato. Unripe fruit will ripen at home, on the counter, out of direct sunlight. Ripe fruit will keep in the refrigerator in a plastic bag for up to 3 weeks.

Tamarillos are a good source of vitamins A and C and are low in calories. Half a cup has only 50 calories.

Tamarillos can be served as a vegetable—sliced, marinated in dressing and then added to a salad. They can also be served as a fruit: let them sit in honey for a couple of seconds and serve them on ice cream or yogurt.

No matter how you use tamarillos, they have to be peeled. Either use a vegetable peeler or immerse the fruit in boiling water for about one minute, then plunge the tamarillo into ice water, pierce the skin and slip it off.

Tamarillos in Syrup

This is the easiest and most versatile way to prepare the fruit. It can be served with ice cream or whipped cream or as a condiment with spicy curries.

4 tamarillos, peeled and sliced into 1/4-inch-thick slices
4 tsp sugar
1/2 tsp cinnamon
1/4 tsp cloves
2 tsp lemon juice
Salt and pepper

Arrange the sliced fruit in a shallow baking dish and sprinkle with the sugar, cinnamon, cloves, lemon juice, salt and pepper. Bake at 375F for about 20 minutes or until tender, basting once or twice with the syrup. *Serves 4*

Each serving contains: Cal-52, Prot-1g, Carb-13g, Fib-1g, Tot. Fat-0g, Sat. Fat-0g, Chol-0mg, Sdm-67mg

UGLI FRUIT

Ugli fruit is a superb addition to any salad in which you ordinarily use oranges or to bitter salad greens such as radicchio or Belgian endive. It will turn your fruit salad into a real paradise and is wonderful in gelatin desserts, too.

Although ugli fruit are indeed ugly, especially in the eyes of North Americans who take so much stock in the appearance of things, they are seed-free, juicy and tartly-sweet. Ugli fruit are about the size of a grapefruit, having rather loose, extremely rough, badly disfigured skin, and can range from light green to yellow-orange in color. Once you get your thumb under it, however, the skin virtually falls away, revealing a gorgeous, warm, orange-colored flesh. Because the juice sacs are bigger than in ordinary citrus fruit, the flesh of an ugli is particularly luscious.

Ugli fruit is available from January to early June. Look for fruit that is heavy for its size, showing no indication of dryness at the stem end. Although the fruit should have a little give, don't worry about the outer appearance of the fruit. If it didn't look awful, it wouldn't be named ugli fruit, would it? Surface scarring, uneven coloring, dappling, patchiness . . . it's all part of this creature. The smaller fruits tend to be more flavorful and often sweeter.

You can store the fruit in the refrigerator for up to 3 weeks. If you plan to use them within a couple of days, leave them on the counter; their thick skin offers good protection against drying out.

Ugli fruit is a good source of vitamin C and fiber and has about the same number of calories as grapefruit.

Use ugli fruit as you would a grapefruit or an orange. Eat half for breakfast or take one with you for lunch. And take lots of paper napkins; although this fruit is delicious and easy to eat out of hand, its juiciness makes it a messy fruit to eat, especially because the sections tend to split easily. Ugli fruit is delicious solo—don't feel you have to do anything to it but eat it!

WHITE SAPOTE

The world of tropical fruit is rather confusing when it comes to the names of various fruit: feijoa is wrongly called *pineapple guava*, granadilla is actually a kind of *passion fruit*, the notorious cactus pear is also known as *prickly pear*, *Indian fig* and *tuna* among other things, and the cherimoya is sometimes called *sherbet fruit* or *custard apple*. Apparently the white sapote is another fruit whose name is in dispute and calling this particular fruit simply *sapote* is incorrect.

Sapote, which comes from the Mexican *zapote*, simply means soft fruit—a dangerously vague description. So use its proper name: *white sapote*. Mind you, unless you live in Mexico or have an unusually stubborn fruit supplier, asking for sapote will probably get you a white sapote.

The white sapote has a delicate, extra-sweet, mild flavor with a hint of something tropical—a combination of peach, apricot and banana. The fruit has no core but it does have a collection of 2 to 6 inedible seeds scattered throughout the flesh.

The white sapote is a superb fruit. It is nondescript on the outside, looking rather like a green cooking apple with a slight point at the blossom end. Its pale cream-colored flesh is light textured, almost buttery, smooth, soft and very juicy. It has a delicate, extra-sweet, mild flavor with a hint of something tropical—a combination of peach or apricot and banana. The fruit has no core, but it does have a collection of seeds, between 2 and 6, scattered throughout the flesh. In size, the fruit is between an orange and a grapefruit. Its thin, edible, easily bruised skin is green but sometimes turns yellow when ripe, when it will yield to gentle pressure like a ripe plum.

It is tricky to determine exactly when white sapotes will be available in your markets, but look for them between August and November; they tend to peak in September. Buy the fruit while it is still firm and let it ripen at home, on the counter, out of direct sunlight. But don't turn your back on this fruit, because it ripens very quickly, sometimes in only a day or two and in no more than 3 days. Once ripened, the fruit may be refrigerated in a plastic or paper bag for the better part of a week.

White sapotes are a good source of potassium, vitamin C, iron and fiber. One medium-size fruit has about 135 calories.

The skin of a white sapote is edible, though it may be slightly tart. Sapotes are delicious eaten out of hand like an apple; just bear in mind that the seeds are inedible. You can also peel the fruit, slice it and dip it in lemon juice to prevent darkening.

The sapote should not be cooked. It is delicious in fruit salads, especially in combination with strawberries and kiwi. The fruit is excellent sliced and served with a squeeze of lime or lemon juice, and topped with cream or whipped cream. Purée the fruit and blend it with orange juice for a different and delicious drink. Or use the fruit purée as a sauce for other fruit.

Sapote Shake

When was the last time you had a sapote milkshake?

1 cup white sapote pieces, peeled and seeded

1 cup vanilla yogurt

1/2 cup orange juice

2 Tbsp honey

1/4 tsp ginger

1 egg

Put all the ingredients into a blender or food processor and blend until smooth. *Serves 2 generously*

Each serving contains: Cal-288, Prot-10g, Carb-60g, Fib-2g, Tot. Fat-3g, Sat. Fat-1g, Chol-109mg, Sdm-112mg

INDEX